Persuasion

SPEECH AND BEHAVIORAL CHANGE

THE BOBBS-MERRILL SERIES IN *Speech Communication*

RUSSEL R. WINDES, *Editor*

Queens College of the City University of New York

GARY CRONKHITE

Illinois State University

Persuasion

SPEECH AND BEHAVIORAL CHANGE

The Bobbs-Merrill Company, Inc.

INDIANAPOLIS AND NEW YORK

Editor's foreword

An understanding of the theories and art of persuasion is a subject fundamental to the study of speech communication; most basic books in the discipline deal with the nature and structure of the "speech to persuade" and with the persuasive effects of messages. Until recently, most texts did not incorporate empirical research, which casts doubt on many of the common-sense assumptions of centuries of rhetorical theory. Those books which have used the conclusions of empirical research have often presented partially tested hypotheses as recently discovered truths. While certitude may provide security for the lecturer and satiate students' cravings for quotable dicta, any book which presents conclusions **about** persuasion may well miss the dynamic nature of the subject.

If the study of persuasion is seen, not as a body of rules which, if followed, lead inevitably to power and influence, but as a set of unanswered (and sometimes unasked) questions and a series of techniques for ferreting out answers and directions, then the proper shape of a text on persuasion becomes clearer. Emphasis shifts from what has been discovered about persuasion to the question of how persuasive effects can best be described and tested. Saying this is not to deny any pragmatic or functional purposes or results. A study of questions, technology, and effects will probably yield greater control and skill, through knowledge, than will rote memorization of largely unverified rules and axioms and the application of clichés in fairly meaningless situations.

Professor Cronkhite's book explores the nature and problems of persuasion by delineating the processes of communication research. The discussion is divided into three parts. First, there is a presentation in synthetic form of hypotheses which communication researchers have put forward, including an excellent treatment of the vexing problem: How ought the subject of persuasion be defined? Second, Professor Cronkhite outlines crucial disagreements between theoreticians, thereby indicating areas and problems where additional research is necessary. This debate over hypotheses is followed, in a third section, by a discussion of research approaches. Two theses are keys to his treatment of research: a methodology borrowed from techniques of psychologists and social-psychologists; an approach which is essentially described behaviorally and measured experimentally. Thus the student is introduced to relevant material from other disciplines; he better understands how a communication researcher goes about his work; he comprehends persuasion as a behavioral study. Such a point-of-view should doubtless be presented early to the student of persuasion for his guided consideration, since it is an argument with fundamental ramifications for the study of speech communication.

Persuasion is an introductory text in the best sense of the word. The student is forearmed with ways of placing theories of persuasion in perspective and with ways of evaluating those theories. The book, however, is neither definitive nor conclusive. Students will find in this description of the contentions, problems, and methods of thought of scholars of persuasion a significant guide and strong incentive for further study in persuasion.

Russel R. Windes

Contents

3. *Psychological theories of persuasion* 49

4. *The paradigm of persuasion* 74

Persuasion

SPEECH AND BEHAVIORAL CHANGE

ONE

A definition of persuasion

For an author to announce that he will "define" a word such as "persuasion" might be considered painfully presumptuous. If one listens to the semanticists, "general" or otherwise, or to the linguists, "psycho" or otherwise, he knows that the "real" meaning of a word is unique to a given individual at a given time in a given set of circumstances. The definition offered by a dictionary is only an attempt to provide a mold which will synthesize, compromise, or encompass all these unique meanings, vaguely specifying their common collateral and their outer limits. For a single individual to attempt such a feat without benefit of a systematic survey of the ways in which the word has been used would suggest an inordinate degree of self-esteem. That is not the intent of this chapter.

Neither is it intended to prescribe what the word "should" mean in order to maintain logic and purity in the language, for that seems equally presumptuous. The purpose of this chapter is simply to qualify the term "persuasion" as it will be used here. That term has been used to describe the focus of this book, and if it remained unqualified the reader might be led to expect too much for his money.

As a starting point, consider the simple definition of "persuasion" provided by Merriam-Webster's **New Collegiate Dictionary:** the "act of influencing the mind by arguments and reasons." That definition does not totally describe the focus of this book, however. I would like to qualify, in reverse order, the three specifications of this definition: (3) persuasion is an act, (2) it influences the mind, and (1) it does so by means of arguments and reasons.

The means of persuasion

Most people would not label a phenomenon as "persuasion" unless it involved communication. Occasionally one hears the statement, "He persuaded himself," but that use seems almost metaphorical. Also, the statement seems to imply that "he" is "communicating" with "himself," again probably in a metaphorical sense. The phenomenon of "self-persuasion," which will be dealt with later in the book, is the effect of a speaker's assertions upon himself, and certainly involves communication. Granted that the term "persuasion" is sometimes applied in situations which do not involve communication between individuals, nevertheless the existence of communication between individuals will be considered a necessary or defining characteristic of "persuasion" for the purposes of this book.

To say that "persuasion" necessarily involves communication is not to say much, however, for "communication" is at least as difficult to define. Does one neuron "communicate" with another? Does it "persuade" the other? Do amoebas "communicate" and "persuade"? Does thunder "communicate" the message that rain is on the way and "persuade" the hearer to seek shelter? Does the cawing of crows and the sound of the beaver's tail slapping the water "communicate" the message that danger is approaching and "persuade" the other forest animals to take appropriate evasive action? Certainly the terms are used in that sense. Without pausing to debate the merits of such usage, I would merely like to specify that, again for the purposes of this book, "persuasion" must involve the manipulation of "symbols," in the sense in which Morris (1955)* uses that term. That is, "persuasion" does not occur when a sign which constitutes a mere signal, a natural response to or accompaniment of an event, fortuitously "communicates" a message which produces a change in behavior on the part of the observer. The sign which "persuades" has the characteristics of a symbol: it is deliberately and arbitrarily specified as a sign of its significate (the thing for which it stands), and does not necessarily bear any natural relationship to that significate. Thus thunder **signals**

* Reference material is listed at the end of each chapter.

the approach of rain, but does not **symbolize;** thus it does not "persuade" in the present sense. Neurons and amoebas certainly **signal** each other, but there is no evidence that they symbolize and thus "persuade." The cases of the crow and the beaver are less clear. If one believes that the cawing and tail-slapping are signs which the animals have arbitrarily agreed will symbolize the approach of danger, one might still say they constitute "persuasion." However, if one believes they are merely **responses** to the approach of danger, which the other animals have learned to interpret, as they have learned to interpret the rustling of leaves, then no "persuasion" occurs in the present sense.

It becomes a nice question, then, whether such things as the massing of Red Chinese troops on the Indian border or the burning of a cross on a new neighbor's lawn constitute "persuasion." Do girls in bikinis clustered around the Aston-Martin stand at an auto show "persuade" potential customers? Again, without entering the fray, I will merely say that this book will be concerned primarily with verbal "persuasion," treating non-verbal elements only insofar as they complement the verbal. To be even more restrictive, the primary focus here will be upon oral rather than written persuasion, although many of the experiments cited have been conducted with written messages, and much of what will be said can be applied to situations in which the message is written. As suggested earlier, the book will deal with the phenomenon of "self-persuasion," since it seems to be an integral part of the persuasive process. Further, most of the analysis will be general enough to apply to both audience and small group situations.

The discussion to this point should prompt the inference that the use of force will not be considered a part of "persuasion." Minnick's example, "For nothing doth persuade reluctant man or maid so thoroughly as a bullet through the brain," certainly suggests that the term "persuasion" is sometimes applied to the use of force; but as Minnick (1957) indicates, the use seems metaphorical rather than literal. Festinger, on the basis of his research on the effects of a *fait accompli* (see Festinger, Rieken, and Schachter, 1955), and Bettelheim (1958), on the basis of research on "identification with the aggressor," have argued that the use of force **does** change attitudes, but since it does not necessitate symbol manipulation it will not be included.

More interesting is the question of whether the use of **threat** or

coercion constitutes "persuasion." Frankly, the first temptation was to exclude it. However, Kelman (1961) has raised an interesting question, theorizing that threat affects behavior but attitude and belief do not necessarily change. Further, it is sometimes difficult to decide when a speaker is threatening to take action which an audience will regret if they do not comply and when he is simply warning them of consequences which will ensue if they do not accept his proposition. Did President Kennedy **persuade** Khrushchev to withdraw Russian missiles from Cuba, for example? Again, whether one cares to call it "persuasion," the use of verbal threat will be compared to types of influence which are more conventionally labeled "persuasion."

Thus, in order to be considered an instance of "persuasion" for present purposes, a phenomenon must involve not only communication but also the use of symbol manipulation. Further, the focus of the book will be upon "persuasion" which is primarily verbal, with special attention to that which is oral. This means that instances of the use of force will be excluded from our definition of persuasion, but phenomena which might be classified as instances of threat, self-persuasion, or group discussion will be included.

The effects of persuasion

The definition used as the starting point for this discussion specified that an act must "influence the mind" in order to qualify as "persuasion." Without quibbling unduly over the use of the term "mind," which does not occupy a very esteemed place in the contemporary literature of psychology, that specification will be cautiously accepted. However, the discerning reader may have noticed that this book is titled **Persuasion: Speech and *Behavioral* Change.** Does this indicate that the author is deliberately limiting this present discussion to that "persuasion" which not only "influences the mind" but influences behavior as well, or does it imply that **any** "persuasion" which "influences the mind" necessarily influences behavior as well? The answer is a qualified "neither," which should set some sort of record for evasive ambiguity.

This question of the relation between "attitudes" and "behavior" has plagued social psychologists for some time. The well-known study by LaPiere (1934), conducted in the middle thirties, seemed to show that "attitudes" bore no necessary relation to "actions." If this were true, it might make the job of defining "persuasion" somewhat more difficult, at least if one were to define the word by reference to effects. Certainly some resolution of the problem is necessary before one can specify the effects or intended effects of persuasion.

LaPiere traveled through the United States with a Chinese couple. The trio was accommodated in 66 hotels and 184 restaurants and was refused only once due to the couple's race. After the trip, LaPiere mailed questionnaires to the hotels and restaurants asking whether they would accept Chinese guests. The replies were overwhelmingly negative with 92 percent of the restaurants and 91 percent of the hotels claiming they would not accommodate Chinese.

This, although probably the most often cited, is not by any means the only study which seemed to indicate a disparity between "attitude" and "behavior." The evidence prompted Arthur Cohen (1964) to make this recent statement:

> Most of the investigators whose work we have examined make the broad assumption that since attitudes are evaluative predispositions, they have consequences for the way people act toward others, for the programs they actually undertake, and for the manner in which they carry them out. Thus attitudes are always seen as precursors of behavior, as determinants of how a person will actually behave in his daily affairs. . . . Until experimental research demonstrates that attitude change has consequences for subsequent behavior, we cannot be certain that our procedures for inducing change do anything more than cause cognitive realignments. [pp. 137 and 138]

A recent article by Leon Festinger (1964) also deals with this general problem, although from a slightly different point of view. His argument is that, while "attitudes" do seem to be related to "behavior" under certain carefully controlled conditions, there is not much evidence that "attitude" **change** is related to "behavior" **change.** As evidence that "attitudes" bear a demonstrable relation to "behavior," he cites the experiment by DeFleur and Westie (1958), in which 23 college students having the most favorable attitudes toward Negroes and 23 having the most unfavorable attitudes toward Negroes were selected from an initial group of 250. Each student was then asked to have his picture taken with a Negro of the opposite sex. If he agreed, he also was asked to sign a "photo release statement" which was designed to indicate the extent to which he was willing to have the photograph used as publicity. The liberal group showed greater willingness to have the photograph taken and widely publicized than did the bigoted group. The difference, while small, was statistically significant.

Festinger does not waste much time rejoicing, however. He immediately points to three studies which he believes indicate that "attitude" **change** is not very useful in predicting "behavior" **change.**

Maccoby, et al. (1962), for example, interviewed mothers concerning the age at which toilet training should begin. Half of these mothers then received a communication arguing that toilet training should be delayed. All were again interviewed, and the group receiving the communication was found to have changed attitudes significantly in the expected direction. A later interview, however, revealed that the mothers receiving the communication actually trained their own children **earlier** than did the mothers who received no communication.

Festinger also cited a study by Fleishmann, et al. (1955), in which a group of foremen in industry had been given a two-week training course designed to persuade them that they should show greater personal warmth when dealing with subordinates. Questionnaires administered before and immediately after the two-week period showed that the program was effective in changing attitudes, but independent ratings of subsequent behavior did not differ significantly from ratings of a control group which had not been involved in the program.

Finally, Festinger argues that the Janis and Feshbach (1953) experiment, in which subjects heard either a strong fear appeal or a mild fear appeal for better dental hygiene, can be reinterpreted to support his thesis. His contention is that the questionnaire which Janis and Feshbach administered immediately after the communication, with which they intended to measure "anxiety," could be considered an "attitude" test of sorts, while their criterion measure, the reports of the subjects of improvements in their dental hygiene, could be considered an indication of "behavior" change. The test showed that subjects who heard the strong fear appeal were more "anxious" (or more favorable toward improved dental hygiene, by Festinger's interpretation) but did not improve their dental hygiene as much as did subjects who heard the weak fear appeal.

Festinger's explanation for all this is that individuals hearing a message contrary to their own opinions may show an immediate attitude change, but may later seek support for their original opinions. Thus their subsequent behavior may not only not change, but may actually be the opposite of that urged by the communication.

The conclusion Festinger reaches seems quite reasonable. The problem is that neither the conclusion nor the studies on which it is based have any necessary relevance to the relation between "attitude" change and "behavior" change. Note that in all three studies "attitudes" were measured shortly after the communication, but "behavior" was observed much later—more than a year later, in one case. It may well be that, had "attitudes" also been tested at the later date, they would also have been found to revert and to be in line with "behavior" at that time. An experiment by Biddle (1966) has since demonstrated that "attitudes" toward legalized wiretapping showed a significant correlation of .65 with the "behavior" of signing a petition urging that action be taken, **when both "attitudes"** and **"behavior" were observed immediately after a speech on the topic.**

Since the experiments cited by Festinger seem to have confounded the effect of the time of testing so as to provide no real answer to the question of whether "attitudes" predict "behavior," and since there are some fairly obvious methodological problems in the LaPiere study, it probably would be possible to deprecate the experimental evidence and avoid the basic question entirely. However, I am convinced that there **are** many times that "attitudes" do not predict "behavior" in the sense in which those terms have heretofore been used in the psychological literature. I would prefer to analyze the question at issue here in order to arrive at a restatement of the basic problem, and then attempt to provide some explanations of difficulties which still remain.

To ask whether "attitudes" predict "overt behavior" is to ask a rather strange question, because **we have no measure of "attitudes" except "overt behavior."** An attitude test response is certainly behavior, and is certainly overt as well, although it may not require quite as much energy as a lynching. On the other hand, to participate in a lynching can certainly be interpreted as a response to an attitude test, in that an observer is certainly likely to infer that the participants hold certain attitudes toward their victims and toward law enforcement. That is, **"overt behavior" may be viewed as an attitude test response.**

From this point of view, the question may be rephrased: To what extent does behavioral response to any given formal structured paper-and-pencil attitude test correlate with behavioral response in an unstructured situation? The problem of low correlation looks somewhat different if approached as a problem of low correlation between two tests.

First, in the case of the study by LaPiere, the lack of correlation may be explained on the basis of "item difficulty" (see Segall, 1964). Briefly, we know that because an individual correctly answers an easy item on an IQ test, for example, is no indication that he will correctly answer a more difficult item. No one sees any inconsistency in the fact that the one item is answered correctly and the other incorrectly. Similarly, one might conceive of the "attitude" questionnaire in the LePiere study as being an easy item to pass, but it may have been much more difficult to refuse to accommodate the Chinese couple when they appeared in person. Thus it should hardly be viewed as inconsistent that nearly all respondents "passed" the easy item but about 92% "failed" the more difficult item. What would have indicated inconsistency would have been a number of establishments answering "yes" on the questionnaire but refusing to accept the Chinese couple when they appeared in person. This combination does not appear in LaPiere's data, so there is no evidence of inconsistency.

Secondly, two test items are likely to show high agreement if they impose very similar conditions upon the subject. A test of verbal intelligence, for example, may accurately predict success in college to the extent that it duplicates the conditions the subject will encounter in college and measures the success of his responses to such conditions. The LaPiere questionnaire was not very successful in duplicating the conditions of the actual confrontation.

For one thing, as is rather customary with paper-and-pencil attitude tests, the observed questionnaire behavior was elicited by a printed verbal stimulus, probably the word "Chinese." Doob (1947) has advanced the theory that "attitudes" are learned mediating responses which are elicited by a given stimulus and which in turn serve as stimuli to elicit an overt response. In his terms, the mediating responses elicited by the printed word "Chinese" may have been quite different from those elicited by the Chinese couple in person, and consequently the overt response was quite different. Somewhat similarly, the structural theorists have distinguished between "beliefs" about an attitude object and "attitudes" toward both the attitude object and the attributes which it is believed to possess (see Rosenberg, 1960, for example). In these terms, the stereotyped attributes which the respondents believed Chinese to possess may have been quite different from those actually possessed by the Chinese who presented themselves at the desk. Whereas the respondents may have believed that Chinese in general are dirty and inscrutable, and may have responded to those attributes, the specific Chinese couple were clean, candid, and generally pleasant. This is the explanation LaPiere himself chose, by the way. Put another way, the stimuli used to elicit the responses were different in the two cases, so of course the responses were different. Attitude tests usually use stereotypes as stimuli. It should not be surprising that a **stereotype** which is believed to possess attributes A, B, and C may elicit a response which differs from that elicited by a **specific stimulus** or stimulus complex, which may or may not possess attributes A, B, and C, but probably does possess additional attributes D through N.

Finally, in cases in which the results of a paper-and-pencil attitude test do not successfully predict other and more overt behavior, the temptation is to assume that the fault lies with the paper-and-pencil test. To the contrary, what has been termed "overt behavior"—behavior in the unstructured "real life" situation—is often a very poor test of attitudes.

For one thing, the reliability of behavior in a "real life" situation could not be expected to be very high (see Fishbein, 1965). It is, after all, a **one-item** test of attitude, and one-item tests are notoriously unreliable. Reliability of a test increases as a function of the number of items in the test, assuming that the quality of the items remains constant (Guilford, 1954, p. 391). Those who construct paper-and-pencil attitude tests invariably include several scales or items. Consequently an individual's score on a given attitude test at a given time is usually a fair indication of his score on the same test at some later time, and may even be a decent predictor of his score on a different attitude test. Behavior in "real life" is not usually so consistent. A member of the Ku Klux Klan on a visit to New York might still sit next to a Negro on a crowded bus due to numerous other factors present in the situation: The seat may be the only one available; he may be conforming to social pressure; or he may prefer the company of a Negro to the company of a "Damyankee." Despite the antipathy of the Ku Klux Klan for Jews, he might sit next to a Jew simply because he did not recognize the person to be Jewish. From observing many instances of an individual's behavior in response to Negroes, one might eventually infer that the individual likes or dislikes Negros, and might be able to predict his future behavior. If one observes enough responses, he may even be able to predict that the individual will receive a low score on a paper-and-pencil test of attitude toward Negroes. But if that prediction is incorrect, the inference need not be that the paper-and-pencil test is at fault; the low reliability of the "real life" item may be responsible.

Hovland and Sherif (1961) write that an attitude is inferred from a persistent and characteristic mode of reaction to a stimulus or stimulus class. Those of us who would purge scientific analysis of all mythology would prefer to say that attitude **is** a persistent and characteristic mode of reaction to a stimulus or stimulus class. This definition, of course, would be purely for the purpose of scientific description. The intent is not to state categorically that "attitudes" do not exist as feelings within an individual; the argument is that such a thing has no present operational utility, and is in danger of becoming the latest in a disheartening series of pseudo-explanations which have included the "theories" of "phlogiston," "faculties," and "drives." Not long after theorists begin to talk about a concept which has no specified operational definition, or talk about a concept as if it were separable from its operational definition, they are overcome by the temptation to explain phenomena by labeling them. Thus fire was at one time "caused" by the presence of "phlogiston," a man was moved to action by the operation of his "will," a rat explored a maze because he had an exploratory "drive." If this definition were allowed to persist, an audience would be said to reject a speaker because of their unfavorable "attitudes" toward him.

Even with this modification, the definition allows the theorist too much freedom to explain by labeling, because it speaks of a mode of reaction to a **stimulus class.** Some psychologists have become involved in a needless uproar just because they thought subjects **ought** to put the printed word "Chinese" and a neat couple with yellow skin into the same stimulus class and thus ought to respond to them similarly. Why define the word "attitude" so as to allow such subjectivity? I would prefer to define an "attitude" as **a cluster of evaluative or approach-avoidance behavior.** If two different situations show a consistent contingent relationship, they constitute an attitude. That is if, given a subject who performs behavior A in situation X, I know there is a high degree of probability that the same subject will perform behavior B in situation Y, **this constitutes an attitude.**

The question at issue thus becomes an empirical one—the extent to which one can predict evaluative or approach-avoidance behavior in one situation from evaluative or approach-avoidance behavior in another. Ultimately it is probably the extent to which the stimulus complexes (including exteroceptive and interoceptive cues, when identifiable) are similar, and the extent to which activation levels are similar, that determine the extent to which behavior in one situation is predictive of behavior in another. To the extent that the stimulus complexes and activation levels are different, accurate prediction depends on the observer's ability to make allowances for such differences.

Note that this approach obviates the whole question of whether "attitudes" predict "behavior," and does the same for the question of whether an act must influence behavior as well as the "mind" in order to qualify as persuasion. Recall Cohen's statement that "until experimental research demonstrates that attitude change has consequences for subsequent behavior, we cannot be certain that our procedures for inducing change do anything more than cause cognitive realignment."

This proposed approach is based on the assumption that we know nothing about cognitive realignment **except** through inference from changes in behavior, whether "our procedures for inducing change" have induced no more than the listener's willingness to nod his head in assent to the speaker's plea or no less than his willingness to lose his head in support of the speaker's cause.

Another issue which inevitably arises in any discussion of the meaning of "persuasion" concerns the distinction between informative and persuasive communication. It is difficult to conceive of a communication which would not change evaluative or approach-avoidance behavior in some way, and the point of view thus far expressed has been that symbol manipulation which causes behavior change constitutes persuasion. Examples of communications which are "purely informative" in this sense are hard to come by. Yet most people would agree that certain communications are more informative and less persuasive than others.

I would prefer to speak of the "informative" and "persuasive" **elements** or **dimensions** of a communication. To the extent that a communication introduces items of information new to the audience, one might label that communication "informative." To the extent that the communication produces change in the evaluative or approach-avoidance behavior of an audience, one might label it "persuasive." Thus a given communication is not likely to be purely informative, since it will be almost certain to change **some** evaluative or approach-avoidance behavior on the part of the audience, even if the change is in audience evaluation of the speaker. On the other hand, it is simply inconceivable that evaluative behavior of an audience could be changed by a communication which imparts no information; to say that a communication imparts no information seems to be a contradiction in terms. This approach allows for communications which are highly informative and highly persuasive, not very informative but highly persuasive, not very persuasive but highly informative, and for the overwhelming number of communications which are neither very informative nor very persuasive.

The locus of persuasion

Fotheringham (1966) has noted that both dictionary definitions and expert usage have applied the term "persuasion" to four phenomena: (1) the **intent,** (2) the **ability,** (3) the **discourse,** and (4) the **effects.** No deep analysis seems necessary here, for I will be interested in "persuasion" by any of these four definitions. If a speaker **intends** to alter the evaluative behavior of his audience but fails, it will be of interest to know why he failed. If a speaker has the **ability** to alter evaluative behavior, it will be interesting to analyze that ability. If **discourse** contains elements which alter or are intended to alter evaluative behavior, it will be of interest to identify and analyze those elements. Finally, any time the manipulation of symbols achieves the **effect** of altering evaluative behavior, it is persuasive by the proposed definition. It would be easy to get involved in a heated argument about the wisdom and propriety of using the term "persuasion" to cover all four of these phenomena. Such an argument might be interesting, but it certainly is not necessary. Each of these four phenomena will be dealt with at some time in this book. Personally, I would prefer to reserve the term "persuasion" for that situation in which a communication actually produces some change in evaluative or approach-avoidance behavior. Thus I will speak of the **intent** to persuade and the **ability** to persuade. When it becomes necessary to distinguish the act from its effect, I will use the terms "persuasive **discourse**" and "persuasive **effects.**"

Finally, despite all the modesty professed at the outset of this chapter, the reader will probably notice that the author has presented a fairly specific description of the class of phenomena to which the term "persuasion" should be applied, so the definition may as well be formalized. For the purposes of this book, then, **"persuasion" will refer to the act of manipulating symbols so as to produce changes in the evaluative or approach-avoidance behavior of those who interpret the symbols.** The remainder of the title, "Speech and Behavioral Change," should be taken to mean that the primary concern will be with **oral** persuasion.

REFERENCES

Bettelheim, Bruno. "Individual and Mass Behavior in Extreme Situations," **Readings in Social Psychology,** 3rd ed., Eleanor E. Maccoby, Theodore M. Newcomb, and Eugene L. Hartley, eds. New York: Henry Holt, 1958, pp. 300–310.

Biddle, Phillips R. "An Experimental Study of Ethos and Appeal for Over-Behavior in Persuasion." Unpublished doctoral dissertation, University of Illinois, 1966.

Cohen, Arthur R. **Attitude Change and Social Influence.** New York: Basic Books, 1964, pp. 137, 138.

De Fleur, M. L., and F. R. Westie. "Verbal Attitudes and Overt Act: An Experiment on the Salience of Attitudes," **American Sociological Review,** 23 (1958), 667–673.

Doob, Leonard. "The Behavior of Attitudes," **Psychological Review,** 54 (1947), 135–156.

Festinger, Leon. "Behavioral Support for Opinion Change," **Public Opinion Quarterly,** 28 (1964), 404–417.

———, Henry W. Rieken, and Stanley Schachter. "When Prophecy Fails," **Readings in Social Psychology,** 3rd ed., Eleanor E. Maccoby, Theodore M. Newcomb, and Eugene L. Hartley, eds. New York: Henry Holt, 1958, pp. 156–163.

Fishbein, Martin. This explanation was suggested in a lecture in a seminar in attitude change conducted at the University of Illinois, Spring 1965.

Fleishman, E., E. Harris, and H. Burtt. **Leadership and Supervision in Industry.** Columbus: Ohio State University, Bureau of Educational Research, 1955.

Fotheringham, Wallace C. **Perspectives on Persuasion.** Boston: Allyn and Bacon, 1966.

Guilford, J. P. **Psychometric Methods.** New York: McGraw-Hill, 1954, p. 391.

Hovland, Carl I., and Muzafer Sherif. **Social Judgment.** New Haven: Yale University Press, 1961.

Janis, Irving L., and Seymour Feshbach. "Effects of Fear-Arousing Communications," **Journal of Abnormal and Social Psychology,** 48 (1953), 78–92.

Kelman, Herbert C. "Processes of Opinion Change," **Public Opinion Quarterly,** 25 (1961), 57–78.

LaPiere, Richard T. "Attitudes versus Actions," **Social Forces,** 13 (1934), 230–237.

Maccoby, Nathan, A. K. Romney, J. S. Adams, and Eleanor E. Maccoby.

"Critical Periods," **Seeking and Accepting Information.** Stanford: Stanford University Press. Paris-Stanford Studies in Communication, Institute for Communication Research, 1962.

Minnick, Wayne C. **The Art of Persuasion.** Boston: Houghton Mifflin, 1957, p. 3.

Morris, Charles. **Signs, Language, and Behavior.** New York: George Braziller, 1955, pp. 23–27.

Rosenberg, Milton J. "A Structural Theory of Attitude Dynamics," **Public Opinion Quarterly,** 24 (1960), 319–340.

Segall, M. H. This explanation was suggested in a lecture in a seminar on attitude change, conducted at the University of Iowa, Spring 1964.

TWO

Rhetorical theories of persuasion

Like "persuasion," the term "theory" has been used in a great variety of ways. However, since "theory" is not the focus of this book, there is no need to dwell on its definition. When used here, the term "theory" will apply to a generalization about (or an explanation of) the relationships among observable phenomena, which encompasses all the data but goes beyond the data to provide new and testable predictions. This definition is not offered as "correct." It is merely a description of the sort of thing to be surveyed in this chapter. The word "theory" is used only as a shorthand symbol for the longer description.

The emphasis on **observable** phenomena and **testable** predictions excludes from the description much of the early writing on the topic of "rhetoric." A great deal of what was written in the classical, medieval, and early Renaissance periods dealt with **classification** of the factors involved in persuasion and with the **morality** of these factors and the morality of persuasion or rhetoric as a whole. Such considerations, while they may be of interest, do not qualify as theoretical considerations in the present sense. Classification is basic to a theory, of course, but a system which merely classifies without specifying relationships among the categories falls short of a theory by this definition. Moral pronouncements, on the other hand, often deal with phenomena which are hypothetical rather than observable, and seldom make testable predictions.

Many of these writers do make specific predictions about the ways in which an audience will respond to certain methods of persuasion, but these predictions appear to be based more upon past observation than upon analysis of the underlying causes. Admittedly, it may be possible to derive a fairly comprehensive rationale from an author's explicit statements. Aristotle's theory of the "good," for example, is certainly reflected in his **Rhetoric,** although never explicitly stated there.

It is probably accurate to say, then, that until publication of Campbell's **Philosophy of Rhetoric** in the eighteenth century, there was no explicit exposition of a comprehensive theory of persuasion. If nothing else, judicious use of such a statement should allow one to start arguments almost at will at speech department cocktail parties. It is not the purpose of this chapter to attempt support for the statement, but one would do well to keep it in mind while considering the major writers who dealt with the subject of persuasion before the eighteenth century.

Classical theories of persuasion

For the classical writers, the art of persuasion as it has been defined here was the art of rhetoric. Plato, for example, in his **Phaedrus,** represented Socrates as saying, "Is not rhetoric, taken generally, a universal art of enchanting the mind by arguments, which is practiced not only in courts of law and in public assemblies, but in private houses also, having to do with all matters, great as well as small?" Aristotle, in his **Rhetoric**, defined rhetoric somewhat similarly as "the faculty of discerning all the available means of persuasion."

Yet Plato, in his two rhetorical treatises, the **Gorgias** and the **Phaedrus,** made no attempt to explain the operation of persuasion. In fact, the primary concern in both of these works is more with the question of the ethics of rhetoric or persuasion than with the question of how persuasion may be accomplished. The earlier of the two dialogues, the **Gorgias**, amounts to an attack on rhetoric as an "artifice of persuasion," the "shadow of politics." Plato, using a surrogate Socrates as his mouthpiece, argues that rhetoric, by giving speakers the power to make the good appear evil and evil appear good, does a disservice to both speaker and audience. He admits in passing that it is conceivable for rhetoric to be used for the real good of both speaker and audience, but doubts that such a thing ever happens. In the

Phaedrus, Plato contrasts this evil rhetoric with a rhetoric which he outlines, in which the speaker is a combination of philosopher, logician, psychologist, and statesman and aims at the greatest good for his audience.

In the latter part of the **Phaedrus,** Plato engages in a little discussion of the principles by which persuasion may be accomplished, but the discussion seems almost incidental to his primary purpose. There is no attempt to explain **why** these principles operate, although the following passage seems to suggest he had such a theory:

> Oratory is the art of enchanting the soul, and therefore he who would be an orator has to learn the difference of human souls . . . they are so many and of such a nature, and from them come the differences between man and man. Having proceeded thus far in his analysis, he will next divide speeches into their different classes: . . . 'Such and such persons,' he will say, 'are affected by this or that kind of speech in this or that way,' and he will tell you why. The pupil must have a good theoretical notion of them first, and then he must have experience of them in actual life, and be able to follow them with all his senses about him, or he will never get beyond the precepts of his masters. But when he understands what persons are persuaded by what arguments, and sees the person about whom he was speaking in the abstract actually before him, and knows that it is he, and can say to himself, 'This is the man or this is the character who ought to have a certain argument applied to him in order to convince him of a certain opinion'; . . . he who knows all this and knows also when he should speak and when he should refrain, and when he should use pithy sayings, pathetic appeals, sensational effects, and all the other modes of speech which he has learned; . . . when, I say, he knows the times and seasons of all these things, then and not till then, he is the perfect master of his art. [Plato, **Phaedrus,** 271]

Aristotle's approach was considerably different. In more scientific fashion, he viewed the act of persuasion as a phenomenon of the physical world, and set about to describe it as he would any other. He considered the art of rhetoric to be a tool, amoral in itself, and useful to the moral and immoral alike. He outlined a system for classifying the various elements involved in the persuasive situation, and made many statements about which means of persuasion are most effective. Most of these statements appear to have been derived from observation, and many are capable of being tested experimentally. A comprehensive explanation of the way in which persuasion operates is not given in the **Rhetoric**, however. That is not to say that there should have been one. There is a school of thought, represented especially by B. F. Skinner, which holds that the social sciences are not even now ready for theories, that we should be doing much more observation and much less theorizing. If that is true today, it was much more true in Aristotle's time.

If there is anything that approaches a comprehensive theory in the **Rhetoric**, it is this: A speaker is most effective when he uses those lines of reasoning characteristically accepted by the types of persons represented in his audience to appeal to those motives which characteristically move these persons. This is reminiscent of the passage cited earlier from Plato's **Phaedrus,** but Aristotle develops the point throughout the entire **Rhetoric.** He describes the things that constitute happiness, virtue, and justice for most people; he describes the emotions of people in general and the means by which they may be aroused; he analyzes the attitudes and modes of thought characteristic of persons of different ages and circumstances; he considers the types of reasoning most likely to be accepted by audiences in general; and he has something to say about the types of language and organization which will be generally most appealing. Unfortunately, like so many "theories," this one is close to a tautology: It is not very informative to say that, in order to be most effective with his audience, a speaker must use those means of persuasion most effective with his audience. It is useful, however, to emphasize that those lines of argument which the speaker considers most "valid" may not be those most likely to persuade an audience, and those which persuade one audience may not persuade another. The accomplished speaker may view this as a rather primitive truism, but it is a basic principle of persuasion which beginning speakers seem to learn rather slowly, especially when their audiences consist of other students similar to themselves and to each other. Aristotle's **Rhetoric** represents, at the least, a very early elaboration of this fundamental principle.

The rhetorical works of Cicero were practical handbooks for the speaker who intended to be persuasive. Like Aristotle, Cicero did not have a great deal to say about the ethics of persuasion. He himself was a very successful speaker, and the methods of persuasion which he suggested in **De Inventione, De Oratore,** the **Orator,** the **Brutus,** and **De Partitione Oratoria** are probably those which he believed were responsible for his own success. He wrote at one point in **De Oratore:**

I believe the force of all the precepts is this, not that orators by following them have gained distinction for eloquence, but that certain men
have observed what men of eloquence have done of their own accord
and have deduced the precepts therefrom. Thus eloquence is not born
of the theoretical system; rather the system is born of eloquence (I,
xxxii, 146).

The scheme of classification that Cicero used was more elaborate
than that of Aristotle, and his analysis of the means by which persuasion may be accomplished was more thorough and specific. However, he made no attempt to explain **how** persuasion operates; specifying the means by which it is accomplished seems to have been
enough. The same may be said for Quintilian, whose analysis followed
Cicero's in both time and form, and is not only thorough and specific
but exhaustive and exhausting.

To say that Aristotle, Cicero, and Quintilian have no **comprehensive** explanations of how persuasion takes place may be somewhat
misleading, however. Certainly all three authors make statements
about how persuasion may be achieved, and one may derive testable
predictions from some of these statements. Without pretending to
be exhaustive, or even very thorough for that matter, I would like to
briefly survey the rhetorical systems of these three major classical
writers. The influence of their systems has been of tremendous importance. The study of rhetoric or persuasion until at least the
eighteenth century is not much more than a study of the ways in
which succeeding writers rearranged and rephrased essentially the
same material. Even today, writers in the field of speech tend to
judge new treatments of persuasion by comparing them to and con-
trasting them with the works of Aristotle, Cicero, and Quintilian.

Ehninger (1963) has pointed out that "at least eight characteristics
remained stable enough to warrant description" during the classical
period of rhetorical theory, generally considered to extend from late
in the seventh century B.C. into the fifth century A.D.

First, the art of persuasion was considered to consist of the "five
great arts," "canons," or "officia" of invention, disposition, style,
memory, and delivery. "Invention" was the art of discovering arguments which could be used to persuade a specific audience. Aristotle,
for instance, wrote that the speaker must persuade by use of "enthymemes" and "examples," which were analogous to the deduction and
induction of logic, but were adapted to the requirements of the per-

suasive situation and to the specific audience. "Disposition" was the art of arranging or organizing arguments in the speech. "Style," or "elocutio," was the art of choosing and using language effectively. "Memory," usually treated in more detail then than now, was the art of recalling one's ideas vividly "at the moment of utterance," to borrow Bryant and Wallace's phrase. "Delivery," or "pronuntiatio," was the art of presenting the speech with effective use of voice, body, and toga.

Second, Ehninger points to two characteristic patterns by which classical rhetorical treatises were organized: according to the five canons just mentioned, or according to the customary parts of the speech, which were usually called the exordium or introduction, narration of the facts of the case, confirmation or proof, refutation, and peroration or conclusion.

Third, classical writers classified speeches according to the occasion or circumstance in which they were delivered: The deliberative speech was delivered before the legislative or popular assembly and generally urged a course of future action; the forensic speech was delivered in the court of law; and the epideictic speech was delivered on special ceremonial occasions and was generally commemorative, designed to praise or condemn individuals or past actions.

Fourth, Ehninger notes that three modes of artistic proof were generally distinguished, those being termed by Aristotle "ethos," "logos," and "pathos." These three might be considered subdivisions of the art of invention, and were considered to be quite distinct from one another, in theory if not in practice. "Ethos," or ethical proof, was persuasion by the moral force and character of the speaker, "logos" was persuasion by the logic of argument, and "pathos" was persuasion by appeal to the emotions. When Ehninger writes of these as modes of "artistic" proof, he refers to another distinction generally maintained by classical authors: that between "artistic" proofs, developed by the speaker within the speech, and "inartistic" proofs, those which are available before the speech, such as documents and prior testimony. Some writers did not classify "ethos" as totally artistic, incidentally; they considered the prior reputation of the speaker, since it is available before the speech, to be inartistic.

Fifth, the apparent intent of the classical theorists was to devise a system of analysis which the less capable and less inspired speaker could apply to any question and have some assurance that he would come up with arguments or amplification. Ehninger describes this system as consisting "first, of a scheme for cataloguing disputable questions; second, of the **status**; third, of the topics; and, fourth, of a description of the stages through which a dispute passes in approaching resolution." These systems were generally rather complicated, and differed from one author to another. The student who is interested in a detailed explanation would do well to consult the articles of Dieter (1950) and Hultzen (1958). If the question could be classified as one relating to common argument, the speaker should then, according to Cicero and Quintilian, attempt to determine whether it rests upon an issue of fact, definition, or quality. If, for example, a man is alleged to have murdered his wife, one would try to decide which of the following is the crucial issue:

1. What act did the man actually commit?
2. Did that act constitute murder?
3. Was the act justified?

The crucial issue would be termed the **status** or **stasis,** the point at which the argument initially (and temporarily) comes to rest, the initial point of clash. Out of this initial confrontation, a new line of argument may develop, and a new crucial issue or point of **stasis** will develop. Thus, if the prosecution initially alleges that the man killed his wife and the act constituted murder, but the defense argues that the act was justified, the argument comes to rest on the question, "Was the act justified?" The prosecution might then argue that one is never justified in killing, and if the defense chose to refute this directly, the new point at issue would become, "Is a man ever justified in killing?" The system of the "topics" or "places" was essentially a list of the questions one might ask oneself in analyzing a question, the "topics" one might survey, or the "places" in which one might look for arguments or amplification. Quintilian, for example, lists the questions as "Why? or Where? or When? or How? or By what means?" Cicero's list includes the "places" of definition, contrast, similarity, dissimilarity, consistency, inconsistency, conjunction, repugnancy, cause and effect, and a number of others. The idea of the topics, as with the system of the **status,** was to provide a system by which a speaker could assure himself that he had performed an exhaustive analysis of the subject.

The remaining three characteristics of classical rhetoric as listed by Ehninger do not seem relevant to the present purpose. Briefly, he argues: Sixth, that the classical rhetoricians viewed rhetoric as totally concerned with persuasion; Seventh, maintained careful distinctions among the canons; Eighth, maintained a careful distinction between rhetoric and poetic.

Looking back at these major characteristics of classical rhetoric, it seems obvious that the primary concern was with a system of classifying the various questions which a speaker must face when he prepares and delivers a speech. These systems of classification, useful as they may be, do not constitute comprehensive explanations of or generalizations about the way in which persuasion operates. Thus, while they may be "theories" in a loose and popular sense, they are not "theories" in the technical sense in which I am using that term.

On the other hand, it is true that most of the classical writers made some specific, testable generalizations concerning the ways in which a speaker may most effectively persuade. I have already mentioned some of Aristotle's generalizations. Cicero also made testable predictions, as when he wrote that listeners are persuaded by evidence of the speaker's character and that the strongest arguments should be placed first and last. Quintilian argued that it is never effective to attack an argument which one's opponent has not mentioned, and believed that an idea may be emphasized by a pause. While these are specific predictions, they appear to be isolated from one another; there is no coherent articulation of a guiding principle, theory, or generalization from which they are derived. Consequently, even in looking at the specific recommendations of the classical authors, one is unable to conclude that they articulated any comprehensive theory in the present sense. Again, that is not to condemn them; there are many contemporary critics who contend that the field of persuasion is presently suffering from a superfluity of theories and a lack of basic research.

This survey has been rather cursory, and the reader has been asked to accept by faith some contentions too complicated to demonstrate in the available space. The student who is mildly interested and skeptical may wish to refer to more detailed accounts of the classical period, which can be found in a chapter in Clark's (1957) book titled "The Precepts of Rhetoric," in the first five chapters of Baldwin's (1924) volume, and in Kennedy's (1963) excellent and more recent treatment. The really careful student might profitably consult the primary sources themselves.

In the early fifth century A.D., St. Augustine wrote **De Doctrina Chris-**

tiana, of which the fourth book treated rhetorical theory. St. Augustine acknowledged Cicero as his source for this work, however, and it contains nothing that would qualify as a theory of persuasion. Similarly, Alcuin's rhetoric to Charlemagne, written in 794, is clearly Ciceronian in inspiration, and is not theoretical in the present sense.

Persuasion after the eclipse

The eclipse of learning that occurred between the eighth and thirteenth centuries apparently cast its shadow on the art of persuasion as well, for little is known of rhetorical theory during that time. Even the rhetorical treatises produced during the thirteenth, fourteenth, and fifteenth centuries were for the most part fragmentary and limited in scope. The English rhetorics of the sixteenth and seventeenth centuries, however, became more complete. They are described in Howell's (1961) treatment of logic and rhetoric in England during that period.

Howell describes the period from 1500 to 1700 as having consisted of three movements: the renaissance of "traditional," classical, and primarily Ciceronian rhetoric; a revolt against traditional rhetoric; and a movement which "pointed toward a new rhetoric."

The "traditional" rhetorics, while they all may be judged as depending heavily on Cicero, exhibited three distinct patterns. The first of these patterns consists of those rhetorics most faithful to Cicero, in that they treated most or all of the five canons of invention, disposition, style, memory, and delivery, placing the emphasis upon invention. The culmination of this approach appeared in Thomas Wilson's **The Arte of Rhetorique** published in 1553. Howell characterizes it as "giving an English version of Ciceronian theory," and the resemblance to Cicero's works is so close as to make what has been said about Cicero's approach apply almost equally well to that of Wilson.

The second of the traditional patterns Howell terms the stylistic, which treated all or most of the five canons, but emphasized style to the neglect of the others. The later stylistic rhetorics devoted a great deal of space to listing and describing the figures of speech. Henry Peacham's **Garden of Eloquence,** for example, published in 1577, which Howell says "brings to full maturity the English stylistic theory of rhetoric," describes 191 separate devices by which language may be embellished. Again, these elaborate systems of classification, while they included some predictions about the relative effectiveness of the various schemes and tropes, did not provide comprehensive explanations of the manner in which they operate to produce persuasion.

The third of Howell's traditional patterns is termed the "Formulary." In his words, "Formulary rhetoric is made up of compositions drawn to illustrate rhetorical principles and presented as models for students to imitate. . . ." The basis of these works was in the Ciceronian approach, and the illustrations, of course, added nothing theoretical to that approach.

A Frenchman by the name of Peter Ramus initiated the revolt against traditional rhetoric of which Howell speaks, as a part of his plan for reorganizing the liberal arts. The revolt, however, was not much more than a reorganization of the traditional subject matter of rhetoric, and does not seem to be of basic concern to those interested in theories of persuasion. Essentially what Ramus and his student Talaeus proposed was that the canons of invention and disposition be considered a part of the discipline of logic, that treatment of delivery and the figures of language be made the province of rhetoric, and that treatment of memory in relation to public speaking be eliminated from the system. Rhetoricians since have been rather unhappy about this arrangement, since it eliminated from rhetoric what they and the classical authors have generally considered to be its heart: the study of invention. Thus rhetoric for a time became a study not of **what** to say, but of how to say it. This image of the rhetorician as being unconcerned with the truth of the ideas he advocates has led to his being maligned from the time of Plato to the present day, for it makes rhetoric appear to be an art of sham and trickery. The fact that such a view prevailed in England during the late sixteenth and most of the seventeenth centuries is of historical interest, but from the point of view of the theorist in persuasion the controversy seems to be primarily semantic. Certainly the speaker interested in persuading an audience must construct rational arguments and arrange them effectively, as well as phrase and deliver them.

New alternatives to the classical theories

During the seventeenth century, rhetoric turned slowly back toward the traditional approach based on Cicero's works. More important to this survey of pre-theories of persuasion, however, was the appearance of Francis Bacon's **The Advancement of Learning** and **De augmentis scientarium** early in the seventeenth century. The sections of these works devoted to rhetoric and to the "soul" presented what appears to be the first important new analysis of persuasion to appear after the classical period.

Bacon's first division of the soul is into the rational, "which is divine; the other of the irrational, which is in common with brutes." He argues that the irrational soul "is only the instrument of the rational soul. . . ." Another concept, "imagination," is introduced at this point. The term seems to cover most of the modern concept of "perception" and its closely allied "association." The senses themselves, however, are discussed separately from "imagination," so it does not cover all that may be included in the modern use of the term "perception." This "imagination" Bacon describes as the "director and driver of voluntary motion," which would sound astonishingly contemporary if it were rendered: "The perception and association of stimuli provide the cues and drives which direct and motivate behavior." This motivation, which Bacon apparently believed to have a physiological basis, so determines action that ". . . when the image which is the object of the motion is withdrawn the motion itself is immediately interrupted and stopped." This specific relation of reason and emotion is defined by Bacon as a function of imagination, which serves as a messenger between the understanding and reason on the one hand and the will, appetite, and affections on the other. He writes, ". . . this Janus of imagination has two faces. . . ," there is one "face toward reason" and another "face toward action."

When Bacon writes: "The duty and office of Rhetoric is to apply Reason to the Imagination for the better moving of the Will," he seems to be suggesting that rhetoric occupies a place between logic and ethics analogous to that which imagination occupies between reason and emotion. If the relationship is not explicit in the definition, it is certainly made clear in the following passage:

> For the end of logic is to teach a form of argument to secure reason, and not to entrap it; the end likewise of moral philosophy [ethics] is to procure the affections to fight on the side of reason, and not to invade it; the end of rhetoric is to fill the imagination with observations and images, to second reason, and not to oppress it. [**De aug.,** VI, IX, 132]

Bacon is not very clear as to what he means by "logic," however. In the passage just quoted, and in several others, he seems to use the term to refer to the art of argument, whereas at another point in **De**

augmentis scientarium he uses it to refer to what he had called the four Intellectual Arts in **The Advancement of Learning**. One of the Intellectual Arts includes rhetoric as a subdivision, which would seem to make rhetoric a **part** of logic. I have chosen to assume that in most cases Bacon uses the term "logic" to refer to the art of argument before a reasoning audience, apparently including invention and judgment.

Thus Bacon believed reason to be generally in command of man's nature, and considered it the duty of rhetoric to maintain that state of affairs. Because of "the violence of the passions," however, rhetoric must attend to that face of the imagination which overlooks the will, appetite, and affections. As Bacon expresses it:

> Again, if the affections themselves were brought to order, and pliant and obedient to reason, it is true there would be no great use of persuasions and insinuations to give access to the mind, but naked and simple propositions and proofs would be enough. But the affections do on the contrary make such secessions and raise such mutinies and seditions . . . that reason would become captive and servile, if eloquence of persuasions did not win the imagination from the affections' part, and contract a confederacy between the reason and imagination against them. [**De aug.**, VI, IX, 133]

It is interesting to compare this with Aristotle's statement in **De Anima,** 433a 24–26, that " . . . mind is never found producing movement without appetite . . . but appetite can originate movement contrary to calculation."

The distinction between reason and emotion and the function of rhetoric in relation to it may be most clearly seen in the following passage:

> For it must be observed that the affections themselves carry ever an appetite to the apparent good, and have this in common with reason; but the difference is that the affection beholds principally the good which is present; reason looks beyond and beholds likewise the future and sum of all. And therefore the present filling the imagination more, reason is commonly vanquished and overcome. But after eloquence and force of persuasion have made things future and remote appear as present, then upon the revolt of the imagination, reason prevaileth. [**De aug.**, VI, IX, 133–134]

In contemporary terms, Bacon might be said to believe that the motivation of behavior is dependent upon the salience of stimuli and therefore tends to be determined by stimuli which are proximate in time and space; reasoning behavior is that which is elicited at least in part by stimuli remote in time and space; and it is "the duty and office of rhetoric" to make these remote stimuli more salient by symbolic representation. Again, it is interesting to compare this with a statement from Aristotle's **De Anima,** 433b8–10, ". . . while mind bids us hold back because of what is future, desire is influenced by what is just at hand. . . . "

Many of Bacon's pronouncements, especially when rephrased in the idiom of contemporary psychology, sound remarkably current. One sometimes wonders if modern psychologists and rhetoricians have made more than occasional improvement upon his theory of the role of communication in relation to reason and emotion.

However, Bacon labored under a considerable handicap. He fastened upon both the vocabulary and the metaphor of the doctrine of the faculties, which attributed different types of behavior to different "faculties" of man's nature, such as the will, imagination, intellect, and emotions. As an explanation, this doctrine was teleological; that is, it was hardly any explanation at all. To attribute man's propensity to reason, for example, to a "faculty" called the "intellect," tells nothing further about how the process operates; it is simply using a label to avoid a true explanation. This is essentially the same as attributing the behavior to the ministrations of a benevolent entelechy: "We act that way because we were meant to act that way." An ancient "theory" of combustion was that wood burns because of the presence of "phlogiston." This sport of pseudo-explanation is not totally out of vogue, however, so we cannot be too severe with Bacon. It hasn't been too long since McDougall was attributing all kinds of behaviors to the operation of "instincts." An even more contemporary myth is that the fascination of organisms with novel stimulation is due to an "exploratory drive," which is no great improvement over faculty psychology. A second difficulty of the doctrine of the faculties is that it pictures man's nature as composed of entities operating independently, whereas since John Dewey it has been the fashion to emphasize man's unity.

If Bacon was guilty of "explaining" by merely labeling, he did not have a "theory" in the present, technical sense, because his "explanation" would not go beyond the data to make predictions. There is no denying that he does make some predictions, and others can be de-

rived from his pronouncements. The basic, comprehensive explanation, however, that persuasion is attributable to the operation of un-
defined and unobservable "faculties," does not seem to yield any de-
rivable predictions, is consequently untestable in the form in which
Bacon stated it, and therefore fails to meet the requirements of the
present definition. That is not to say that his scheme lacks utility
as a framework for thinking about and teaching persuasion.

Bacon also seems to be open to the charge that he vivisects a
living, breathing, unified organism into a multiplicity of entities operating independently. His treatment is no worse than those of some
modern speech textbooks which treat the parts of a speech as if each
had a separate function appealing to separate elements in a psychological sequence, nor is it worse than those which deal with speeches
to inform, arouse, or activate. Still, it could be more sophisticated.

The reader interested in a more complete description of Bacon's
specific suggestions as to how the speaker may persuade should refer
to a book by Karl Wallace (1943). The enumeration of these suggestions
is not really within the scope of this chapter.

Strictly speaking, my intention in this chapter has been to survey
comprehensive explanations of how persuasion operates rather than to
survey ideas of what a speaker should do in order to persuade successfully. Occasionally, however, it is impossible to maintain that
distinction, and at other times I have digressed because I felt the
reader needed to know what writers such as Plato, Aristotle, Cicero, and
Quintilian **were** saying in order to understand why their systems were
not theories in the present sense. At this point I feel it is wise to consider a controversy that arose over what was primarily a question of
the means by which a speaker may find those arguments which are
most effective. What may appear to be a brief digression seems justi-
fiable in that it deals with an important development in the history of
rhetorical "theory" in the nontechnical sense.

Invention, for the classical authors, was a process of discovering
lines of argument, and was thought to be accomplished by a careful
search of a catalogue of "topics" or "places." The writers surveyed so
far took little issue with this notion. Bacon argued that the process is
totally a matter of discovery or even recollection rather than invention;
he compared it to the pursuit of a deer in an enclosed park. However,
he did not challenge its usefulness. The first really damaging attack
upon the system occurred in Bernard Lamy's **Art of Speaking,** often

called the **Port-Royal Rhetoric,** first published in English in 1676. Lamy argues that a speaker who understands his subject and is well informed has no need of the topics, because he will perceive the crucial issues and will know the most effective lines of argument. He disagreed with the notion that amplification should consist of many arguments derived from the topics or "commonplaces":

> . . . To persuade, we need but one Argument, if it be solid and strong, and that Eloquence consists in clearing of that, and making it perspicuous. All those feeble Arguments . . . deriv'd from Commonplaces, are like ill Weeds that choke the Corn." [pt. V, p. 106]

Fénelon's **Dialogues on Eloquence,** first published in English in 1722, was a more forceful and cogent attack on traditional logic and invention in rhetoric, but the general point of view was similar.

Somewhat analogous was an attack on the catalogue of figures of speech which had its beginning in the classical period and grew until it contained 191 items by 1577. During the seventeenth century, probably assisted by Bacon's notion that rhetoric should be clear in order to aid transmission of information in the sciences, there developed a demand for less embellishment of language, and a preference for plain style and the language of the layman. For example, Joseph Glanvill's attack in **An Essay Concerning Preaching,** published in 1678, complained that "there is a bastard kind of eloquence that is crept into the Pulpit, which consists in affectations of wit and finery, flourishes, metaphors, and cadencies."

Another development, of more importance historically than theoretically, was the revival of interest in Aristotle's **Rhetoric** which began about this time and seems to have culminated in the rhetorics of Lawson and Ward in the early eighteenth century.

Ehninger (1963) has argued that the rhetorics of Campbell and Blair in the late eighteenth century and that of Whately in the early nineteenth century "stand as the great watershed that divides earlier from modern rhetorical thought." He contends that these three rhetorical treatises represent a significant break from classical theory and that they have exerted considerable influence upon modern theory.

Blair's chief contribution to rhetoric was to greatly broaden its scope, overtly advocating treatment of expository as well as persuasive discourse, and including criticism of written and even poetic communication. Again, this is of historical interest to rhetoricians, but hardly concerns one whose specific focus is upon persuasion.

In **The Philosophy of Rhetoric** of George Campbell, published in 1776, Campbell propounded what Ehninger has called a "psycho-epistemological" theory of persuasion, the first, I believe, which is clearly a theory in the present sense, with the possible exception of Bacon's treatment.

Ehninger lists a number of ways in which Campbell's rhetoric differs from classical theory. It is not organized by either the canons or the parts of the speech, but rather "through an abstract analysis of how men think and know, how they are aroused and stirred to action. . . ." Campbell does not classify speeches as deliberative, forensic, or epideictic, according to the function of the "judge" or audience, but instead classifies them according to the purpose of the speaker. He does indicate much more clearly than did the classical authors that the forms of proof (logos, pathos, and ethos in Aristotle's system) work together to achieve persuasion; the speaker must first dwell upon audience motives and then demonstrate how they may be satisfied. He does not propose any artificial scheme for finding arguments. In fact, he does not treat "invention" in any one place in his rhetoric, and what discussion there is of the means by which arguments are composed and chosen is heavily oriented toward analysis of the way in which the listener thinks. Campbell gives a considerably different view of ethos or ethical appeal, arguing that the force of the speaker's character in persuasion depends not upon his "essential goodness," but upon the audience's subjective observation and evaluation of him. He denies that the syllogism is useful in discovering arguments or in advancing them.

Finally, Ehninger concludes his list of Campbell's departures from classical doctrine by saying that his theory of how persuasion operates depends on two crucial concepts: the "lively" idea and the "vivacity" of testimony. Since this is what I consider to be the first testable explanation of how persuasion operates, I would like to consider it in more detail than does Ehninger.

First, I would say that the two basic tenets of Campbell's theory differ slightly from Ehninger's statement of them: The first is that belief depends upon the "vivacity" of an idea, and the second is that a certain vivacity is inherent in or instinctively attached to certain propositions, which may then be used as the basis for establishing others.

Campbell divided the means of knowledge into two major types, intuitive and deductive. He believed deduction depends upon the mediation of inference through a third term, while intuition occurs as soon as the terms of the proposition are understood, requiring no inference.

Intuitive knowledge is said to be based upon intellection, consciousness, or common sense. Intellection often seems to be no more than a process of definition, as "all the points on the circumference of a circle are equidistant from the center," but sometimes may be more useful, as in the statement "twice five is ten." Knowledge from consciousness might be exemplified by the simple awareness of a patch of color. Knowledge from common sense is derived from certain intuitive axioms, without which Campbell says any sort of reasoning would be impossible, as exemplified by the statements: "There are material substances independent of the mind's conceptions," "The future will resemble the past," "Whatever has a beginning has a cause," and "The clear representations of my memory, in regard to past events are indubitably true." The axioms of common sense are of particular importance to us and will be dealt with in more detail later, as it is on this point that Campbell disagrees with Hume.

Deductive knowledge is said to be composed of two types, demonstration and moral evidence. Demonstration consists simply of a chain of self-evident axioms leading to a conclusion. It is distinguished from intuition by the fact that it is a chain, and thus depends upon inference mediated by intervening terms.

None of the types discussed thus far give any indication of matters of fact or of the relations between things. All but consciousness deal with abstractions, and therefore are not applicable to specific matters of fact, and consciousness provides data concerning only the present moment in time, and thus cannot provide the basis for any other knowledge.

It is moral evidence that provides knowledge of specific cases, and its scope is probably greater than the others combined; it is the basis of speculation concerning objects and occurrences remote in time or space and thus not perceptible. It is composed of three types: experience, analogy, and testimony. Another type, the calculation of chances, is also discussed under this division, although Campbell believed it to be a combination of demonstration and moral evidence.

Campbell does not use the word "experience" in any esoteric sense, so it should suffice to say that he believes the certainty of conclusions from experience depends both upon the number of examples observed and upon the uniformity of these examples. His discussion of analogy provides a third criterion, for he considers it a less direct form of experience, the strength of which is proportionate to the amount of resemblance. Testimony is "a serious intimation from another, of any fact or observation, as being what he remembers to have seen, or heard, or experienced." Its ability to induce belief is said to be drawn primarily from an instinctive human inclination to believe what is told, in the absence of contradictory facts, and only secondarily from experience with the veracity of others. It is held to be even more effective than experience. The calculation of chances is used when the causes are not so well known as to make the outcome predictable. It is partly demonstration, as illustrated by our calculation of the probabilities involved in a roll of dice, but may also be based upon experience, as when an insurance company calculates its probabilities.

Most students have considered Thomas Reid and John Locke to be Campbell's primary sources. Lloyd Bitzer, however, has brilliantly and systematically demonstrated that Campbell depended primarily upon Hume.

He has offered convincing evidence that, while Hume does not divide his discussion of intuitive evidence, Campbell apparently follows his lead when speaking of intellection and of consciousness. He contends successfully that Campbell's ideas of the common sense axioms, while undoubtedly inspired by Reid's, differ from them more than they agree. Campbell and Hume are found to make the same divisions in deduction, while Locke and Reid do not. While the ideas of demonstration are very similar in the works of all four men, they are not given as much emphasis by Campbell and Hume. Bitzer continues to argue convincingly that Campbell's general idea of moral evidence is drawn from Hume, and specifically that their treatments of experience, analogy, and the calculation of chances are almost identical.

His argument attempting to establish the similarity of their beliefs with regard to testimony, however, is not so inspired. He argues that Campbell "grants nearly everything that Hume demands." Now it is true that Campbell briefly suggests that testimony depends in some measure upon experience, as we have already seen, and that this is probably some concession to Hume. However, this had been a major point of controversy between the two before the **Rhetoric** was published, and two quotations will illustrate that Campbell had not succumbed:

. . . testimony, antecedently to experience, hath a natural influence on
belief . . .

. . . it must be owned, that in what regards single facts, testimony is more
adequate evidence than any conclusions from experience.

The disagreement is important only insofar as it indicates that
Campbell was prepared to disagree with Hume when the occasion demanded, and not so quick to acquiesce as Bitzer seems to think. As we
will see in a moment, Campbell took occasion to differ again at a more
crucial point, and again on the ground that the affirmation of instinct
is adequate evidence of truth without any reference to experience.

Both men agree that it is only moral evidence that allows us to make
inferences about things in the real world. **Moral evidence induces
belief through an instinctive process, by which a natural vivacity is
imparted independently of either sense or reason.** A basic disagreement develops at this point, however. Campbell and Hume agree that
the axioms of common sense (upon which moral evidence depends)
are instinctive and affirmed by the vivacity imparted to them by nature.
Campbell argues, however, that **this vivacity is adequate proof of their
truth,** that "such instincts are no other than the oracles of eternal
wisdom," and thus escapes skepticism at the last moment. Hume believes the axioms are questions of fact which are to be decided by
experience. Since they **cannot** be decided by experience, **there is no
real evidence of their truth.**

Thus Campbell finally relied on the vivacity instinctively attached
to common sense axioms as a source of truth. It is possible to argue
that belief in these axioms is not necessarily instinctive, and it should
be possible to test the question by empirical observation. Four of the
axioms mentioned by Campbell are these: (1) The future will resemble
the past; (2) whatever has a beginning has a cause; (3) the clear
representations of my memory are . . . indubitably true; and (4) there
are material substances independent of the mind's conceptions. The
question here is not whether the axioms are true or false, but whether
an individual's belief in them is a product of learning or is instinctive.
There is, for example, no reason to believe that a newborn infant ever
expects its earliest sense impressions to be repeated. Not many hours
of life pass, however, before certain of these sensations **are** repeated,
and thus the expectation may be learned. Campbell therefore has no
justification for attributing to instinct our propensity to expect re-
currence of sense impressions.

Similar arguments could be constructed with regard to the other axioms. The important thing here, however, is not that the theory is probably wrong; it is that Campbell has given an explicit explanation of the way in which persuasion operates, and one which may be tested, albeit with some difficulty.

Joseph Priestley, best known for his discovery of oxygen, also contributed greatly to the eighteenth-century rhetorical atmosphere. Like Campbell, he was persuaded by associational psychology. However, again like Campbell, his was an associational psychology which depended heavily upon the older psychology of the faculties, so that he writes of the passions, judgment, and imagination as relatively separate entities.

His rhetorical work, titled **A Course of Lectures on Oratory and Criticism,** was first published in 1761. Organized by the classical canons and traditional in treatment of some matters, this work might lead one to miss at first glance the fact that Priestley's rhetoric, like Campbell's, is more modern than classical. His concept of the function of rhetorical invention is similar to that of Bacon, for example. He writes that rhetorical invention is a process of recalling and selecting what has been discovered by other means. Thus his system of topics, rather traditional in appearance, is more a mnemonic device for the speaker than a system for **inventing** arguments. Consistent with his belief in the psychology of association, and depending especially upon his devotion to the "scientific method" as expressed by Bacon and Newton, he proposes two possible (but not necessarily alternative) patterns of argumentative organization: One may proceed from assumptions, granted by the audience, to their logical conclusions, or one may describe the process of investigation, which the speaker followed in reaching the conclusion, on the assumption that the audience will follow the same path. Priestley excludes ethical and emotional proof from his discussion of invention, where Aristotle originally discussed them, and introduces them as a part of his discussion of style, which includes whatever "affects the passions, judgment, and imagination." These are affected most by vivid representation so that the idea of reality occurs again by means of association.

As Bevilacqua and Murphy (1965) point out in their introduction to the recent reprint of Priestley's rhetoric, this notion of "vivid representation" which transported the audience into "ideal presence" is adopted quite directly from Henry Home's (Lord Kames) **Elements of**

Criticism, another eighteenth-century rhetorical work which may also have influenced Campbell. While Kames's work is hardly a treatise on persuasion, two things are worth noting about it: (1) he advanced the theory that the passions may be aroused by "vivid representation," as mentioned above, describing a large number of ways in which this "vivid representation" could be achieved; and (2) he was guilty of a "proliferation of innate causes for rhetorical effects," to quote Bevilacqua and Murphy again—that is, he attributed the efficacy of the rhetorical devices he recommended to the operation of something like McDougall's later instincts. Priestley argued that the devices operated instead by means of the principle of association. Campbell, as already noted, finally turned to the operation of instinct to explain persuasion, but he at least reduced the number of propositions affirmed by instinctive vivacity, whereas Kames postulated new instincts almost as fast as he encountered new rhetorical phenomena in need of explanation.

The approach formulated by Richard Whately in his **Elements of Rhetoric,** published in 1828, did not present any audience-oriented theory regarding the process of persuasion. For Whately, rhetoric was a part of logic, and the syllogism was the means by which it operated. The book gives the impression that it was intended as an essay on how persuasion **should** operate in order to produce a critical decision, rather than a description or explanation of how persuasion **does** operate. The description of the rules by which a dispute ought to be conducted, including especially the concepts of presumption and burden of proof and the tests of evidence and reasoning, would be more familiar to the student of the theory of argument than to the student of persuasion or rhetoric in general.

Three ideas in the book are especially important. The first of these is Whately's treatment of what the ancients called "ethos." In the **Elements of Rhetoric,** "ethos" is considered a part of pathos or emotional proof, since audience attitudes toward the speaker are "affections." Second, "testimony" is considered to be a sign of the occurrence of an event. Thus it is neither "inartificial" and outside the province of rhetoric, as the classical authors considered it, nor does it owe its efficacy to the operation of instinct, as Campbell believed.

The third and most important concept is that of "presumption" and its mirror image, "burden of proof." The concept is important to Whately because of his specification that the disputant who enjoys the presumption is not obligated to respond to the charges of his opponent until those charges have been so established that they will stand in the absence of contradiction. That the concept has contemporary importance is evidenced by the fact that modern textbooks in argumentation and debate invariably treat it as basic to the theory of argument, and it has been the subject of numerous recent articles in speech journals.

The use of the concept of presumption was and is fairly straightforward and well established by convention in legal argument, but Whately's attempt to adapt it to the field of extralegal argument is quite confusing. In legal argument, the defendant is said to be "presumed" innocent until proven guilty, and the one against whom a civil suit is brought is said to have the "presumption" until his opponent discharges the "burden of proof" by establishing a "prima facie case." In another sense, certain facts are "presumed" to follow from certain others. For example, a man seven years absent is "presumed" dead, although such a presumption is capable of being refuted. Some of these presumptions rest on legal definitions, however, and are thus incontestable, as the presumption that a child of less than seven years cannot commit a crime.

Bishop Whately's adaptation of the concept of presumption to extralegal argument is, strangely enough, quite useful to the adherent of an established religion such as that of the Anglican Church. He says there is a "habitual presumption" or "deference" which is accorded to an individual of good reputation, or to morality, "rectitude," orthodoxy, the "true, right, or expedient," or to "whatever accords with the natural laws of providence." Obviously difficulties are encountered when one tries to decide **before an argument** which side is moral, right and expedient, and it is especially difficult since this assignment of presumption depends in part, at least, on the attitudes of the audience or of people in general, which are not always accessible. A second type of presumption is described by Whately when he writes, "There is a presumption in favor of every **existing** institution," and this seems to be implied in his statement that presumption means a "preoccupation of the ground." This idea that the status quo always has the presumption and the individual who attacks the present system always has the burden of proof has been adopted by most contemporary textbooks in argumentation and debate. It creates some real problems when applied to "real-life" argument, however, since the status quo cannot always be identified. I have argued elsewhere (Cronkhite, 1966) that it is much more useful to require the party initiating a dispute to undertake the burden of proving his assertion. It is useful to remember, however, that there are at least three possible burdens which may fall upon an advocate: the burden of opposing audience consensus, the burden of opposing the inertia of the present system, and the burden of proving one's assertions.

Twentieth century theories

Almost a century later, in 1915, James A. Winans published his textbook titled **Public Speaking,** which seems to be based primarily upon the theory of attention of the psychologist William James. His approach seems to be an application to the public speaking situation of the "foundation principle of persuasion" that "what holds attention determines action." One of his central statements is that "persuasion is the process of inducing others to give fair, favorable, or undivided attention to propositions." Thus attention is used to define persuasion; it is specified as the ultimate goal of persuasion. If it sounds somewhat strange to make attention rather than belief the goal of persuasion, Winans clarifies the relationship somewhat when he writes: "Our belief and attention are the same fact." Much of Winans' book, of course, is devoted to instruction on how the speaker may get and hold audience attention.

Up to this point, 2500 years after the birthdate of rhetorical theory, it was still quite popular to distinguish between something like "logical argument," which ostensibly produces "conviction," and "emotional appeal," which is said to produce "persuasion" as well. However, Winans' book was hardly in print when this conventional distinction collided headlong with the apostles of John Dewey. Winans, in time-honored style, had used the terms "conviction" and "persuasion" in what Mary Yost and Charles Woolbert took to be two separate senses. Actually, Winans himself went so far as to suggest that the dichotomy was artificial. It would seem that this might have been enough to have excused him from the controversy, but it was not. The attack may have occurred just because his was the most recent prominent textbook at the time the controversy erupted. Whatever the reason, Woolbert set upon his book with such single-mindedness of purpose that the whole affair has come to be known as the Winans-Woolbert controversy.

Mary Yost fired the opening round in the **Quarterly Journal of Public Speaking** of April 1917:

Almost all the textbooks state that an argument effects its end by means of **conviction** and **persuasion**. With some variation in wording in the different books, the definitions of each term are practically the same; **conviction is an appeal to the reason, persuasion, an appeal to the emotions.**

Now this explanation of the terms **conviction** and **persuasion** was formulated when the belief held sway that the mind was divided into three compartments, the reason, the emotions, the will—roughly the assumptions of the old faculty psychology. Today, however, the leading psychologists have found these assumptions inadequate to explain the phenomena of the mind. A conception of the mind as an organic unit performing a particular function—reasoning, feeling, willing—as may be demanded by the situation the individual is meeting, has taken the place of the more rigid, formal idea. [110-111]

Charles Woolbert followed this in the next issue of the **Journal** with the contention that all the distinctions between "conviction" and "persuasion," "emotion" and " intellect," or "thought" and "action" were psychologically unsound and pedagogically undesirable. He began by arguing that any mental state produces action, even if it is only increased respiration and circulation. Thus he argued that the rhetoricians of the day were incorrect in saying that conviction produces only a decision, while persuasion produces action. He rejected other bases for the distinction also, including those based on the perceptibility, complexity, effort, duration, and rationality of the action involved.

Woolbert's attack upon the "conviction-persuasion duality" was long overdue, despite the fact that, when it came, the book that bore its brunt was probably the least offensive of those extant at the time. The controversy has sparked occasional rumblings in the speech journals since that time. Rowell, in 1934, attempted, unsuccessfully I believe, to refute Woolbert's arguments. Ruechelle, in 1958, attempted to demonstrate that neither laymen nor experts are capable of distinguishing between "emotional" and "intellectual" appeals. This, of course, amounts to an attempt to prove the null hypothesis, which is impossible due to the logic of experimental design, and was consequently doomed to failure. Further, since he allowed the speakers themselves to generate their ideas of what is "emotional" and "intellectual," he was testing their ability to produce distinctly different types of appeals as much as he was testing the ability of his judges to identify them.

The distinction certainly hasn't been abandoned in contemporary speech textbooks, although these textbooks usually use new terms for the two types of argument. Even Yost and Woolbert did not totally abandon the distinction: Yost used the terms "logic" and "emotion," and Woolbert continued to distinguish between "emotion" and an "intellectual type of activity." There is also evidence that, under some circumstances, listeners agree very well upon what is "emotional appeal" as distinguished from "logical argument." However, modern speech textbooks have for the most part abandoned the notion that these appeal to separate "faculties." Further, as I have argued elsewhere, an increase in the logic of a speech need not imply a decrease in its emotionality, or vice versa. The best persuasive speech is probably one which is both as logical and as emotional as possible. I will have more to say about this in the chapter describing the paradigm of persuasion.

This attack upon the conviction-persuasion duality was not Woolbert's only contribution to the theory of persuasion. He also wrote a series of three articles for the **Quarterly Journal of Speech Education** in which he set forth a theory of persuasion which was fairly sophisticated for its time.

Actually, Woolbert's view would make persuasion identical with verbal communication. He begins by arguing that all verbal communication aims at action or response, that all response is muscular and involves acceptance. This view will sound rather familiar to the reader of the first chapter of this book. He continues to point out that acceptance necessarily involves propositions, and specifies the aim of all persuasion to be gaining acceptance of propositions. Thus all verbal communication apparently involves persuasion. The propositions used in persuasion are sufficient if accepted by the audience. The speaker must analyze audience motives carefully and must choose a proposition which, if accepted, will bring the action desired. Such propositions, he says, contain both logical and emotional elements. The speaker must base his appeals on audience "stimulators," which seem identical to what we now call "drives." These are divided into two classes: "inner stimulators," by which he clearly means basic or biological drives, and "outer stimulators," which are what we now call secondary, social, or learned drives or needs. All in all the theory shows a sophistication beyond its time, and one has the feeling that rhetorical theory might have profited considerably from an even closer

alliance with sound principles of behavioral psychology had not Woolbert died at such an early age.

One notices a behavioral emphasis in the writings of I. A. Richards,
too, but Richards would never include his own in any list of theories
dealing with persuasion. His new rhetoric, unlike the traditional rhetorics, would not be concerned with persuasion. He says the traditional
rhetoric was "an offspring of dispute," which is a "puppy war with
words," and "an exploitation of a systemmatic set of misunderstand-
ings for warlike purposes." The new rhetoric which Richards favors
"should be a study of misunderstanding and its remedies."

One might reasonably ask, then, why I have chosen to mention
Richards' theory in a survey of theories of persuasion. Very simply, because I believe Richards' theory has a great deal to do with persuasion
as it has been defined here. The purpose of the new rhetoric is to **eliminate ambiguity** and to improve the fidelity of communication. Eliminating ambiguity or misunderstanding is one very potent way of
changing the evaluative behavior of others. By redefining and clarifying an object of audience judgment, it is often possible to cause the
audience to behave differently toward that object, which is the definition of persuasion being used here. This is closely allied to the
technique of "differentiation," described in the next chapter, which
some psychologists suggest is a very potent means of resolving cognitive conflict and inducing attitude change. Consider, for example, an
individual who would define "diplomatic recognition of Red China"
as a type of submission to Communist demands. If an erstwhile persuader can point out that he agrees with the individual that Communism must be put down at every opportunity, but that he sees
diplomatic recognition of Red China as an effective propaganda tool
for the United States, he has certainly eliminated misunderstanding,
but he has also persuaded the first individual, since that individual
will probably act differently toward the concept of diplomatic
recognition.

Whereas I. A. Richards considerably narrowed the concept of rhetoric
by seeking to purify it of "persuasion" as he used that term, Kenneth
Burke used both "rhetoric" and "persuasion" in senses much more
encompassing than anyone before him. Burke is a philosopher dealing
with language, a one-time Marxist with a fascination for the psychoanalytic approach. He views persuasion and rhetoric as forming an
intrinsic part of all man's language activities, at the very least. Even

more broadly, he contends that there is rhetoric in all the social activities of man, from the affairs of nations interacting with one another down to the communication of an individual with himself. He says there is rhetoric in any situation in which meaning can be said to reside; rhetoric itself is "the use of language as a symbolic means of inducing cooperation in beings that by nature respond to symbols."

Burke begins with the assumption that there is a generic "divisiveness" between men, and believes that men are constantly striving to bridge that divisiveness. This social cohesion is achieved through the strategy of identification; men become less divisive insofar as they become more similar in goals, language, appearance, modes of thought, and all other identifiable characteristics. Rhetoric and persuasion "include those areas in which some form of identification takes place." It becomes difficult at this point to determine whether the identification produces the persuasion or the persuasion produces the identification, until one gradually becomes aware that, for Burke, identification and persuasion are identical. Thus the missionaries' first feeble efforts to communicate with an African tribesman are persuasive through the strategy of identification in that they represent attempts to bridge the gulf created between them by their differences in language and culture.

Burke is much more traditional when he turns to description of the overt means by which a persuader operates, for his analysis is drawn quite directly from Aristotle. However, he reinterprets Aristotle's precepts, in that he explains them in terms of his own concept of identification. As Day (1960) has pointed out, the logical, ethical, and pathetic proofs, enthymemes, and examples, are all "stylistic identifications." As Burke puts it, "You persuade a man only insofar as you talk his language by speech, gesture, tonality, order, image, attitude, idea, identifying your ways with his."

One final approach from the rhetorical tradition, before turning to the literature of psychology, is that of the English philosopher Stephen Toulmin. Toulmin, in his book **The Uses of Argument,** contends that argument does not proceed in any syllogistic form, and offers what he believes is a more complete and useful analysis of argument. His view is that argument begins with the statement of a **claim,** such as the statement: "Ann must not be a Catholic." The individual hearing the claim, if he does not accept it, will probably indicate that he would like to know why, whereupon the speaker is expected to furnish what Toulmin calls **data:** "She is divorced." The listener, of course, may not be familiar with the rules of the Catholic Church, and consequently may fail to see any relation between the data and the claim. If this turns out to be true, the speaker must furnish a **warrant** which specifies that relationship, such as the statement: "A woman cannot be a Catholic and be divorced." The listener may expect some proof that the warrant is true, in which case the speaker must produce **support for the warrant.** Further, Toulmin takes into account the fact that the speaker may not wish to argue that his claim is universal and totally probable, so he makes provision for a **qualifier** within the claim, which might be represented by the statement: "Ann is **probably** not a Catholic." The qualifier can specify the probability, as in the statement: "There is a .90 probability that Ann is not a Catholic." Finally, one of the reasons why the claim may be qualified is that the warrant may have exceptions, so Toulmin includes what he calls a **rebuttal** which allows for such exceptions, as: "A woman cannot be Catholic and be divorced **unless she was divorced before she was converted.**"

If the Toulmin model is used to encompass an entire argument, it has an obvious shortcoming: Both the data and the warrant may require support and may, in effect, become claims in new units of proof. If this major modification is made as suggested in the chapter describing the paradigm of persuasion, the Toulmin model appears to have great utility in describing a part of the process of persuasion.

REFERENCES

Alcuin. **De Rhetorica.** Written in 794. A translation is available: Wilbur Samuel Howell. **The Rhetoric of Alcuin and Charlemagne.** Princeton: Princeton University Press, 1941.

Aristotle. **De Anima. The Basic Works of Aristotle,** Richard McKeon, ed. New York: Random House, 1941.

————. **Rhetoric.** John Henry Freese, trans. Cambridge: Harvard University Press, 1926.

————. **Rhetoric.** Lane Cooper, trans. New York: D. Appleton Century, 1932.

————. **Rhetoric and Poetic.** W. Rhys Roberts, trans. New York: Random House, 1954. Also partially reprinted in **The Basic Works of Aristotle,** Richard McKeon, ed. New York: Random House, 1941.

Augustine, Saint, **De Doctrina Christiana,** 4, Sister Therese, trans. Washington, 1928. Originally written about 426 A.D.

Bacon, Francis. **The Advancement of Learning,** James Spedding, Robert Leslie Ellis, and Douglas Denon Heath, eds. New York: Hurd and Houghton, 1870.

Baldwin, Charles Sears. **Ancient Rhetoric and Poetic.** New York: Macmillan, 1924. Reprint, Gloucester, Mass.: Peter Smith, 1959, chap. 1–5.

Bitzer, Lloyd F. "The Lively Idea: A Study of Hume's Influence on George Campbell's **Philosophy of Rhetoric.**" Unpublished doctoral dissertation, University of Iowa, 1962.

Blair, Hugh. **Lectures on Rhetoric and Belles Lettres.** London and Edinburgh, 1783.

Bryant, Donald C., and Karl R. Wallace. **Fundamentals of Public Speaking.** New York: Appleton-Century-Crofts, 1960.

Burke, Kenneth. **A Rhetoric of Motives.** Chicago: Prentice-Hall, 1950. See also: Marie Hochmuth. "Kenneth Burke and the 'New Rhetoric,'" **Quarterly Journal of Speech,** 38 (1952), 133–144; and Dennis G. Day. "Persuasion and the Concepts of Identification," **Quarterly Journal of Speech,** 46 (1960), 270–273.

Campbell, George. **The Philosophy of Rhetoric.** Reprint, Lloyd Bitzer, ed. Carbondale: Southern Illinois University Press, 1963. Originally published in London and Edinburgh, 1776.

Cicero. **Brutus.** G. I. Hendrickson, trans. Cambridge: Harvard University Press, 1939.

————. **Orator.** H. M. Hubbell, trans. Cambridge: Harvard University Press, 1939.

———. **De Oratore.** E. W. Sutton and H. Rackham, trans. Cambridge: Harvard University Press, 1942. 2 Vols.

———. **De Partitione Oratoria.** H. Rackham, trans. Cambridge: Harvard University Press, 1948.

———. **De Inventione.** H. M. Hubbell, trans. Cambridge: Harvard University Press, 1949.

Clark, Donald Lemen. **Rhetoric in Greco-Roman Education.** New York: Columbia University Press, 1947, chap. 4.

Cronkhite, Gary. "The Locus of Presumption," **Central States Speech Journal** 17, (1966), 270–276.

Day, Dennis G. "Persuasion and the Concepts of Identification," **Quarterly Journal of Speech,** 46 (1960), 270–273.

Dieter, Otto. "Stasis," **Speech Monographs,** 17 (1950), 345–369.

Ehninger, Douglas. "Campbell, Blair, and Whately Revisited," **Southern Speech Journal,** 28 (1963), 169–182.

Fénelon, Francois. **Dialogues sur L'Eloquence.** First published in French, 1717, and in English **(Dialogues on Eloquence),** 1722.

Glanvill, Joseph. **An Essay Concerning Preaching.** First published in London, 1678.

Home, Henry (Lord Kames). **Elements of Criticism.** Edinburgh, 1762.

Howell, Wilbur Samuel. **Logic and Rhetoric in England, 1500–1700.** New York: Russell and Russell, 1961.

Hultzen, Lee S. "Status in Deliberative Analysis," **The Rhetorical Idiom.** Donald C. Bryant, ed. Ithaca: Cornell University Press, 1958, pp. 97–123.

Hume, David. **A Treatise of Human Nature.** Originally published, 1739–1740.

———. **An Enquiry Concerning Human Understanding.** Originally Published, 1748.

Kennedy, George. **The Art of Persuasion in Greece.** Princeton: Princeton University Press, 1963.

Lamy, Bernard. **De l'Art de Parler.** First published in French, 1675, and in English **(The Art of Speaking),** London, 1676.

Lawson, John. **Lectures Concerning Oratory.** Dublin, 1758.

Locke, John. **An Essay Concerning Human Understanding.** Originally published, 1690.

Peacham, Henry. **The Garden of Eloquence.** London, 1577.

Plato. **Gorgias.** W. C. Helmbold, trans. Indianapolis: Bobbs-Merrill, 1952.

———. **Phaedrus.** R. Hackforth, trans. Cambridge, Eng.: Cambridge University Press, 1952.

———. **Phaedrus and Gorgias** in **The Dialogues of Plato,** B. Jowett, trans. New York: Random House, 1892, Vol. 1.

Priestley, Joseph. **A Course of Lectures on Oratory and Criticism.** Reprint,

Vincent M. Bevilacqua and Richard Murphy, eds. Carbondale: Southern Illinois University Press, 1965. Originally published in London, 1777.

Quintilian. **Institutio Oratoria.** H. E. Butler, trans. Cambridge: Harvard University Press, 1920, 4 vols.

Ramus, Peter. **Institutiones Dialecticae.** First published in Paris, 1543.

Reid, Thomas. **An Enquiry Into the Human Mind on the Principles of Common Sense.** Originally published, 1764.

Richards, I. A. **The Philosophy of Rhetoric.** New York: Oxford University Press, 1936. See also: Marie Hochmuth. "I. A. Richards and the 'New Rhetoric,'" **Quarterly Journal of Speech,** 44 (1958) 1–16.

Rowell, Edward Z. "The Conviction-Persuasion Duality," **Quarterly Journal of Speech,** 20 (1934), 469–482.

Ruechelle, Randall C. "An Experimental Study of Audience Recognition of Emotional and Intellectual Appeals in Persuasion," **Speech Monographs,** 25 (1958), 49–58.

Taleus, Audomarus. **Institutiones Oratoriae.** First published in Paris, 1544.

Toulmin, Stephen. **The Uses of Argument.** Cambridge, Eng.: Cambridge University Press, 1959.

Wallace, Karl R. **Francis Bacon on Communication and Rhetoric.** Chapel Hill: University of North Carolina Press, 1943.

Ward, John. **A System of Oratory.** London, 1759.

Whately, Richard. **Elements of Rhetoric.** Reprint, Douglas Ehninger, ed. Carbondale: Southern Illinois University Press, 1963. Originally published in London, 1828.

Wilson, Thomas. **The Arte of Rhetorique.** First published in London, 1553; the more complete edition, 1560.

Winans, James A. **Public Speaking.** New York: Century, 1915.

Woolbert, Charles. "Conviction and Persuasion: Some Considerations of Theory," **Quarterly Journal of Public Speaking,** 3 (1917), 249–264.

———. "Persuasion: Principles and Method, Part I," **Quarterly Journal of Speech,** 5 (1919), 12–25.

———. "Persuasion: Principles and Method, Part II," **Quarterly Journal of Speech,** 5 (1919), 101–119.

———. "Persuasion: Principles and Method, Part III," **Quarterly Journal of Speech,** 5 (1919), 212–238.

Yost, Mary. "Argument from the Point-of-View of Sociology," **Quarterly Journal of Public Speaking,** 3 (1917), 109–127.

THREE

Psychological theories of persuasion

The second chapter might have been subtitled, "Speaker-Oriented Theories of Persuasion," for the field of rhetoric has traditionally been concerned with the question of what a speaker may do in order to influence an audience. The question of how the speaker's actions operate to affect an audience is, of course, a large part of that question, and is certainly given a great deal of consideration in most rhetorical theories, but the point of view, with the exception of the most recent theories, has generally been that of the speaker. Theorists operating from psychological backgrounds, on the other hand, generally take the point of view of an observer of the process. Since they are not usually concerned with the speaker-audience situation, they center upon the question of how attitude change occurs, often without even differentiating between the audience and the small-group situations. Consequently the student of psychological theories who is interested in learning to persuade must make his own inferences about what he must do to achieve persuasion. The fields of rhetoric and psychology have a great deal to offer each other in this area, and it is unfortunate that their communication has been hampered in many universities by the rigidity of departmental organization. The growth of interdepartmental groups interested in communication is certainly to be applauded. Psychologists are being exposed to the "rhetorical correlates" of attitude change, and rhetoricians are building their theories on more contemporary theories of human behavior—and both approaches are improved. There is still a considerable division between the two disciplines, however, so that, whereas the student of psychology may have found himself on unfamiliar ground in reading the second chapter, the student of rhetoric may feel a sense of disorientation in reading the third. Hopefully, both may profit from perseverance.

Heider's balance theory

One of the earliest and most basic of the psychologically oriented theories of attitude change was that of Fritz Heider, whose earliest comprehensive explanation was published in 1946. Heider considers the situation in which an individual, whom I shall refer to as the first person, is confronted by a second person and an object of judgment, although this object of judgment might be a third person. Heider attempts to explain how the first person relates his attitudes toward the second person and toward the object of judgment. He assumes, first, that the first person has attitudes toward the second person and toward the object, which may be either favorable or unfavorable. His second assumption is that the first person knows or thinks he knows that the attitude of the second person toward the object is either favorable or unfavorable. If all three of these attitudes are favorable, or if any two are unfavorable and the third favorable, the situation is said to be in a state of "balance," and no attitude change is predicted on the part of person one. However, if any two of the attitudes are favorable and the third is unfavorable, or if all three are unfavorable, a state of imbalance is said to exist, and it is predicted that the first person will change his own attitudes, attempt to cause the second person to change his attitude about the object, or will change his perception of the second person's attitude toward the object.

If the favorable and unfavorable attitudes are represented, respectively, by positive and negative signs, as in the following diagrams, and if one multiplies the signs algebraically, the balanced situations will yield positive products and the unbalanced situations will yield negative products.

Clearly, some of these unbalanced situations are more balanced than others. One may be concerned if a valued friend does not share his likes and dislikes. However, he may not be at all disconcerted to find that he and an enemy like some of the same things, any more

Balanced Situations   **Unbalanced Situations**

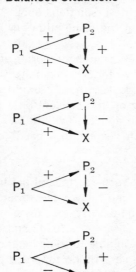
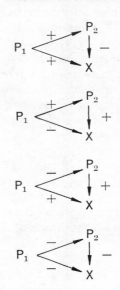

than he is disturbed to find that they dislike some of the same things.

There are more important shortcomings of the formulation, however. One of these is that it does not cover those situations involving more than two persons and an object of judgment, and another is that it cannot be used to predict which of the available means an individual will use to bring the situation into balance. Cartwright and Harary (1956) have attempted to solve both of these problems by extending the diagrams to include more complex situations and by applying the theory of linear graphs to predict which of the links an individual will be most likely to change. An explanation of the Cartwright and Harary extension is beyond the limitations of this chapter, and probably beyond the limitations of this writer as well, so the interested reader is urged to refer to the article itself.

The congruity hypothesis

Another problem with the Heider model is that attitudes are represented as either favorable or unfavorable, without allowance for degrees of favor or disfavor. Charles Osgood and Percy Tannenbaum have stated what they call the "congruity hypothesis," by means of which they attempt to make more specific predictions about the direction and extent of attitude change in the same situation Heider described.

The method used by Osgood and Tannenbaum in measuring attitude change is described in more detail in Chapter Six. Generally, Osgood and Tannenbaum conceive of an individual's attitude toward a concept as being represented by his rating of that concept on a seven-point scale ranging from "good" at one end to "bad" at the other. Thus if the subject checks the position nearest the "good" end of

the scale when asked to rate a concept such as "federal aid to education," it is assumed that he is extremely favorable toward that concept; if he checks the middle position he is assumed to be neutral; and if he checks one of the positions toward the "bad" end of the scale his attitude is assumed to be unfavorable to some degree.

Now suppose a subject has a favorable attitude toward a person such as Eugene McCarthy and an unfavorable attitude toward a concept such as withdrawing troops from Vietnam. He then comes upon information causing him to believe that McCarthy **favors** withdrawing troops. The effect of such an **associative bond** in most situations is to draw the ratings of the source (McCarthy) and the concept (withdrawal of troops) closer together, although that is not always true. In this case, one would predict on the basis of the congruity hypothesis that the subject will come to have a somewhat less favorable attitude toward McCarthy and a somewhat more favorable attitude toward withdrawal of troops from Vietnam. If the subject had learned that McCarthy did **not** favor troop withdrawal, one would say a **dissociative** bond had been established. The principle of congruity was devised to predict the direction and extent of attitude change in such situations.

The basic principle of congruity is that "changes in evaluation are always in the direction of increased congruity. . . ." Congruity is then defined by the following statement:

> Whenever one object of judgment is associated with another by an assertion, its congruent position along the evaluative dimension is always equal in degree of polarization (d) to the other object of judgment and in either the same (positive assertion) or opposite (negative assertion) evaluative direction.

Suppose, for example, that McCarthy is rated two spaces toward the favorable end of an evaluative scale such as the "good-bad" scale, that rating being represented as +2, troop withdrawal is rated one space toward the unfavorable end (−1), and McCarthy says he favors troop withdrawal. The "congruent position" toward which McCarthy's rating will move will be "equal in polarization" (one space from neutral) and in the same direction as the other object of judgment. Thus, while McCarthy's initial rating was +2, the "congruent position" toward which it will move will be −1. Thus audience attitudes should become less favorable toward McCarthy. This rating, of course, will not move all the way to its congruent position. For one thing, the rating of the concept will be doing some of the moving to facilitate a state of congruity. The congruent position for the concept, initially rated at −1, will be equal in polarization and in the same direction as the source, that is, +2. Thus audience attitudes should become more favorable toward troop withdrawal.

Suppose, however, that the ratings are the same as in this example, but McCarthy says he opposes troop withdrawal. The congruent position for each object of judgment is still equal in polarization to the position of the other, but since the assertion is negative, opposite in direction. The congruent position for McCarthy would be +1, so that audience attitudes toward him would become somewhat less favorable than the initial +2. The congruent position for troop withdrawal would be −2, so that audience attitudes should become less favorable toward troop withdrawal as well. This particular prediction, by the way, is very difficult to explain. It is difficult to accept the notion that a well-liked speaker can lose favor with an audience by condemning things which they mildly dislike.

In describing their system by which the extent of attitude change is predicted, Osgood and Tannenbaum first describe what they term the "pressure toward congruity," which they represent in their formulas with the letter P. The pressure toward congruity is equal to the difference in attitude scale units between the initial rating of the object of judgment and the point on the rating scale at which it would be totally congruent with the other object of judgment. This difference in scale units is given a positive (+) sign if the pressure is toward favorable attitude change, and a negative sign if the pressure is toward unfavorable change. If McCarthy (+2) makes a favorable statement about troop withdrawal (−1), the congruent position for his rating is

−1, and the pressure toward congruity is the difference between +2 and −1, or −3. The sign is negative because the pressure is toward unfavorable change.

A second specification is that "the total pressure toward congruity is distributed between the objects of judgment associated by an assertion in inverse proportion to their separate degrees of polarization." That is, the more "polarized" or extreme the attitude, the more difficult it is to change. This "degree of polarization" is represented in the formula below by the letter "d." The subscripts "$_c$" and "$_s$" designate "concept" and "source" values. Degree of polarization is, specifically,

Attitude change toward source   **Attitude change toward concept**

$$AC_s = \frac{|d_c|}{|d_s| + |d_c|} \, P_s \pm i \qquad AC_c = \frac{|d_s|}{|d_s| + |d_c|} \, P_c \pm i \pm A$$

the difference in attitude scale units between the neutral point and the point at which the object of judgment is rated. The upright bars indicate that this value is to be the **absolute magnitude** of the difference without regard to sign.

Two qualifying factors are included in these formulas. The first is the "correction for incredulity," represented by a lower case "i," which applies to both formulas. This correction is based on the assumption that there are certain circumstances under which a listener is unlikely to believe that the source made the assertion about the concept. This is especially true when the "pressure for congruity" is very high, but might also be true if the listener distrusted the speaker or experimenter who told him that the source made the assertion. The second qualifying factor springs from the empirical finding that the source in a paradigm such as this does not change as much as the concept; another way of saying it is that the assertion itself seems to carry some weight. Consequently an "assertion constant," represented by "A" in the formula and given the same sign as the assertion, is added to the formula used for predicting attitude change toward the concept.

Two objections seem worth mentioning. One of these is that attitudes differ not only in their extremity on a scale, they may differ also in something which might be called their "tenacity." For example, there are at least two types of individuals who might mark the neutral point on an attitude scale. One of these is the type who knows nothing about the concept and is consequently neutral toward it. The other is the type who has surveyed the evidence on both sides quite thoroughly and has concluded that he cannot make a decision. The first of these types should be a pushover for the first item of relevant information that comes along, but the second type is going to defy any attempt to move him off the neutral point. Similarly, as Brown (1962) suggests in his excellent review of this and other attitude change theories, an individual may know a great deal about the source but little about the concept, or vice versa, so that one of the two items is anchored in a mass of information while the other is not. The theory might well be refined by taking this tenacity into account. The explanation may, in fact, account for Tannenbaum's discovery that neutral attitudes are considerably more resistant to change than his model would predict.

The second objection may be only a qualification, but needs to be noted. That is that the congruity hypothesis makes no attempt to take the **message** into account. In order to obtain the reported correlation of .91 between predicted and obtained scores, Tannenbaum had to use quite bare assertions which did no more than relate the source to the concept. When message content is carefully controlled so that it produces no variance in attitude change among subjects, the congruity hypothesis appears capable of accounting for most of the remaining variance. However, when the source produces a message of any complexity, a much more complex model such as that suggested in Chapter Four will be required to predict attitude change among subjects. An example of the difficulties which may occur when the congruity hypothesis alone is applied to a situation involving a message with more than minimal content is an experiment (Stochowiak and Moss, 1965) in which the experimenter had his source argue in favor of the Negro and was surprised to find that his subjects changed attitude more negatively toward the source and less positively toward the Negro than would have been predicted by application of the congruity principle. Looking at the message the source used, it is not difficult to see why. In arguing for the Negro, the source also argued for interracial marriage, among other things, which is quite a different concept, and one toward which most subjects undoubtedly had attitudes more negative than those toward Negroes. The experimenter, however, failed to measure audience attitudes toward this as well as a number of other concepts inadvertently included in the message. The congruity hypothesis may be extended to cover all the concepts which a speaker associated with himself in a complex message, but it cannot take into account audience attitudes toward all the other concepts which the message causes to become associated with the primary concept, as well as all the individual words, phrases, and peculiarities of delivery, each of which becomes an additional concept in itself, and each of which becomes associated to some extent with both the speaker and the primary concept. Bettinghaus' (1959) dissertation demonstrated that the addition of even a few of these factors produced a significant improvement in predictability in the speech situation, for example.

Despite its shortcomings, the model has produced a great deal of fruitful research. Tannenbaum (1966) has more recently demonstrated that audience attitudes may generalize from one concept to another unrelated to it except by mediation of a source making statements about both. This "principle of mediated generalization" should prove to be a very useful extension of the basic congruity principle.

Leon Festinger's theory of cognitive dissonance (1957) applies to a much broader range of situations than do the models of Heider or of Osgood and Tannenbaum. Further, Festinger's theory is a rather general theory of human (and even animal) behavior. It is only partially concerned with attitude change as **one** of the means by which dissonance can be reduced, and only occasionally concerned with the persuasive situation as **one** of the situations in which dissonance can occur. Brehm and Cohen, two of Festinger's sometimes wayward disciples, have even argued that a dissonance analysis does not apply in the straightforward persuasive situation unless the listener perceives that he has deliberately chosen to expose himself to the persuasive message.

The theory of cognitive dissonance

Festinger points out that it is possible for "cognitions" (by which he apparently means anything which can be known, including beliefs and attitudes) to be in irrelevant, consonant, or dissonant relations to one another. What he means by an irrelevant relation is actually no relation at all. He writes: "Two cognitive elements are in a dissonant relation if, considering these two alone, the obverse of one element follows from the other . . ." and "in a consonant relation if, considering these two alone, one element follows from the other."

He then lists a number of situations which, as he puts it, "imply dissonance." The first of these is the situation in which a choice has been made between two or more alternatives. After the choice, all the attractions of the rejected alternatives and all the dissatisfactions with the chosen alternative are dissonant with the knowledge that the choice has been made. Obviously, dissonance will be greatest when the choice is an important one, all the alternatives are very attractive, and when the alternatives are so dissimilar as to make compromise impossible. Typically, an individual who has made an irrevocable choice will reduce dissonance by seeking evidence that his choice was the correct one, by maximizing the advantages and minimizing the disadvantages of the chosen alternative.

The example usually cited to illustrate this phenomenon is the finding that an individual who has recently purchased a new automobile tends to seek out advertisements for the make of automobile he chose. Brehm and Cohen (1962) have devoted a great deal of effort to the investigation of these choice situations, and have made the element of choice central to their version of dissonance theory. This type of situation is important to the persuader when he begins to analyze his audience, for he must realize that certain individuals in his audience may be so committed to an alternative other than the one he is urging that they will seize every opportunity to avoid, reject, or refute his message. This topic will be covered in more detail in a later chapter concerned with audience analysis. For the present, let it suffice to say that the situation is not hopeless; the evidence does not seem to support such a simple dissonance analysis, although it may support a more complex revision which Festinger has offered.

A second situation which "implies dissonance" might really be considered a subcategory of the first: "Dissonance almost always exists after an attempt has been made, by offering rewards or threatening punishment, to elicit behavior that is at variance with private opinion." If the individual performs the behavior, the knowledge that he has done so is dissonant with the realization that he believes otherwise. If he does not perform the behavior, the attractiveness of the reward or the distastefulness of the punishment is now dissonant with the realization that the reward is now unattainable or the punishment unavoidable. Again, dissonance will be greatest when the belief is an important one, when the reward offered or the punishment threatened is just strong enough that the behavior is barely elicited or almost elicited, and when the behavior is most obviously at variance with the belief. If the individual performs the behavior, he will seek to reduce dissonance by minimizing the importance of the belief, changing the belief, and by maximizing his perception of the threatened punishment or offered reward. If he does not perform the behavior, he will reduce dissonance by minimizing his perception of the lost reward or the impending punishment. An experiment by Festinger and Carlsmith (1959) has been offered as an illustration of this situation. Subjects, after performing a tedious task for one hour and rating those tasks, were hired to represent the tasks to other "subjects" as interesting. Some were paid one dollar, some were paid twenty dollars, and some subjects were not asked to lie at all. Subjects who were paid only one dollar came to view the tasks as more interesting than before, and their attitude change was greater than that of subjects who were paid twenty dollars, while attitude change was least on the part of subjects who did not lie at all. Festinger's explanation is that subjects who were paid twenty dollars felt their behavior was more nearly justified and consequently had less dissonance to resolve by subsequent attitude change. Again, the analysis has not been totally supported by other research, but the effect does seem to occur under certain circumstances, as I will note later. This phenomenon has at least two implications for the persuader. One of these is the possibility of something which might be called rhetorical "overkill": the greatest attitude change may be obtained by giving an audience **just enough** justification to elicit the desired behavior, so that they will feel compelled to reduce their own dissonance by further attitude change. Another implication is that, if one can induce an individual to argue in favor of a point of view to which he does not subscribe, and offers him only minimal justification for his behavior, he will be likely to persuade himself.

A third situation which Festinger lists as dissonant is that in which an individual is exposed to information which contradicts beliefs he holds. Dissonance in this situation will be greatest if the belief is important, if the information **directly** contradicts the belief, and if the information is incontestable. The individual will attempt to reduce dissonance by coming to view the belief as less important, by finding a way in which the belief and the information can be viewed as compatible, by contesting the evidence and, if all these avenues are closed, by changing the belief. The relevance of this situation to the persuasive situation seems obvious.

Actually, this third type of dissonant situation probably can be most

profitably discussed in relation to the fourth: that in which an individual encounters someone who disagrees with him. Again, this **is** the
persuasive situation. The dissonance is greatest if the person who
disagrees is liked and respected, and if the disagreement is important
and extensive. Dissonance will be reduced by attempting to convert
the other person, by changing one's attitude toward the other person,
by minimizing the importance or extent of the disagreement, by seeking new and consonant information, including others who agree with
one's own view or, if none of these means are available, by changing
one's own belief or attitude. These last two situations are among those
listed by Festinger, but Brehm and Cohen have argued that they are not
dissonant unless the individual has **chosen** to expose himself to the
contradictory information or opinion. Festinger apparently maintains
his original opinion, however, for he has argued as late as 1964 that
the mere knowledge that a contradictory opinion exists produces dissonance, even if the individual does not expose himself to it. The difference may or may not lie in semantics, but in any event "dissonance"
is Festinger's word.

Chapanis and Chapanis (1964) have raised some objections to dissonance theory and to much of the research cited in support of it. They
object to the research on the grounds that most of the results can be
explained without reference to dissonance theory, and have raised
questions about the experimental methodology employed in many
cases. Most damaging to the theory is their observation that it is so
vague that it can be used to explain almost any outcome of an experiment; indeed, they point to at least one case in which Festinger **did**
use it to explain all possible outcomes of an experiment. This, of
course, makes it not very useful for purposes of prediction.

As I have argued elsewhere (Cronkhite, 1966a, 1966b), one major
problem is that these "predictions" are not predictions logically derived from some basic premise, which is what is usually expected of a
theory. Instead, they seem to be **definitions of terms in the basic premise,** and these definitions can be changed as often as necessary. According to Chapanis and Chapanis: "The basic premise [of dissonance
theory] is that discrepant cognitions create tension which the individual strives to reduce by making his cognitions more consistent." Thus
there are three entities in the theory which need to be labeled: (1) the
discrepant cognitions, (2) the state of tension, and (3) the behavior
used to reduce the tension. Unfortunately, Festinger has confused

matters by applying the term "dissonance" to the state of cognitive discrepancy as well as to the state of tension presumably aroused. Experiments studying post-decision behavior, especially Brehm and Cohen, have created further confusion by inferring the presence of the tension sometimes from the existence of a situation in which the elements are presumed to be discrepant and sometimes from behavior presumed to be tension-reducing, but hardly anyone has bothered to find out if any state of tension actually intervenes. The experiments which have been conducted have been of two types. Some have been designed to determine what types of situations are dissonant, in which case the experimenters have assumed that those situations are most dissonant which produce the most of what they presume to be dissonance-reducing behavior. Others have been designed to find out what types of behavior are dissonance-reducing, in which case the experimenters put subjects in situations presumed to be dissonant and observed the resultant behavior. This is clearly circular. Such experiments have produced some knowledge of which types of situations produce which types of behavior, but have not confronted the question of whether any state of discomfort, drive, or tension intervenes, which is, after all, the basic premise of the theory. The first step in clearing up the theory is to use three separate terms such as "dissonant situations," "dissonance-produced arousal," and "dissonance-reducing behavior." The second step is to find operational definitions of all three terms, including especially an independent measure of "dissonance-produced arousal." Then it should be possible to begin testing the basic premise. I have reported, in the articles previously cited, some attempts to do that. Let it suffice to say that the experimental evidence has not yet lent much support to the theory.

Brown's principle of differentiation

Roger Brown (1962), along with his excellent review of the congruity, dissonance, and structural models, has added a new emphasis to the theory of attitude change: the principle of differentiation. The point of the first part of his paper appears to be that a major vehicle for resolving conflict, incongruity, dissonance, and the like is differentiation of a global stimulus into $stimulus_1$, and $stimulus_2$. This is very convenient when it can be accomplished. An individual who holds favorable attitudes toward a stimulus S may experience some psychological discomfort if he discovers that S has some negative attributes. However, if he can differentiate S into S_1 and S_2, he can maintain his favorable attitude toward S_2 while adopting a negative attitude toward S_1. A white Southerner who believes Negroes to be mentally inferior, lazy, and dirty, for example, encounters one who is bright, industrious, and neat. Without taking the more painful route of openly (or even covertly) admitting that he was wrong, he can simply differentiate between educated and uneducated Negroes. The principle is not new with Brown, but the strong emphasis upon it certainly is.

Structural theories

A number of writers have continued further from the original Heider formulation to present more complex models of the individual's "cognitive structure." Brown (1962) has labeled these "balance" models. However, to avoid confusion with Heider's system, I will refer to them as structural models. They are distinguishable from other theories in that they maintain fairly careful distinctions between "attitudes" and "beliefs," although they do not all use the same terms. They also specify quite similar relationships between attitudes and beliefs (or between the "cognitive" and "affective" components) and generally argue that an individual will act so as to maintain a consistent cognitive structure.

McGuire's rational-syllogistic analysis. McGuire (1960) suggested there are two types of cognitive consistency. One of these he labels "logical thinking" and describes it as a tendency for an individual's beliefs to be consistent with each other. To be "consistent" in this case is to be related to each other in ways which can be validated by application of the rules of formal logic, so that an individual expressing belief in related major and minor premises may be expected to express belief in the conclusion which is deduced from them. The extent of the belief in the conclusion is not expected to be that which the rules of formal logic would dictate, however, for the cognitive process is modified by demand for a second type of consistency. This McGuire labels "wishful thinking," and describes it as the tendency for a person's beliefs to be consistent with his desires. Thus an individual's belief that members of an organization such as Students for a Democratic Society are Communists may depend in part upon his belief that radical left-wing groups are Communistic and upon his knowledge that SDS is a radical left-wing group, but will depend also on the extent to which he wants to believe that SDS members are Communists. McGuire measured on a scale of probability the extent to which subjects favored and believed in syllogistic premises and conclusions presented in random order. He also exposed subjects to persuasive messages arguing that the minor premises were likely. To predict the strength of a subject's belief in a given conclusion, McGuire multiplied the probabilities that subject assigned to the premises leading to that conclusion. He found that scores thus predicted were correlated +.48 with the subject's actual scores, but this correlation of predictability improved to +.85 when "wishful thinking" was taken into account.

Rosenberg's affective-cognitive consistency. The model proposed by Rosenberg as it is most recently described (Rosenberg, 1960, 1965) begins with the assumptions that an individual has cognitive elements which may be described as his perceptions of objects, persons, and ideas, and that there are relationships between these cognitive elements which can be positive, negative, or null. The relationships may be relationships of liking (p), indifference (o), or disliking (n), or they may be causal: **a** causes **b** (p), **a** is unrelated to **b** (o), or **a** prevents **b** (n). The individual also feels states of affect toward the cognitive elements themselves which may be favorable (+), unfavorable (−), or neutral (o). Rosenberg uses the term "attitude" to cover both of these components, which he terms the "cognitive" and "affective." However, these "cognitive" and "affective" components appear to be identical to what Fishbein (1965) has called "beliefs" and "attitudes."

Rosenberg postulates the existence of a human need for affective-cognitive consistency. He advances three propositions: (1) As long as the affective and cognitive components are consistent, attitude will remain in a stable state. (2) When an individual hears a persuasive communication, or when his attitude structure is otherwise altered beyond his "tolerance limit," the attitude structure will be reorganized. (3) This reorganization may be achieved through one of three alternatives: (a) rejection of the communication or information, (b) "fragmentation" of the attitude, or (c) attitude change. Another assumption supported by subsequent research is that individuals will choose that avenue of attitude change which requires fewest alterations of affective and cognitive elements. As Brown (1962) points out, this analysis adds a further specification to the conditions necessary before reorganization will occur: The individual must realize that an inconsistency exists. This model, as the other structural models, allows one to consider a multiplicity of cognitive elements and their relationships, whereas the systems of Heider, Osgood and Tannenbaum, and Festinger can be used to deal with only two cognitive elements and the relationship between them.

Rosenberg reports an interesting experiment which illustrates his conception of the way in which attitude structure operates. He first measured subjects' affect toward a number of concepts such as "increased foreign aid," "increased U.S. prestige," and "increased taxation," as well as their perceptions of the relationships between these concepts. Typically, a subject who favored increased foreign aid believed that it would lead to increased United States prestige but would not lead to increased taxation. He then hypnotized as many subjects as were susceptible and left them with post-hypnotic suggestions such as instructions to feel nauseated upon encountering the expression "foreign aid." Needless to say, his subjects were not so favorable as before toward the concept of foreign aid. This new negative affect, however, was inconsistent with the belief that increased foreign aid leads to increased United States prestige. Some subjects came to believe that increased foreign aid would not cause increased United States prestige but would cause increased taxation; other subjects came to view the topic as less important and no longer wanted to think about it. Further, they gave very imaginative explanations for their newfound beliefs.

Brown (1962) has pointed out, by the way, that the model proposed by Abelson and Rosenberg (1958) is very similar to this one except that a relationship is stated "in terms of a relation between Ego and something else rather than simply in terms of single-valued elements. . . ." Since the Abelson and Rosenberg model is more complex but seems to lead to essentially the same predictions, I have not chosen to give it separate treatment.

Fishbein's attitude-belief distinction. Fishbein and Raven presented their operational distinction between beliefs and attitudes in 1962, although it was a year later before Fishbein gave a very clear and complete explanation of the way in which the two concepts may be integrated into a view of cognitive structure. In his most recent explanation of his approach, Fishbein (1965) gives a very clear and concise explanation of the verbal distinction in his opening paragraph:

Two persons who are equally opposed to segregation may have quite different conceptions of its nature, causes, and consequences and may hold different views concerning the actions that should be taken to eliminate segregation. In the language of this paper, these two persons are said to have the **same attitudes** toward segregation but to hold **different beliefs** about it. Attitudes are learned predispositions to respond to an object or class of objects in a favorable or unfavorable way. Beliefs, on the other hand, are hypotheses concerning the nature of these objects and the types of actions that should be taken with respect to them [p. 107].

Operationally, Fishbein uses as his measure of attitude the evaluative dimension of Osgood's semantic differential, described briefly earlier in this chapter and described in detail in the sixth chapter. This measure is composed of a number of seven-point scales having evaluative adjectives opposite in meaning at opposite ends of the scales as typified by the "good-bad" scale. A subject's rating of a concept on a set of such scales is Fishbein's operational definition of the subject's attitude toward the concept. However, Fishbein's basic premise is that a subject's attitude toward one concept is based upon the attributes the subject believes are related to it. A belief may be measured by asking a subject to indicate the strength of his belief in assertions about the existence of relationships between the concept and its attributes. The measuring instruments consist of scales of the semantic differential type, these having probability-related adjectives opposite in meaning at opposite ends of the scales. Typical adjective pairs might be "likely-unlikely" and "true-false."

The formula which expresses the crux of Fishbein's theory is:

$$A_o = \sum_{i=1}^{N} B_i a_i$$

where "A" represents the attitude toward an object, person, or idea, "B" represents the strength of the belief that attribute "i" is related to the attitude object, and "a_i" represents the individual's attitude toward the attribute. The formula indicates that the attitude toward each attribute is to be multiplied by the strength of the belief that it is related to the attitude object; and the sum of all these multiplications, including a multiplication for each attribute believed to be related to the attitude object, can be used to predict the strength of the attitude toward the attitude object itself. This is similar to the Rosenberg formulation, but allows for degrees of attitude and belief strength.

This system is so similar to one devised by the present author to deal with the persuasive situation that most of its implications are better discussed in the next chapter where the paradigm of persuasion is described. There are two comments which seem useful at this point. The first is to draw attention to Fishbein's note that no "need for consistency" is implied or intended in his theory, stated as it is in strictly behavioral terms. This is a fresh and welcome change from the theories surveyed to this point. I have already complained of the difficulties one encounters in theories which include mythical states of an organism given no specified operational definitions. When an individual is forced, by a persuasive message or some other event, to relate a new attribute to an old attitude object, and then is asked to indicate his attitude toward the object, any attitude change which occurs may be explained either by the fact that the individual has **learned** to associate a new attribute and his attitude toward it with an old attitude object or by the fact that he has formed one new concept out of two prior concepts. Postulating a **drive** to account for the change seems totally unnecessary.

Second, the formula contains a specification which may not be immediately apparent. Suppose a given attitude object has ten relevant and important attributes. After making the ten multiplications called for, one might proceed in one of two ways: by adding the ten products and dividing by ten, on the assumption that a subject's attitude toward the attitude object is equal to the **average** of his attitudes toward its attributes, or by merely adding without averaging, on the assumption that a subject's attitude toward the attitude object is equal to the **sum** of his attitudes toward its attributes. Fishbein's model is a **summation** rather than an **averaging** model.

At first glance this might not appear important. If all subjects have (or are assumed to have) the same number of beliefs about the attitude object, both systems would lead to the same predictions about the relative strengths of their attitudes toward the object. However, the summation approach would generally predict wider variance in attitudes among individuals who have more beliefs about the object. Averaging serves as a correction for the number of beliefs, whereas mere summation does not. Further, from the summation approach one would infer that an individual's attitude toward the attitude object may be more extreme than his attitude toward any of its attributes. Finally, and of greatest interest to me, is the situation in which a moderately favorable item of information is added to the beliefs of an individual already very favorable toward the attitude object. Clearly contradictory predictions are to be derived from the two approaches in this case. From the averaging model one would predict that the subject's new attitude will be **less** favorable than before, whereas use of the summation model will yield the prediction that the subject's attitude will be **more** favorable than before. These questions are obviously to be decided empirically. So far the research evidence appears to be overwhelmingly in favor of the summation approach, but most of that research has been done by Fishbein and his colleagues (see Anderson and Fishbein [1965], for example). The important thing is that Fishbein has made clear and unequivocal predictions which are amenable to experimental verification, which is not true of all the theories surveyed in this chapter.

A personality-oriented theory

There are a number of theories relating various personality traits such as authoritarianism, dogmatism, cognitive complexity, and need for achievement to an individual's response to persuasion. Some of these, especially Rokeach's elaborate concept of dogmatism, come close to being full-fledged theories of persuasion. These individual personality variables are treated, however, in the chapter which deals with audience analysis. It seems more efficient, therefore, to leave the explanation of such concepts as dogmatism and cognitive complexity to that later chapter and to treat here only those theories of personality which give a more encompassing view of the process of attitude change. It seems profitable to survey two such theories.

The classic Summer 1960 issue of **Public Opinion Quarterly** devoted exclusively to papers dealing with attitude change contained a lead article by Daniel Katz titled "The Functional Approach to the Study of Attitudes." Actually, the article contained more than an attempt to explain attitudes and attitude change in terms of personality theory; it was an attempt to integrate into a common framework that type of theory as well as the other theories surveyed in this chapter. The attempt was remarkably successful. The personality-oriented theory was outlined in that article as a part of the overall framework, but was given more detailed treatment in an article by Sarnoff published in the same issue.

Katz acknowledges as one of the antecedents of his approach the system of Smith, Bruner, and White (1956). Those writers proceeded on the assumption that man "is an organism, a system of life processes that somehow maintains its identity in active interplay with its environment," and the assumption that "behavior occurs as an interaction between striving organism and environment." Man's attitudes develop as a part of this struggle and are used by man as at least one means of adapting to his environment. They serve as **mediators** between the internal demands of the organism and the reality of his external environment. More specifically, they serve the functions of object appraisal, social adjustment, and externalization (resolution of internal problems by translation into action).

Katz's approach is quite similar. Defining "attitude" so as to include "affect" as well as "cognition" or "belief," he argues that the general approach to a theory of attitude and attitude-change should be exemplified by the question, "What **functions** does a given attitude perform for an individual?" He notes four major types of functions which attitudes may perform, and discusses the conditions which lead to the formation, arousal, and change of attitudes performing each function. Attitudes, he says, may perform the functions of adjustment, ego defense, value expression, and knowledge.

Attitudes performing the function of adjustment develop so as to be useful in "need satisfaction" for the purpose of "maximizing external rewards and minimizing punishments." These attitudes are "activated" or become salient upon the activation of the needs with which the attitude was designed to cope. Such attitudes may change when need deprivation is prolonged, when new needs or new levels of aspiration occur, when new systems of rewards and punishment are encountered, or when the individual is directed toward "new and better paths for need satisfaction."

Attitudes performing the function of ego defense originate in response to a need to protect oneself against internal conflicts and against external threats, especially to the ego. Such attitudes become especially salient when the individual is threatened or frustrated, when he hears someone appeal "to hatred and repressed impulses," or when he is exposed to "authoritarian suggestion." The attitudes may change if the threat is removed, if the individual is allowed successful aggression or "catharsis," or if he comes to recognize and acknowledge his defense mechanisms.

Attitudes serving the function of value expression are developed for the purpose of "maintaining self-identity; enhancing favorable self-image; self-expression and self-determination." They may be aroused upon the presentation of cues associated with the individual's values, or in response to "appeals to [the] individual to reassert [his] self-image," or when the individual faces "ambiguities which threaten [his] self-concept."

Finally, those attitudes which serve the knowledge function are developed in response to a "need for understanding, for meaningful cognitive organization, for consistency and clarity." They are especially salient when the information on which they are based is especially salient. They may change if new or more meaningful information becomes available.

For illustration, consider the situation in which a white, southern boy attends an integrated, northern college. His attitude toward Negroes has heretofore served the function of adjustment, since it has maximized social rewards and minimized social punishment. If the boy comes from a poor southern family, the attitude may have served the function of ego defense as well, in that it has developed as a defense against the threat of Negro competition for jobs (external threat) and perhaps in response to a need to feel superior to **someone**. Further, if the boy has a clear conception of himself as a white southerner, it may also serve the function of value expression, in that the attitude helps him to maintain his identity. Finally, it probably serves the knowledge function, for the majority of poor southern Negroes seen by the boy may have been dirty and lazy.

His attitude may actually be intensified during his first year or two at the integrated northern college. He may find himself in competition with Negroes for grades and part-time jobs. His early contact with aggressive, intelligent, ambitious Negroes may threaten him with defeat by the one class to whom he had previously felt superior. Certainly he will become more aware of his identity as a southerner; his identity will be emphasized by observation of northern speech and mannerisms in those around him, and by the other students, who will almost certainly call attention to his own speech and mannerisms. Thus the old attitude may be aroused to unusual intensity, being called upon to serve its ego-defense and value-expressive functions in a time of crisis. It will probably no longer serve its adjustment function, however, in that it will now maximize social punishment and minimize social reward. This will be a source of conflict, and the boy may try to overcome it by writing to his family and friends at home in search of social support, and he may seek the friendship of other southerners at school. The old attitude will not serve the knowledge function either, in that he now sees Negroes who are definitely not dirty and lazy. He will probably try to minimize this conflict by searching for examples of college-educated Negroes who are inferior, by recalling with greater vividness the inferiority of Negroes at home, by discovering a Negro ghetto in a nearby city, and by differentiating between the mass of dirty, lazy Negroes and the few educated "exceptions." The well-meaning individual who attempts to persuade him by offering evidence that the Negro is the intellectual equal of the white man and is dirty and lazy, when he is, only because of the paternalistic treatment accorded him by whites will be doomed to failure and probably worse, for his argument will increase rather than decrease the boy's tension.

Hopefully, as the southerner moves into his junior or senior year, he may feel more secure. Some academic and social success may make him feel less threatened by Negro competition. At the same time, he may begin to see himself as a reasonable, urbane, educated northern college student, and may feel a need to adopt values and attitudes consistent with his new self-image. As this begins to occur, he will be likely to write home less often and to become less inclined toward friendship with other southerners; he may discover that his first more tolerant opinions are given considerable social approval by his northern friends, and may be gratified by it. He may also find comforting evidence that Negroes and whites do not differ in intellect or motivation, since that information is consistent with his new attitude. His new attitude may become even more intense than those of his northern friends, since its **arousal conditions,** stemming from the conflict of his old attitude and environment with the new, will be more salient for him. The important part of this illustration is the suggestion that **the attitude would never have changed if it had not ceased to perform the functions for which it was designed.**

This analysis by Katz seems to me to be the most comprehensive and sophisticated presently available. Its framework encompasses the consistency theories and makes room for behavioral and learning theories and seems to provide some additional insights, especially in the categories of ego-defense and value expression, that the other theories either lack or fail to emphasize. The personality-oriented approach can certainly profit from increased behavioral emphasis and from some healthy skepticism about the multitude of tests used to measure the vast array of symptoms hypothesized to accompany various personality syndromes, as I will argue in a later chapter. But Katz and Sarnoff have done an excellent job of analyzing and synthesizing the bases for attitude development and change.

Etcetera

Two other theories deserve mention at this point: the judgmental approach of Hovland and Sherif and Kelman's analysis of the process of persuasion into the processes of compliance, identification, and internalization.

Hovland and Sherif have attempted to explain the relation between an individual's initial attitude and his responses to messages urging varying degrees of attitude change. In the most recent and clearest of Sherif's explanations (Sherif, Sherif, and Nebergall, 1965), he theorizes that an individual has a range of attitude positions around his own attitude, called a "region of acceptance," a "region of noncommitment" further removed from his own attitude, and a "region of rejection" even further removed. Attitudinal statements falling within the region of acceptance will be accepted, and will also be perceived as lying closer to the individual's own attitude than they actually do. Attitude statements falling in the region of noncommitment may be neither accepted nor rejected, and will not be misperceived. Attitude statements falling in the region of rejection will be rejected, their discrepancy from the individual's own attitude will be perceived as greater than it actually is, and the individual may actually change attitude in the direction opposite that desired by the communicator. Probably the most important specification is that individuals with an extremely favorable or unfavorable attitude toward a given concept have much narrower latitudes of acceptance and noncommitment, and much broader latitudes of rejection. Since the chapter dealing with audience analysis contains one section on the effects of the initial attitude of the audience, a more detailed treatment of this theory is presented there.

Kelman has described a view of three "processes of social influence" which may constitute a theory of persuasion in their own right. He refers to the process of "compliance," in which the communicator has the power to demand compliance, but points out that such compliance will continue only so long as the communicator is able to enforce his demands. A second process is the process of "identification," which depends upon the attractiveness of the communicator, and attitude change in this situation is predicted to last only so long as the listener's relationship to the communicator is satisfying to the listener. The third process is that of "internalization," in which the communicator's influence depends upon his credibility, and attitude change in this situation is predicted to last so long as the individual continues to perceive the communicator's recommendations as facilitating satisfaction of his needs and realization of his values.

For a really detailed analysis of most of these theories and the related research, the reader is urged to consult the book by Insko (1967). The collections of articles edited by Feldman (1966) and by Fishbein (1967) are also recommended.

REFERENCES

Abelson, Robert P., and Milton J. Rosenberg. "Symbolic Psychologic: A Model of Attitudinal Cognition," **Behavioral Science,** 3 (1958), 1–13.

Bettinghaus, Erwin. "The Operation of Congruity in an Oral Communication Situation." Unpublished doctoral dissertation, University of Illinois, 1959.

Brehm, Jack W., and Arthur R. Cohen. **Explorations in Cognitive Dissonance.** New York: Wiley, 1962.

Brown, Roger. **Social Psychology.** New York: Free Press, 1962, chap. 11.

Cartwright, D., and F. Harary. "Structural Balance: A Generalization of Heider's Theory," **Psychological Review,** 63 (1956), 277–293.

Chapanis, Natalie P., and Alphonse Chapanis. "Cognitive Dissonance: Five Years Later," **Psychological Bulletin,** 61 (1964), 1–22.

Cronkhite, Gary. "Toward a Real Test of Dissonance Theory," **Quarterly Journal of Speech,** 52 (1966a), 172–178.

———. "Autonomic Correlates of Dissonance and Attitude Change," **Speech Monographs,** 33 (1966b), 392–399.

Feldman, Shel. **Cognitive Consistency: Motivational Antecedents and Behavioral Consequents.** New York: Academic Press, 1966.

Festinger, Leon. **A Theory of Cognitive Dissonance.** Evanston: Row, Peterson, 1957.

———, ed. **Conflict, Decision, and Dissonance.** Stanford: Stanford University Press, 1964.

———, and J. Carlsmith. "Cognitive Consequences of Forced Compliance," **Journal of Abnormal and Social Psychology,** 58 (1959), 203–210.

Fishbein, Martin. "An Investigation of the Relationships Between Beliefs About an Object and the Attitude Toward the Object," **Human Relations,** 16 (1963), 233–239.

———. "A Consideration of Beliefs, Attitudes, and Their Relationship," **Current Studies in Social Psychology.** Ivan D. Steiner and Martin Fishbein, eds. New York: Holt, Rinehart, and Winston, 1965, pp. 107–120.

———. **Readings in Attitude Theory and Measurement.** New York: Wiley, 1967.

———, and B. H. Raven. "The AB Scales: An Operational Definition of Belief and Attitude," **Human Relations,** 15 (1962), 35–44.

Heider, F. "Attitudes and Cognitive Organization," **Journal of Psychology,** 21 (1946), 107–112.

Hovland, Carl I., and Muzafer Sherif. **Social Judgment.** New Haven: Yale University Press, 1961.

72

Insko, Chester A. **Theories of Attitude Change.** New York: Appleton-Century-Crofts, 1967.

Katz, Daniel. "The Functional Approach to the Study of Attitudes," **Public Opinion Quarterly,** 24 (1960), 163–204.

Kelman, Herbert C. "Processes of Opinion Change," **Public Opinion Quarterly,** 25, (1961), 57–78.

McGuire, William J. "A Syllogistic Analysis of Cognitive Relationships," **Attitude Organization and Change.** M. J. Rosenberg, et al., eds. New Haven: Yale University Press, 1960.

Osgood, Charles E., George A. Suci, and Percy H. Tannenbaum. **The Measurement of Meaning.** Urbana: University of Illinois Press, 1957.

Osgood and Percy H. Tannenbaum. "The Principle of Congruity in the Prediction of Attitude Change," **Psychological Review,** 62 (1955), 42–55.

Rosenberg, Milton J. "Cognitive Structure and Attitudinal Effect," **Journal of Abnormal and Social Psychology,** 53 (1956), 367–372.

————. "A Structural Theory of Attitude Dynamics," **Public Opinion Quarterly,** 24 (1960), 319–340.

————. "Inconsistency Arousal and Reduction in Attitude Change," **Current Studies in Social Psychology.** Ivan D. Steiner and Martin Fishbein, eds. New York: Holt, Rinehart, and Winston, 1965, pp. 121–134.

————, and Robert P. Abelson. "An Analysis of Cognitive Balancing," **Attitude Organization and Change.** M. J. Rosenberg, et al. eds. New Haven: Yale University Press, 1960, pp. 112–163.

Sarnoff, Irving. "Psychoanalytic Theory and Social Attitudes," **Public Opinion Quarterly,** 24 (1960), 251–279.

Sherif, Muzafer, Carolyn W. Sherif, and Roger E. Nebergall. **Attitude and Attitude Change.** Philadelphia: W. B. Saunders, 1965.

Smith, M. B., Jerome S. Bruner, and R. W. White. **Opinions and Personality.** New York: Wiley, 1956.

Stachowiak, J., and C. Moss. "Hypnotic Alterations of Social Attitudes," **Journal of Personality and Social Psychology,** 2 (1965), 77–83.

Tannenbaum, Percy H. "Mediated Generalization of Attitude Change via the Principle of Congruity," **Journal of Personality and Social Psychology,** 3 (1966), 493–500.

FOUR

The paradigm of persuasion

The basic paradigm

The basic paradigm of classical conditioning is that in which a novel or at least relatively neutral stimulus (the conditioned stimulus) is presented to an organism and is followed almost immediately by a stimulus (the unconditioned stimulus) which is already capable of eliciting a specific behavioral response (the unconditioned response). After repeated pairings of the two stimuli, the previously neutral stimulus begins to elicit from the organism a behavioral response similar to that previously elicited only by the unconditioned stimulus. The example encountered by every student of general psychology is the experiment in which Pavlov rang a bell shortly before blowing meat powder into a dog's mouth. The dog initially salivated in response to the meat powder, of course, but he soon came to salivate also in response to the bell alone, whereas the bell initially produced only an alerting or orienting response.

Let me grant at the outset that the situation in which persuasion occurs is vastly more complex than this. However, the situation in which learning occurs is vastly more complex than the paradigms of classical conditioning, operant conditioning, and all the other basic paradigms described in the literature of psychology. Yet psychologists have learned a great deal about more complex forms of human behavior by first isolating these basic situations. In fact, they made very little progress toward understanding human behavior before they began this microscopic analysis.

The basic paradigm of persuasion may be viewed as that situation in which a persuader attempts to cause a listener to perceive a relationship between two stimuli. One of these stimuli is one which is either relatively neutral, in that it elicits few and very weak responses from the listener or, more likely, is one that elicits from the listener behavior which the persuader wishes to change. I have called this the "object concept" or "object stimulus," since it may be viewed as the object of the persuasion (Cronkhite, 1964). It is very similar to what Fishbein has termed the "attitude object" (see Chapters Three and Six). For example, a persuader might be interested in changing a listener's behavior toward "United States military aid," in which case "United States military aid" would be the "object concept" or "object stimulus."

If he wishes the listener's behavior to be a more favorable evaluation of "United States military aid," he may choose a second stimulus (the "motivational stimulus" or "motivational concept") which the listener already evaluates favorably, and will attempt to cause the listener to perceive a positive relationship between the object stimulus and the motivational stimulus. He may, instead, choose a motivational stimulus which the listener evaluates unfavorably and try to demonstrate a negative relationship between the motivational stimulus and the object stimulus. He might, for example, argue that "United States military aid" increases United States prestige and decreases the likelihood of war. If he were opposed to United States military aid, he would argue the opposite: that it decreases United States prestige and increases the likelihood of war.

Two operations are involved: The individual who wishes to persuade another must choose motivational concepts which consistently elicit strong behavior from the listener, and he must demonstrate that those motivational concepts are clearly related to the object concept, so that his listener will respond to the object concept as intensely and consistently as he does toward the motivational concept. This differs from classical conditioning, in that a listener may come to perceive a **negative** relation between the two stimuli, so that his response to the object stimulus will be the **opposite** of his response to the motivational stimulus, as when the persuader argues that United States military aid will **decrease** the likelihood of war. This difference is not so great as might at first appear, however, since the persuader is in effect arguing that United States military aid will **increase** the likelihood of **peace.** A second qualification is also necessary. The listener probably already believes that the object concept is related to various other concepts, and some of these beliefs may cause him to resist persuasion. Consequently the persuader will often argue that there is **no** relation between two stimuli. For example, he may know his listener believes United States military aid causes increased taxation. Since such a belief is opposed to his cause, he might argue that United States military aid does **not** increase taxation; that the United States would have to increase its own defensive forces if it did not aid its allies in building theirs.

The process of choosing motivational stimuli or concepts to be associated with the object concept is quite complex, because there are so many types of motivational stimuli. What we usually call the "ideas" or "arguments" in a persuasive message make use of concepts of the first type. These are concepts such as "war," "United States prestige," and "increased taxation" which the persuader intentionally and obviously argues are related to the object concept.

The persuader will seldom stop when he has demonstrated (for example) that withdrawal of United States military assistance will lead to some global concept such as war. His listener's attitude toward war may not be intense enough. If he perceives this to be true he will intensify the attitude toward war by arguing that war will lead, in turn, to other concepts toward which the audience has even more intense attitudes. He may argue that the type of limited conventional war which would result from withdrawal of United States military assistance will be likely to lead to nuclear war or to the interruption of the listener's career by causing him to be drafted, or even to the death of the listener or those close to him. To the extent that the listener comes to perceive a relationship between war and his own suffering, he will be motivated to avoid war. To the extent that he is motivated to avoid war and to the extent that he perceives that withdrawal of United States military assistance will lead to war, he will be motivated to avoid withdrawal of United States military assistance. The success of the persuader will depend upon his having a complete and accurate catalog of his listener's attitudes toward a large number of such concepts.

Another type of motivational concept can be derived from the personality-oriented analysis surveyed in the preceding chapter. When a persuader uses these motivational concepts, he will usually be much more subtle in his argument, since the listener will probably not respond and may even rebel if he realizes what the persuader is attempting to do. This is doubtless the sort of argument other writers refer to as "propaganda techniques" and "suggestion." Many writers have considered these devices "unethical." I would rather not address myself to that question, since I am not a philosopher or theologian, but I would like to point out that the use of these motivational concepts can be an effective means of persuasion and they do perform useful functions for the listener. Certainly both the persuader and the listener should be aware that they exist.

For example, a persuader may suggest to the listener that his calling for United States disarmament will facilitate his being accepted by a group of liberal pacifists to whom he is attracted, thus performing for him the function of **adjustment.** Such a suggestion is irrelevant to the question of what is good for the United States or the world as a whole, but it is very relevant to what is good for the listener himself. The motivational concept of "acceptance by an attractive group," is then perceived as being related to the object concept, "favoring United States disarmament." The perceptive reader will notice that a subtle shift has occurred in the object concept: The object concept is now the **behavior of favoring United States disarmament** rather than United States disarmament itself. It is even possible for the listener to believe that United States disarmament would be **bad,** but his openly favoring United States disarmament would be **good.** On the surface that appears to be an inconsistency, but it is not, because **the stimuli are different** and consequently the attitudes toward them may be different without being inconsistent. The listener may believe that his **favoring** United States disarmament **will not lead to United States disarmament,** and he probably will be right. Thus he can overtly favor disarmament in order to gain the approbation of the group to which he is attracted and still maintain a negative "private" attitude toward disarmament.

A persuader may describe the person who opposes United States disarmament as a "Birchite," an extreme right-wing "hawk" always opposed to progress, and may describe the person who favors United States disarmament as an educated liberal and progressive humanitarian. If the listener perceives that "favoring United States disarmament" will enable him to feel superior, his choice is obvious. His new attitude will perform the function of ego defense.

Another "functional" motivational concept is "maintenance of identity," and is closely related to the preceding concept. If the persuader knows the listener considers himself to be a liberal, or if the persuader can convince the listener that he is a liberal, he need only point out that "favoring United States disarmament" is a liberal characteristic. To the extent that the listener believes himself to be a liberal and to the extent that he believes "favoring United States disarmament" to be a liberal characteristic, he will alter his own behavior so as to maintain his own identity. The new attitude will serve the function of value expression; the motivational concept is "maintenance of identity."

Katz labeled the fourth function the "knowledge" function, but I think it would be more meaningful to label it the "consistency" function. In a sense the whole paradigm of persuasion might be considered to depend upon some principle of consistency, in that the listener seems to act so as to make his attitudes toward the concepts consistent with his beliefs about the relationships among them. For that matter, one might say that Pavlov's dogs came to respond "consistently" to the two stimuli because they were "consistently" related. For my part, I would rather analyze the paradigm in terms of learning theory and stimulus generalization without postulating any "drive for consistency," but the description of the paradigm itself does not necessarily specify the motive force by which it operates. Still, a persuader may argue that an individual must change his behavior toward the object concept in order for it to be **consistent** with his other behavior. Such an overt appeal seems to put "consistency" in the place of a motivational concept. To make this analysis reasonable, one must assume that the "other behavior" has already been performed or that the individual is already irrevocably committed to perform it, which is the condition of "dissonance" as Brehm and Cohen have described it.

To utilize these four motivational concepts successfully, the persuader must have quite complete knowledge of the functions which his listener's attitudes perform and must be very perceptive and imaginative about the functions new attitudes may perform for him.

The persuader himself may also act as a motivational concept, as may other individuals he cites as being in favor of his proposal. The persuader is, in effect, associating himself with the object concept by making either a favorable or unfavorable assertion about it. To the extent that the listener responds to the persuader, then, he should respond to the concept with which the persuader associates himself. If the persuader dissociates himself from the concept, the listener will respond to the concept in a dissimilar fashion: negatively if he is favorable toward the persuader and favorably if he dislikes the persuader. This situation is the one dealt with by Osgood and Tannenbaum. However, to determine the effect of the listener's liking for the persuader upon his attraction to the concept, I will later recommend a modification of Fishbein's sum-of-products formula rather than the Osgood and Tannenbaum formula. The sum-of-products formula predicts that listener attitudes toward source and concept will always move toward each other if the source's statement is favorable and will always move apart if the source's statement is unfavorable. The congruity hypothesis sometimes predicts otherwise.

Two special notes are necessary. First, it is not only the **persuader** who may act as a motivational concept. He may quote the opinions of other individuals, in which case those individuals also become motivational concepts. Second, the persuader and the individuals he quotes may serve another function in the paradigm. To the extent that they are liked or disliked and express their own attitudes toward the object concept, they may be viewed as motivational concepts themselves, but they also may testify to the existence of a relationship between the object concept and **another** motivational concept. In that case it is the **credibility** of the persuader and his "authorities" that bears upon persuasion rather than the extent to which they are liked or disliked. I will have more to say about this function of the source a little later in the chapter. For now, the reader need only keep in mind that a "source" may operate in two ways to achieve persuasion: he himself may be a motivational concept, and he can testify that another motivational concept is related to the object concept.

The most complex set of motivational concepts is comprised by the units of language of the persuasive message. The listener has some sort of an attitude toward each word in the message, and toward each of the identifiable multiword units as well, and each of these linguistic units bears **some** relation to the object concept. (The approach might be pushed even to the levels of syllables, phonemes, sounds, and letters, but I doubt that such an analysis would be profitable.) The complexity is reduced somewhat by the fact that many of the words, especially the articles, conjunctions, and prepositions, may not elicit attitudes strong enough to be of any importance. On the other hand, the complexity is increased considerably by the fact that many of the words are related to the object concept in very complicated ways, so that the strengths of many links must be measured in order to determine what proportion of the total motivational strength of a given word bears upon the object concept. The analysis, though difficult, is worth doing. Compare the question: "Would you prostitute yourself to vote for Goldwater after he tried to strangle the civil rights bill?" with: "Would you lower yourself to vote for Goldwater after he voted against the civil rights bill?" A really sophisticated analysis of a persuasive message **must** take into account the differences between those two sentences.

Language, of course, bears also upon the listener's perception of the persuader. To measure audience attitude toward a speaker before his speech and then to assume that the initial attitude prevails throughout the speech is to ignore all the information the listener receives about the speaker as he considers the speaker's word choice, language usage, message organization, appearance, gestures, and voice characteristics. Most of these items relate more or less directly to the object concept by virtue of having been presented in the same context if nothing else, but they relate indirectly as well, since they are related to the listener's perception of the speaker which is in turn related to the object concept. Each item is potentially capable of modifying not only the listener's **liking** for the speaker, but may affect the listener's perception of the speaker's credibility as well.

Establishing the relationships

The first job of the persuader then, is to survey the physical and psychological needs of his listeners, find the persons they like and believe, find ways in which he may make himself liked and believed, and find how various language units affect them. All of us carry with us some notions about all of these matters; we have conducted very informal but very extensive surveys in the very process of living and associating with other people. If the persuader is vitally interested in succeeding, he will carry out a more extensive survey of his specific audience. How exhaustive that survey will be will depend, of course, on his motivation, time, and money. He will choose for actual use those motivational concepts which are especially motivating and those which are relevant to the object concept. Once this job is completed—no, actually concurrent with the process of choosing motivational concepts—he will consider how he can go about causing his listeners to believe that the chosen motivational concepts are related to the object concept. He must first know what types of relationships listeners may perceive between two concepts.

Types of relationships. I have chosen to consider these relationships as being of five types, which I will label relationships of contingency, categorization, similarity, approval, and coincidental association. This particular grouping came out of several extended discussions with Bob Davis, presently at the University of Michigan. Mr. Davis was at that time working on a dissertation project at the University of Iowa in which he was attempting to classify published arguments favoring and opposing the mass media. This particular classification scheme appeared to allow reliable categorization of the arguments he found. Obviously two other individuals might have found different categories as useful or more useful, but these seemed to include all the arguments he encountered and seemed to provide fairly clear distinctions.

One distinction needs to be made at this point, although it may be rather rough. It might be useful to distinguish between relationships among physical phenomena (those external to the nervous system, at least) and relationships involving psychological phenomena. Integration of schools may be said to **cause** riots in the South, and for an individual to favor segregation may be said to **cause** more effective ego defense, but the two statements may differ in a way of fundamental importance in analysis of a given persuasive message.

Relationships of contingency are those in which an individual appears to expect the occurrence of one event upon discovery of the occurrence of another event, or infers that the one event has already occurred when he observes the occurrence of the other. This category seems to include those relationships which other writers have termed relationships of "causality" and "sign." The tests of causal and sign reasoning which have been described by myriad other writers are applicable to arguments falling in this category, but it is beyond the scope of this book to describe those tests in detail. Let it suffice to say that the persuader and listener should bear in mind that the contingent occurrence of two events does not indicate that one is necessarily the **cause** of the other. One may mistake the "effect" for the "cause," for example, or may fail to perceive that two events occur together because both are results of another "cause," or may fail to perceive that one event reliably follows either of two "causes," or may fail to perceive a contingent relationship when **two** conditions are necessary to produce a given event. The careful student of persuasion will not simply dismiss these as "fallacies," however, although they are that; nevertheless they are fallacies which persuaders and listeners do commit and seem to enjoy, and they must be included in any accurate description of the process of persuasion.

Relationships of categorization are those in which an individual perceives one concept as **including** the other. The operation of the syllogism depends upon the process of successive categorization, as does the operation of logical definition. The tests of syllogistic reasoning are applicable to arguments of this type, but they have been treated in detail elsewhere and are too complex to be described here. Again, I am dubious about the utility of applying the formal tests of logical validity when describing, assessing, and attempting to predict the psychological efficacy of a persuasive communication. It seems much more useful to find out the relationships which persuaders try to demonstrate and listeners tend to accept. To know that a bit of reasoning is formally invalid does not provide much information to one attempting to describe the process of persuasion.

I would also like to mention in passing that relationships of contingence probably do not differ fundamentally from relationships of categorization, but I am quite sure individuals perceive them as differing; there is little disagreement in assigning arguments to the two different classes.

Listeners may also perceive two concepts to be related in that they are **similar.** The persuader will be successful to the extent that he can demonstrate that the two concepts are similar in all relevant and important respects, and dissimilar only in irrelevant and unimportant respects. If he does his job well, he is justified in expecting audience attitudes toward the motivational concept to generalize to the object concept.

Arguments demonstrating relationships of these first three types are at least potentially "rational" in that, if conducted according to prescribed tests of reasoning, they seem to give adequate justification for the listener to maintain similar attitudes toward the object and motivational concepts. If it can be demonstrated that federal aid to education will **cause** equality of educational opportunity, a rational man will be likely to maintain similar attitudes toward both concepts unless, of course, he believes that federal aid to education is also related to concepts which he **dislikes.** Similarly, if the persuader can demonstrate that allowing a Communist to speak on a university campus is **contained in** the concept of free speech or that it is **by definition** free speech, the rational listener can be expected to become more favorable toward the concept of allowing the Communist to speak, or less favorable toward the concept of free speech, or both. If the persuader shows that voting for Barry Goldwater is actually **similar to** prostitution, the rational listener's attitude toward prostitution may be expected to transfer to the concept of voting for Barry Goldwater, for better or worse.

The next two relationships, however, do not seem to have such a "rational" basis. Yet the experimental evidence clearly indicates that they do work. When a well-liked individual or institution expresses **approval** of a concept, audience liking for the source of the approval does transfer to the concept. The source may be **disliked,** of course, and the relationship may be one of **disapproval,** in which case the predictions are different. Now there seems to be no "rational" reason why a listener should come to like a certain kind of beer just because a well-liked sports hero claims to approve of it. To the extent that the source is an **authority** testifying that the product will satisfy some need of the listener, acceptance of his testimony may be considered "rational," but this is a totally different type of testimony from that I am presently considering. In the present case the only relationship is based on the **approval** or **disapproval** of the source, not upon his authoritative testimony to the existence of a relationship between the object concept and some **other** motivational concept. When the relationship is one of approval, the source **is** the motivational concept. Despite the lack of any apparent "rational" basis, this type of relationship is clearly effective.

One final type of relationship is, if anything, less rational and more difficult to define. Concepts come to be associated with one another merely by virtue of having been encountered in the same context. Some of the words used in a message may become associated with the object concept not because the speaker used them to describe the object concept, but because they occurred in the same context with the object concept. A whole generation of Americans are coming to associate cigarette-smoking with spring days and pleasant beaches, not because they are related by causality, categorization, similarity, or approval, but because they have been presented in the same contexts: simultaneously on the television screen. This type of relationship differs from the others in another way as well: It is a relation of association, never one of dissociation. One concept can **cause** another or **prevent** it; one concept can be **included in** or **excluded from** another; one can be **similar to** or **dissimilar from** another; one can **approve of** or **disapprove of** another; but one concept can never be coincidentally dissociated from another.

Means of demonstrating relationships. Ultimately, the persuader must rely on the experience of the listener in order to gain acceptance for the proposition that any one concept is related to any other. Ultimately he must base his argument on propositions which the listener will accept without further proof because he believes them to be true on the basis of his own past experience. The persuader may not state all the links in the chain running from the claim that two concepts are related to the experiential data on which it rests, but the listener must be satisfied that the claim is somehow verified by his own personal experience. That is not to say that the chain of reasoning will be valid, for the listener may certainly fall into or be led into erroneous deduction, or he may accept inadequate evidence. Neither is it to say that the listener can be given only facts with which he himself is familiar, for it is obvious that listeners often believe the reports of the persuader and of other individuals cited by the persuader. Even belief in testimony, however, depends on the previous experience of the listener upon which he bases his estimate of the veracity of the testimony.

The Toulmin model and the paradigm. Unfortunately, little experimental research has been done to determine how individuals actually reason from one proposition to another, or how they evaluate data to determine the truth of basic propositions. McGuire, as I noted in the previous chapter, has found evidence that listeners base their estimates of the likelihood of a claim or conclusion to some extent upon the likelihood of the propositions supporting it and to some extent upon the desirability of the claim. John Schunk, in a hitherto unpublished dissertation completed at the University of Illinois, has proposed that the Toulmin model (see Chapter Two) be used in the same way McGuire used the syllogism. I personally prefer to use the Toulmin model, since it can be used to cover not only syllogistic but inductive reasoning as well. I would like to consider the assertion that one concept is somehow related to another to be a **claim** in Toulmin's terms. This makes it possible to plug the Toulmin model of "argument" into the basic paradigm of persuasion to give a more complete model which can be pictured as follows:

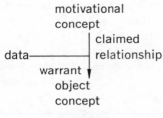

Figure 1

Such a model has the advantage of making clear that **all** arguments are to some extent "emotional," since all concepts elicit **some** degree of motivation or emotionality. It also eliminates the need for talking about "motivational" units of proof as a separate type, as Ehninger and Brockriede have done when dealing with the Toulmin model.

I would like to propose a modification of the Toulmin model which I believe makes it more suitable for describing the process of argument. The model as Toulmin describes it would lead one to believe that the data are to be accepted or rejected by the listener without any further argument. Similarly, while he does provide for what he calls "support for the warrant," he does not make any provision for describing the complex chain of arguments that may be required for its support. Actually, if the listener refuses to accept either data or warrant, the persuader must consider the questioned item to constitute a new claim, and must proceed to construct a unit of proof which will lead to its acceptance. Thus a diagram of a complete argument will very likely consist of several "units of proof" linked together by "warrant-claims" and "data-claims." Further, since it is often necessary to intensify a listener's attitude toward one motivational concept by demonstrating its relation to another motivational concept, and since there is usually more than one motivational concept directly associated with the object concept, a complete diagram of a persuasive message might look like Figure 2.

The picture could be complicated even further, since each claim of relationship, each data-claim, and each warrant-claim probably rests on more than one item of data, so that several chains of proof may impinge on each claim. Obviously the limitations of a two-dimensional diagram make it impossible to picture a message of any complexity. Unfortunately, persuasive messages are complex, and the model-builder has two alternatives: He can make his model simple, so that it can be easily understood and handled, and leave no provision for representing some parts of the real message, or he can build in complexity adequate to picture the real message at the risk of making the model as unmanageable as the reality. I have chosen the latter course, placing my faith in the glorious prospect of computer simulation.

Ehninger and Brockriede classify units of proof in the Toulmin model into three categories: "substantive," "authoritative," and "motivational." I have already noted that this proposed model eliminates the need for "motivational" warrants, but I believe the distinction between "substantive" and "authoritative" units of proof is a useful one. The claim, "withdrawal of United States military aid will cause war," can be supported in two ways. The persuader can offer a "substantive" data-claim such as "similar actions in the past have led to war" and a warrant-claim such as "the future will resemble the past," or he can offer an "authoritative" data-claim such as "the Secretary of Defense says so," and a warrant-claim such as "what the Secretary of Defense says is likely to be true." The listener, of course, may accept neither type of data and neither type of warrant. In that case the persuader will have to engage in further proof until all data-claims and all warrant-claims which are unsupported by further units of proof are accepted by the listener without further proof.

Assessing message impact: the algebraic model*

Fishbein has argued that an individual's attitude toward an attitude object or object concept can be predicted by the formula:

$$A_o = \sum_{i=1}^{N} B_i a_i$$

* I am considerably indebted to Douglas Martin of the Department of Computer Science at the University of Toronto for his assistance with these formulas.

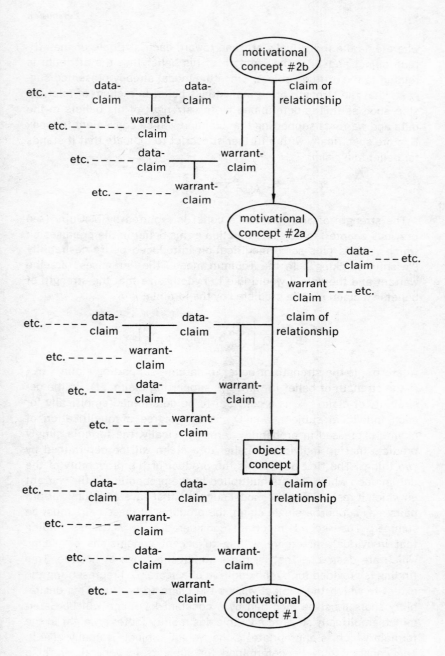

Figure 2

where a_i is the individual's attitude toward each attribute of the attitude object and B_i is the strength of his belief that the attribute is related to the attitude object. Since the model already presented suggests that the strength of an individual's belief in a claim of relationship such as this is determined by the strength of his beliefs in the data and warrants supporting that claim, it will be convenient to index B_i more specifically with a further subscript to indicate that it stands for belief in a *claim:*

$$A_o = \sum_{i=1}^{N} B_{c_i} a_i$$

The strength of an individual's belief is reported by McGuire (see previous chapter) to be some function of his belief in the premises on which it rests plus some modification introduced by its desirability ("wishful thinking"). In the Toulmin model, the "premises" are the warrant and the data. I would like to hypothesize that the strength of belief in a claim may be predicted by the formula:

$$B_{c_i} = Q_{c_i} \left[\sum_{j=1}^{N_i} b_{d_{ij}} b_{w_{ij}} + k_s D_{c_i} \right]$$

where $b_{d_{ij}}$ is the strength of belief in datum $_j$ supporting claim $_i$, $b_{w_{ij}}$ is the strength of belief in warrant $_j$ supporting claim $_i$, D_{c_i} is the desirability of claim $_i$, k_s is a constant to be determined empirically for each individual subject, and Q_{c_i} is the degree of qualification of claim $_i$ expressed in probability terms. Basically, the formula simply predicts that an individual's belief in a claim will be determined by two things. The first of these is the product of the probability of the datum upon which it rests multiplied by the probability of the warrant on which it rests. Since the model suggests that several datum-warrant pairs may support a single claim, the products of these pairs must be summed. The second important consideration is McGuire's finding that individuals are more willing to accept conclusions or claims which are desirable; that is, those which they wish to be true. This finding is provided for by the addition of a score (D_{c_i}) representing the extent to which the subject wishes the claim to be true. This desirability score must be modified by a constant k_s, which will be determined empirically so as to give this desirability factor a weight in the formula which is appropriate to the weight subjects actually give it. The constant may be determined for subjects in general, or for a specific type of subject, or for each specific subject, or even for each specific subject and each specific claim. The more specific the constant, of course, the greater predictability the formula should have. Certainly the constant will differ depending on the scale used to measure desirability.

The qualification (Q_{c_i}) is necessary because the claim may sometimes be qualified. That is, the individual is sometimes presented with a claim such as "there is a .90 probability that federal aid to education will provide more equal educational opportunity." In such a case, the strength of the qualifier ($Q_{c_i} = .90$) is taken into account as shown in the formula. Unfortunately, qualifiers are seldom so specific; one is much more likely to deal with claims such as "federal aid to education will **probably** provide more equal educational opportunity." In that case one must determine the subject's **perception** of the strength of the qualifier. An easier course of action is to eliminate the qualifier whenever possible, in which case $Q_{c_i} = 1$.

It should be obvious that strength of belief in a given item of data ($b_{d_{ij}}$), if not directly measurable, can be estimated by essentially the same formula as that used to estimate strength of belief in a claim, except that the notation must be changed somewhat:

$$b_{d_{ij}} = q_{d_{ij}} \left[\sum_{m=1}^{N_{ij}} b_{d_{ijm}} b_{w_{ijm}} + k_s d_{d_{ij}} \right]$$

The basic assumption involved is that presented in the earlier description of the model: That any item of data may be viewed as a claim in its own right, supported in turn by other data and warrants. The same assumption has been made about any warrant, so that the strength of belief in a warrant should be estimated by the formula:

$$b_{w_{ij}} = q_{w_{ij}} \left[\sum_{h=1}^{N_{ij}} b_{d_{ijh}} b_{w_{ijh}} + k_s d_{w_{ij}} \right]$$

This process of recursive substitution can be continued indefinitely, with appropriate changes in notation.

Returning to the basic formula for attitude change toward a concept, note that formulas have been presented for estimating strength of belief in a claim (B_{c_i}) when it is unknown. Now I would like to turn my attention to the individual's attitudes toward the attributes of the object concept. In this case, one must remember that an "attribute" is an "attribute" only arbitrarily; it has "attributes" of its own, and is capable of being an attitude object. Thus the formula for estimating attitude toward an attribute (a_i) is essentially the same as that for estimating attitude toward an attitude object, and involves only a change of notation:

$$a_i = \sum_{g=1}^{Ni} B_{c_{ig}} a_{ig}$$

Again, this process of recursive substitution can be continued indefinitely, with appropriate changes in notation.

Next I would like to turn to the problem of predicting attitude change from a persuasive message. An individual's attitude toward a concept following a persuasive message will be the sum of four types of belief-attitude combinations. The first type is composed of those attitude-belief combinations in which no change occurs. If the cases are arbitrarily ordered so that this type of case is represented by subscripts 1 to α (i.e., $i = 1$ to α for those cases in which $\Delta a_i = \Delta B_{c_i} = o$), and Δ is used to represent change in a quantity which it precedes, then these cases in which no change occurs may be represented by the expression:

$$\sum_{i=1}^{\alpha} B_{c_i} a_i$$

The second type of case is that in which belief change occurs, but there is no attitude change toward the attributes. If these cases are represented by subscripts $\alpha + 1$ to β (i.e., $i = \alpha + 1$ to β for those cases in which $\Delta a_i = o$ and $\Delta B_{c_i} \neq o$), then the contribution of these cases to overall post-attitude can be represented by the expression:

$$\sum_{i=\alpha+1}^{\beta} a_i (B_{c_i} + \Delta B_{c_i})$$

The third type of case is that in which attitudes toward the attributes change but beliefs do not. If these cases are represented by subscripts $\beta + 1$ to γ (i.e., $i = \beta + 1$ to γ for those cases in which $\Delta a_i \neq o$ and $\Delta B_{c_i} = o$), then the contribution of these cases can be represented by the expression:

$$\sum_{i=\beta+1}^{\gamma} B_{c_i} (a_i + \Delta a_i)$$

The fourth and final type of case is that in which there is change in belief and change in attitudes toward the attributes as well. If these cases are represented by subscripts $\gamma + 1$ to N (i.e., $i = \gamma + 1$ to N for those cases in which $\Delta a_i \neq o$ and $\Delta B_{c_i} \neq o$), then the contribution of these cases can be represented by the expression:

$$\sum_{i=\gamma+1}^{N} (a_i + \Delta a_i)(B_{c_i} + \Delta B_{c_i})$$

If these four expressions are added together, they yield the following formula for estimating an individual's attitude toward a concept after a persuasive message:

$$A'_o = \sum_{i=1}^{\alpha} B_{c_i}a_i + \sum_{i=\alpha+1}^{\beta} a_i(B_{c_i} + \Delta B_{c_i}) + \sum_{i=\beta+1}^{\gamma} B_{c_i}(a_i + \Delta a_i)$$

$$+ \sum_{i=\gamma+1}^{N} (a_i + \Delta a_i)(B_{c_i} + \Delta B_{c_i})$$

An equivalent formula, and one much easier to use, is the following:

$$A'_o = \sum_{i=1}^{N} [B_{c_i}a_i + \Delta B_{c_i}a_i + B_{c_i}\Delta a_i + \Delta B_{c_i}\Delta a_i]$$

Attitude **change** can be estimated by use of a similar formula:

$$\Delta A_o = \sum_{i=1}^{N} [\Delta B_{c_i}a_i + B_{c_i}\Delta a_i + \Delta B_{c_i}\Delta a_i]$$

REFERENCES

Cronkhite, Gary. "Logic, Emotion, and the Paradigm of Persuasion," **Quarterly Journal of Speech,** 50 (1964), 13–18.

Ehninger, Douglas, and Wayne Brockriede. **Decision by Debate.** New York: Dodd, Mead, 1963.

Fishbein, Martin. "A Consideration of Beliefs, Attitudes, and Their Relationship," **Current Studies in Social Psychology.** Ivan D. Steiner and Martin Fishbein, eds. New York: Holt, Rinehart, and Winston, 1965, pp. 107–120.

Katz, Daniel. "The Functional Approach to the Study of Attitudes," **Public Opinion Quarterly,** 24 (1960), 163–204.

McGuire, William J. "A Syllogistic Analysis of Cognitive Relationships," **Attitude Organization and Change.** M. J. Rosenberg, et al., eds. New Haven: Yale University Press, 1960, pp. 65–111.

Schunk, John. "Probability and Desirability Determinants of Relationships Among Beliefs in Rhetorical Propositions." Unpublished doctoral dissertation, University of Illinois, 1967.

Toulmin, Stephen. **The Uses of Argument.** Cambridge, Eng.: Cambridge University Press, 1959.

FIVE

Testing the significance of persuasive effects

In the previous chapters much has been said about the theories of persuasion, that is, about attempts at comprehensive explanations of the way in which persuasion operates. As was pointed out in the second chapter, however, there is another approach to the study of persuasion that is less involved in the testing of comprehensive theories. This is the approach adopted most successfully by Carl Hovland, in which one identifies the choices which the persuader must make as he prepares his message and conducts experiments to determine which of the alternatives is most successful with certain audiences under certain circumstances. One need not abandon theory to pursue this approach. At one extreme, some scholars use just enough experimenting to get from one theory to another; at the other extreme are scholars who use just enough theory to get from one experiment to another. The Hovland approach and the approach to be taken in the remainder of the book are closer to the latter extreme, in which the theories are less comprehensive and the inferences from the experiments are less general.

Chapters Seven and Eight contain a survey of the experimental literature which might be useful to the speaker faced with the choices inherent in preparing and delivering a persuasive communication.

Clevenger (1966), in the volume in this series concerned with audience analysis, speaks of "two important questions: (1) What is useful to know about an audience? (2) How do you use the information once it is in hand?" The latter two chapters of this book will be devoted to answering two questions which closely parallel Clevenger's: (1) What do we know about audience characteristics which affect audience responses to persuasion? (2) What do we know about the ways in which a speaker can achieve persuasion given certain audience characteristics? In answering these questions, I will cite a large number of experiments in which variables have been manipulated and the consequent effects measured. Detailed analysis of the studies will not usually be possible. Hopefully the reader will sometimes be inspired to read the original reports of these experiments. When this occurs, an appreciation of the validity and significance of the experiments will require some knowledge of measurement, experimental method, and statistical inference. It is the purpose of Chapters Five and Six to provide a brief introduction to that material for the reader who is not yet acquainted with it.

Independent and dependent variables

The variable manipulated or controlled by the experimenter is called the "independent" variable. An experimenter may suspect that a speaker who states his major arguments at the outset of a speech will be more effective than one who does not. To test such a hypothesis, the experimenter might compose one introduction which contains a statement of major arguments and one which does not. The differences between the two introductions then constitute the **independent** variable. Another experimenter may suspect that the level of intelligence of the listener makes a difference in the extent to which the listener is persuaded by a given speech. If he has access to IQ scores of a sample of listeners, he may assign those with scores above the average to one group and those with scores below the average to another group, and have them listen to the same persuasive speech under the same conditions. (In fact, in such an experiment, all subjects could listen together to assure that the conditions were similar.) In this case it is the differences between the two **groups** that constitute the independent variable.

The variable which is supposed to depend upon these manipulations is the "dependent" variable. In the examples just given, as in most experiments in persuasion, the dependent variable might be attitude change. The experimenter would choose one of the methods of measuring attitude change, probably one of those described in the following chapter, and would determine whether attitude change does indeed depend upon such differences in speech introductions or audience intelligence.

Other variables may be supposed to intervene between the independent and the dependent variables. For example, it may be that a listener is better able to comprehend a persuasive speech in which the major arguments are stated, and is thus more persuaded by it. In that case, "comprehension" is an **intervening** variable. A variable which is supposed to intervene between the independent and dependent variables is not called an intervening variable unless it is capable of being measured or "operationally defined." If such a variable is hypothesized but cannot be measured, it is called a "hypothetical construct." Of course, what is supposedly unmeasurable at one time, and consequently a hypothetical construct, may come to be measurable, and may then be termed an intervening variable. In the theory of cognitive dissonance, mentioned in the second chapter, "dissonance-produced drive" is a hypothetical construct unless one accepts something like GSR, heart rate, or self-ratings of anxiety as an operational definition of such drive, in which case it may be termed an intervening variable.

Operational definition: reliability and validity

An operational definition of a concept consists in a description of actual operations which constitute or produce that concept. Thus, in the examples given earlier, the introduction containing the statement of major arguments constitutes an operational definition of what the experimenter elsewhere calls "partitioning" or, even more vaguely, "organization." The scores on a specific IQ test, with the circumstances attendant upon and procedures for administration and scoring of the test, constitute the operational definition of "intelligence." Similarly, the differences between pre and post scores on a specific type of attitude test constitute an operational definition of "attitude change."

An operational definition should be precise enough to be **reliable** and should be a careful development of the construct it is supposed to represent, so that it will be valid.

Suppose, for example, the experimenter gives only a vague description of the operations by which one may construct an introduction which "partitions" or states the major arguments of a speech. If other experimenters try to replicate his study, they may produce introductions which differ from his in important ways, and their experiments may produce different results. His operational definition would be said to be unreliable, since it is not reproducible, or does not give consistent results. The IQ test chosen by the experimenter may be a poor one, of inadequate length, possibly. If it were to be administered twice, and the subjects who scored high on it the first time generally were not the same subjects who scored high the second time, the test would be said to be unreliable. The experimenter might make the same error in selecting a test of attitude. Reliability is generally the extent to which an operational definition gives consistent, reproducible results. In the case of a test, it may be measured by the correlation between the scores of subjects on one administration and the scores of the same subjects on a second administration, or by the correlation between scores produced by the odd-numbered items and those produced by the even-numbered items, or by the correlation between scores on the first half of the test and those on the second half. Such a measure is called a "coefficient of reliability." The first method mentioned above, correlating scores on one administration of a test with those on another, produces a coefficient of "test-retest" reliability. Sometimes, to eliminate the effect of experience or learning, an alternate form of the same test will be given at the second administration. The second method mentioned is called the "odd-even" method, and the third is generally called the "split-halves" method. Both these latter methods require that the coefficient of reliability be corrected for length, since reliability depends on length, and these methods in effect give the reliability of only half the test (see Guilford, 1954). Other more sophisticated methods have been developed for measuring reliability without administering a test twice, but they are too complicated to explain here.

The concept of validity is a little more difficult to explain. An operational definition is said to be valid to the extent that it represents that which it is purported to represent. An experimenter might administer a test of attitude toward education and find it quite reliable, but if he used it as an operational definition of "intelligence" one would be inclined to question its validity. If the experimenter in the earlier example hypothesized that greater "organization" in a persuasive speech will produce greater attitude change and offered the introduction which stated the major arguments as his operational definition of greater "organization," one would probably question its validity, for to most people "organization" means something other than or at least something more than an opening statement of the major arguments. There is not much difficulty defining "validity" as long as there is a **concrete** notion of what the operational definition "is purported to represent." A test of scholastic aptitude would be said to be valid to the extent that it predicts success in college; the correlation between scores on a test of scholastic aptitude and college grade-point averages of a group of students would be called a "coefficient of validity." Unfortunately, when attempting to measure attitudes, one has no **concrete** notion of what the test "is purported to represent." In the example just given, college grade-point average was the "criterion" measure. When one measures attitudes, one has no "criterion" measure. Very few in the field would say that overt behavior in an unstructured situation can be used as a criterion measure, and I have already argued that such overt behavior is merely another type of attitude test. How, then, can one say that a given operational definition of a construct such as "attitude" is valid or invalid?

There are at least two possibilities. The easy way out is to say that an attitude test has "content," "face," or "logical" validity, for "the characteristic being tested . . . is by definition precisely the activity in which the subject is asked to engage; thus the thing being tested becomes the job itself." [Goyer, 1965] If one defines an attitude as a tendency to evaluate, then an attitude test which asks subjects to evaluate has a great deal of "face," "content," or "logical" validity. Still, there has been disagreement over the question of whether agreement with a statement such as "Negroes are good fighters" indicates a tendency to evaluate or merely a belief with no evaluative overtones. The concept of "face" validity provides no way to settle such disagreements; indeed, a disagreement such as this is a disagreement about whether the test has face validity.

The second possible way to determine the validity of a test of a construct such as attitude is provided by the concept of "construct" validity. In the view of the advocates of "construct" validity, a construct is valid to the extent that measures which use very dissimilar methods but are purported to measure the same construct actually produce similar results. The more specific requirement is that the dissimilar methods purported to measure the same construct must produce results more similar than those produced by **similar** methods purported to measure **different** constructs (see Campbell and Fiske, 1959). In this view, validity and reliability seem to become opposite poles of the same continuum: Validity becomes the correlation between maximally dissimilar measures of a given construct, while reliability is the correlation between maximally similar measures.

Tests of significance: the rationale

Those not acquainted with statistical procedures often ask what is meant by a statement such as, "The difference was significant at the .05 (or five percent) level." To answer the question directly, the statement may be translated into the English to read, "If no 'real' difference existed, and the experiment were repeated a great many times, a difference as large as that observed would occur only five out of one hundred times by chance." While that translation is a little clearer, it does not usually satisfy the questioner, who usually wants to know how a statistician knows such a difference would occur a given number of times by chance. The answer to that question would fill a small book, but some clarification may be of value here.

Reconsider the example mentioned earlier, the case of an experiment to determine whether a persuasive speech is more effective if the major arguments are stated at the outset. Having prepared the two speeches, the experimenter selects at random two samples of subjects from the population to which he wishes to generalize. He must assume that the differences between the groups in such matters as intelligence, sex, personality traits, alertness and degree of frustration are not systematic; that is, he must assume that the two groups differ only by chance, only because they were randomly chosen. The safest way to accomplish this is to number all subjects and use a table of random numbers to assign them to each group. Because experimenters often use college speech or psychology students as subjects, they often use the members of one or more sections as one group and members of other sections as the other group, keeping the sections intact. That procedure is acceptable if students were originally assigned to the sections at random and if the members of a given section have had no common experiences which will make a difference in their response to the speech they hear. An experimenter using intact classes should give the reader some assurance that the groups differ only at random, and the burden of proof is on him.

Assume for the moment that the two groups are selected at random. Assume further that the differences between the speeches do not "really" produce any difference in the amount of attitude change which occurs. Suppose, in fact, that one were to give **identical** speeches to both groups. The average attitude change in one group would still be greater than that in the other, **by chance.** In fact, it would be a very unusual occurrence if the two groups did **not** differ in their responses to the speech. The question is, how does one know that a difference is large enough that it must be due to the effect of the independent variable rather than to chance?

One never **knows.** One may only estimate the degree of probability that a difference of a given size is due to the experimental differences rather than to chance. He makes this estimate by determining the amount of variation among the attitude change scores **within** each group. That is, he calculates a measure of the extent to which the attitude change scores in group A vary around the mean of the scores in group A and calculates a measure of the extent to which the scores in group B vary around the mean of the scores in group B. These two measures are then used to provide an estimate of the extent to which attitude change scores of subjects will vary **due to chance alone.** (Note that the extent to which the scores in group A differ from each other and from their own average should be due to chance alone, and the same for group B.) This estimate is called an estimate of the **variance within groups** or the **error variance.** It might be called an estimate of the **variance due to chance.**

A second estimate is then computed of the variance **between** groups, or the extent to which attitude change scores for all subjects differ from each other and from their mean, disregarding the fact that they are grouped. Thus, if each group contained fifty subjects, the estimate of the error variance would be obtained from the observed variation of the fifty scores for group A around the mean of the scores in Group A and from the observed variation of the fifty scores for group B around the mean of the scores in group B. This second variance estimate, however, would be obtained from the observed variation of all one hundred scores around the mean of all one hundred scores. This second estimate, the estimate of the variance **between** groups, should contain all the variance due to chance, **plus the variance due to the experimental treatments.**

The next step is to form a ratio between the two variance estimates, dividing the estimate of the error variance into the estimate of the variance between groups. The extent to which the variance between groups exceeds the error variance should be an indication of the amount of variation caused by the experimental treatments. Consequently, the larger the ratio between the variances the more likely it is that the observed differences are partially attributable to the experimental variable. Statisticians have determined, both theoretically and empirically, the probability that a ratio of a given size will occur by chance when there are only random differences between the groups. For example, a **t**-ratio as large as 1.96 will occur by chance only five times out of one hundred. Consequently, if an experiment yields a **t**-ratio as large as 1.96 with a sample size greater than fifty subjects, it is fairly safe to conclude that the difference between the groups is due to something other than chance. Whether the experimenter is justified in concluding that this "something" is purely the experimental variable depends upon the care he has taken in designing and conducting his experiment.

Students who have not heard this explanation before sometimes remain concerned about random variation. They continue to worry about the fact that the experimental group may differ from the control group in average age, average intelligence, etcetera, and may not be solaced by the assurance that these differences are random. They remain unconvinced that the statistical test of significance really takes into account all random variation, and may be tempted to deliberately match the subjects in one group with those in the other. That is, they may think it wise to deliberately assign subjects to groups so that the groups are nearly equal in age and intelligence. To do this defeats the logic of the statistical test. If one deliberately eliminates between-group differences in intelligence, for example, the estimate of the variance between groups will be artificially reduced. There will be no corresponding reduction in the error variance, however, since it is computed from observed variance within each group. With between-group variance reduced and error variance remaining the same, the ratio between the two variances will appear spuriously small, and the experimenter will run a greater risk of failing to find a significant difference between the groups when one actually exists. It is possible to use matched groups in an experiment, or to apply both treatments to all subjects, comparing the response of each subject under one treatment with his response under the other, but special statistics must be used in such cases.

The reader who does not wish to work through the logic of the test of significance in one of the standard statistical textbooks, yet is not quite willing to accept the word of statisticians that what they are doing is acceptable, might be consoled to remember that it is just these random differences in age, intelligence, and personality that make necessary a statistical test of significance. If all human beings were identical and could be assumed to respond identically, only one person would be needed in each group. If the person who heard the statement of major arguments were more persuaded than the person who did not, that would be enough; no test of significance would be necessary. The statistical test of significance is specifically designed to account for individual differences which occur within as well as between groups. One need only be concerned with extraneous differences which occur between groups but not within, and are thus confounded with the experimental variable.

The choice of the level of significance is purely arbitrary. Whether the experimenter will use the .05 or the .01 or the .001 level as indicative of significance is a decision he himself must make, balancing the consequences of concluding there is a difference when none exists against the consequences of failing to find a difference when one does exist. Both the .05 and the .01 levels are used in research in the social sciences, with the .05 level being used most often. Most responsible experimenters do not use the .10 level. It is important that the level of significance be chosen before the experiment is run, since otherwise the temptation will be to choose whatever level of significance one obtains, especially if the experiment must be approved by a graduate committee partial to significant results.

Another important qualification is that one should never conclude that **no** difference exists between two groups or two treatments. It is possible to prove that a difference **does** exist, but if no difference appears, **nothing** is proven. The lack of a difference may be due to sloppiness on the part of the experimenter. The independent variable may not "take": The statement of major arguments may not be clear enough, or the IQ test used may not really discriminate adequately between intelligent and less intelligent subjects. The dependent variable may not be reliably measured: The attitude test may not have accurately identified those subjects having the greatest attitude change. The most one can conclude in the absence of statistical significance is that there is no evidence that a difference exists. The hypothesis that there is no difference is called the "null hypothesis": It can never be proven, only disproven.

It is now rather generally accepted that the experimenter should make specific predictions as to which group or which treatment will produce the most attitude change if he is going to come to any conclusions about the results. The experimenter will usually have some reason for testing a given variable. If it is not a full-blown theory, it will at least be a "hunch" that the variable bears some relation to attitude change. The same theory or "hunch" that leads him to such a conclusion will usually lead him to predict that one treatment will be more effective than the other. Sometimes an experimenter will embark on a "fishing expedition" in which he simply says to himself, "I wonder what would happen if . . ." There is nothing wrong with such research, but when differences appear and the experimenter begins explaining why they appeared, he is obligated to make two things clear to his readers: that his explanations were composed **after the fact,** and that the findings are only indicative of the direction future experiments might reasonably take. Explanations after the fact simply do not have the status of confirmed predictions.

How far may one generalize the results of experimental findings? A great deal has been written on the subject, but no one has come up with a satisfactory answer. Strictly speaking, the findings of an experiment in which the subjects are a sample of students enrolled in a beginning public speech course at the University of Illinois in the third week of the spring semester of 1967 may be generalized to the population of students enrolled in a beginning public speech course at the University of Illinois in the third week of the spring semester of 1967. Beyond that, there are simply no rules to follow when one wishes to generalize. Yet we **do** generalize from our everyday informal observations, and we are at least as justified in generalizing to some extent the findings of carefully controlled experiments. One of the greatest needs and yet one of the most thankless tasks in this field is the replication of experiments using various types of individuals as subjects, various types of speech topics, and systematically varying other elements of the situation so that one can have some idea of how much generalization is justified.

Types of statistics

The statistics which one will most often encounter in reading the experimental literature in persuasion are the **t**-test, the F-test or analysis of variance, and the Pearson product-moment coefficient of correlation (often referred to simply as the Pearson **r**), the rank-order coefficient of correlation (P), the point-biserial coefficient of correlation, and chi-square (χ^2).

Very briefly, the **t**-ratio is generally used to determine whether two group means differ significantly from each other, or whether one group mean differs significantly from zero. It is, somewhat oversimplified, the ratio of the difference between the group means (or the difference between a group mean and zero) to an estimate of the error variance. In experiments in which the size of the sample exceeds about one hundred subjects, this ratio may be referred to as a **z**. The **t**-ratio would be used to determine whether the group hearing the speech containing the statement of major arguments changed attitude more than the control group. One would subtract one group mean from the other and divide by the estimate of the error variance. If one were interested in determining whether the "organized" speech produced any attitude change at all, one would divide an estimate of the error variance for the group hearing that speech into the mean attitude change for that group.

Suppose, however, that the experimenter is interested in the extent to which the listener's intelligence affects persuasion. If he uses only two groups, one of high and one of low intelligence, he can use a **t**-ratio to test the difference between the groups. But suppose he wants to use **three** groups of high, average, and low intelligence. He is now testing, not a difference between two groups, but variation among groups. This requires use of the F-ratio, which is the ratio between an estimate of the variance obtained from the differences among groups and an estimate of the variance obtained from the differences among individual scores within groups. The "groups" need not be composed of different individuals, however. If an experimenter were interested in the effects produced by speeches on three different topics, and didn't care if each subject heard all three speeches, the three groups of scores might be attitude-change scores for the same subjects with regard to different topics. This type of variable is called a "within-subjects" variable, whereas that contained in the previous example was a "between-subjects" variable.

This simple test of differences among the means of groups having different levels of the same characteristic (such as intelligence) or being exposed to several intensities of the same treatment variable (different levels of "language intensity," for example) is called a "simple-randomized" design. Suppose now that the experimenter suspects the success of stating one's main arguments depends on the intelligence of the listener; that is, there is an "interaction" between type of introduction and listener intelligence. He might run two experiments varying the type of introduction using a different level of listener intelligence in each experiment. If he found a significant difference in the experiment using listeners of high intelligence but no significant difference in the experiment using listeners of low intelligence, he could not conclude anything about the **difference between the experiments.** Remember that the lack of a **significant** difference in the one experiment does not justify the conclusion that there is **no** difference.

The proper approach in this case would be to use a multi-factor design. Speeches with two types of introductions would be given to audiences of two (or more) intelligence levels, as illustrated in Figure 3. Then one would first calculate an F-ratio to test the "interaction"

		level of intelligence	
		high	low
type of introduction	main arguments stated	much change	much change
	main arguments not stated	much change	little change

Figure 3

effect; that is, to test the question of whether the effect of the different types of introductions with audiences of high intelligence is different from the effect with audiences of low intelligence. That pattern shown in Figure 3 is one possible pattern of interaction. The statement of major arguments made a difference with audiences of low intelligence but not with audiences of high intelligence. It would also be an interaction effect if the effect were exactly reversed with audiences of different intelligence levels.

If the F-ratio testing the interaction effect is significant, the logic of the design dictates that the experimenter then concern himself only with the "simple effects" of the different types of introductions at **each** level of intelligence. To ask whether a statement of major arguments is generally more effective makes no sense, nor does it make sense to ask whether audiences of low intelligence are more easily persuaded than are audiences of high intelligence, for the effect of one variable has just been found to depend on the other. However, if the F-ratio testing interaction is insignificant, one is justified in testing the significance of the main effect of the type of introduction regardless of audience intelligence and the significance of the main effect of audience intelligence regardless of the type of introduction. Figure 4 illustrates the case in which there is a main effect of type of introduction but no main effect of audience intelligence.

| | | level of intelligence | |
		high	low
type of introduction	main arguments stated	much change	much change
	main arguments not stated	little change	little change

Figure 4

Figure 5 illustrates the case in which both main effects occur. This pattern is sometimes mistakenly called an interaction pattern, but it is not. Note that the two main effects are cumulative, producing the greatest effect when the main arguments are explicitly stated for audiences of low intelligence, and the least effect when the main arguments are not stated for audiences of high intelligence.

		level of intelligence	
		high	low
type of introduction	main arguments stated	moderate change	much change
	main arguments not stated	little change	moderate change

Figure 5

It is possible to test the effects of more than two variables at one time, using designs of three or even more dimensions or factors. When such designs are used, the interpretation of the main effect of each variable is quite straightforward. In interpreting the main effect of any one variable, one simply disregards all the other factors and proceeds as if he were dealing with a simple randomized design. Even when there is interaction between any two variables, interpretation is fairly easy; one proceeds by disregarding all the variables except the two which interact. However, when interaction appears among three or more variables in multi-factor designs, interpretation is difficult. Explaining the interpretation of such interaction is not only beyond the scope of this book, it is beyond the present inclination of the author.

The Pearson product-moment coefficient of correlation (or Pearson r) is a measure of the extent to which one set of scores depends on another set. That is, it is an index of the extent to which an individual's score on one test can be used to predict his score on another test. The coefficient of correlation is represented by numbers ranging from +1.00 to −1.00. If the correlation between two sets of scores is perfect and positive, +1.00, then one knows that the individual receiving the highest score on one test will also receive the highest score on the other. The numbers on the dial of a gasoline pump which show the number of gallons delivered are perfectly and positively correlated with the numbers showing the amount to be paid by the customer. If the correlation between two sets of scores is perfect and negative, −1.00, then one knows that the individual receiving the **highest** score on one test will receive the **lowest** score on the other. The numbers which show how many gallons of gasoline the service station attendant has put into your tank are perfectly and negatively correlated with the amount of change he will give you in return for a ten-dollar bill. If the correlation between two sets of scores is nonexistent, .00, then knowledge that an individual received the highest score on test A gives one no indication whatsoever of the score that same individual will receive on test B.

The Pearson r is useful as an index of reliability or validity. It is the Pearson r calculated between scores on two administrations of the same test (or between alternate forms of the same test) which constitutes **test-retest** reliability, for example. The Pearson r between scores on two tests intended to measure the same thing (two different types of attitude tests, for example) is used as an indication of **test validity.** Another use of the Pearson r can be illustrated by reference to the previous example, in which the experimenter suspected that more intelligent subjects are less easily persuaded. He can divide his subjects into two groups according to whether they are above or below average in intelligence, let them listen to a persuasive speech (or better, several persuasive speeches) and measure their attitude change. If the more intelligent group shows less attitude change, and if that difference is large enough to produce a significant **t**-ratio, the experimenter may conclude his hypothesis is confirmed. An alternative approach would be to form **several** groups of different intelligence levels and measure the attitude change of each group in response to persuasive speeches. Then if the least intelligent group changed attitude more than the group of average intelligence, and the group of average intelligence changed attitude more than the group of high intelligence, and if these differences were large enough to produce a significant **F**-ratio, the experimenter would conclude his hypothesis confirmed. Use of the Pearson r is a third alternative. In this procedure the subjects are not assigned to groups according to intelligence level; in a sense each individual is analogous to a group. Instead of predicting that **groups** of high intelligence will show little attitude change, the experimenter predicts that **individuals** of high intelligence will show little attitude change. Thus, if the coefficient of correlation is negative and large enough to be significant, the experimenter will conclude his hypothesis confirmed.

How large must a Pearson r be in order to be significant? That depends upon the number of **pairs of scores** (usually the number of persons) on which it is based. Once the coefficient is calculated, however, it is quite easy to determine whether it is significant. One simply refers to a table such as that in Guilford's **Psychometric Methods** to find whether the obtained r is large enough to be significant at the chosen level considering the number of subjects used in the experiment. For example, if 25 subjects were used, a correlation coefficient of .39 (or —.39) would be significant at the .05 level and .50 (or —.50) would be significant at the .01 level. If 100 subjects were used, a Pearson r of only .20 (or —.20) would be required for significance at the .05 level, and a Pearson r of .26 (or —.26) would be significant at the .01 level. The fact that a coefficient of correlation of .20 based on 100 subjects is significant at the .05 level does not mean that the "real" correlation is **exactly** .20, however. It means instead that a correlation that high would occur by chance only five times out of one hundred if there were no "real" relation between the variables in the population from which the sample was drawn. That is, it means that the correlation in the sample is large enough that the "real" correlation in the population must be something higher than .00; the "real" correlation may be either higher or lower than the .20 obtained in the sample.

Folklore has it that the Pearson r is inferior to the **t**-ratio or **F**-ratio because the Pearson r gives no indication that differences in one variable "cause" differences in the other; it merely indicates that some relationship exists between the two variables. That is not always true. Look back at the example. As the **t**-ratio and the **F**-ratio are used, they give no more indication of "causality" than does the Pearson r. All three alternatives give essentially the same information. Significant results by any of the three methods would still not allow one to conclude that differences in intelligence "cause" differences in attitude change; the "causality" may be in the opposite direction, or both differences may be due to differences in some third and unidentified factor. **Manipulation** is the key to inferences about "causality." If the experimenter could apply some treatment to one group which made its members more intelligent, and if that group then showed significantly less attitude change, he could conclude that the increased intelligence "caused" the decreased attitude change. Without the manipulation he could make no inferences about "causality" regardless of the statistic used. Thus **t** and **F**-ratios **can,** but do not **necessarily,** allow inferences about "causality." On the other hand, in cases where one is interested only in determining whether a relationship exists, the Pearson r gives not only that information but also an indication of the **strength** of the relationship, which cannot be provided by **t** or **F.**

It is also possible to compute and test for significance a coefficient of multiple correlation or regression (R) which provides information about the extent to which two or more variables are useful in predicting a criterion variable; for example, the extent to which SCAT scores and high school class standing are **together** useful in predicting college grade-point average. One cannot simply add the two predictor scores for each subject and then determine the Pearson r between this new predictor variable and the criterion variable. To do so will give the greater weight to whichever of the two predictors has the greater variation in scores, because its variance will be predominantly reflected in the sums of the two sets of scores. This will give greater "importance" to the variable with greater variance, whereas it may not be the better predictor of success in college. It is possible to determine which is the better of the two predictor variables by determining which one correlates more closely with the criterion measure, and weight the scores accordingly. That procedure, however, ignores the fact that the predictor variables are themselves correlated with one another. If the correlation between the predictor variables is high, so that they are largely redundant, and if one is a much better predictor than the other, it may be better to rely on the one predictor alone. The problem is even more acute when one wishes to select the two or three best predictors from a larger number of predictors. Multiple regression analysis can provide the ideal combination of variables as well as the ideal weight for each variable in a prediction formula.

Factor analysis is another multivariate technique which has become more popular as computers have become more readily available. Suppose one asked a group of subjects to rate a concept such as President Nixon on a set of thirty semantic differential scales. One might then be interested in knowing which scales tended to be mutually predictive; that is, he might wish to know which scales tended to "cluster" into "dimensions" or "factors" so that each scale within a factor showed high correlations with other scales within that factor but was relatively independent of scales outside the factor. This could be done for a few scales by arranging them in a matrix to display the correlation of every scale with every other scale, but such a procedure would become very difficult and subjective when very many scales were used. Factor analysis is essentially a means of determining how many such clusters, factors, or dimensions exist in a matrix of intercorrelations, what is the contribution of each factor to the variance of each scale (or variable), and what is the contribution of each factor to the variance of the total test score. It is especially important that the reader realize how arbitrary are the procedures involved in factor analysis, and how necessary it is that the researcher specify exactly how he intends to analyze the data and what his expectations are **before** he sees any results. It is altogether too easy to use a high-speed computer to search through the data for a chance factor which appears to confirm the researcher's pet theory, and then use a varimax rotation to maximize the variance attributable to that factor. One of the present disadvantages of factor analysis is that modern computers and cooperative computer services make it much easier to do it than to understand it, resulting in a fantasy land where the blind lead the blind and the one-eyed man is an outcast.

The use of "parametric" statistics such as the **t**-ratio, **F**-ratio, and Pearson r depends upon the assumption that the scores being used are "normally distributed." That is, before using these statistics, one should assure himself that the scores he is using are so distributed that the proportion of scores close to the average (mean) score is great, and scores occur less and less frequently at increasing distances from the mean. Specifically, the "distribution" of scores should approximately resemble the type of bell-shaped curve which statisticians call "normal."

Most psychological measures, including most measures of attitude change, do yield scores that are normally distributed. Some, however, do not. College rank in class is one obvious example. In a college class of 25 persons, for example, the "average" rank would be 13, but the rank of 13 would occur no more frequently than the rank of one or 25. Obviously this data, like all rank-ordered data, is not normally distributed. Suppose, as another example, that a sadistic experimenter used as a measure of disbelief in a proposition the number of electric shocks a subject would endure before agreeing with the proposition. If the proposition really had two sides, many subjects would agree with the proposition immediately, and would receive a score of zero. At the other end, assuming the shock to be relatively mild, many subjects might never agree with the proposition. To prevent fatigue and a high electric bill, the experimenter would probably establish an arbitrary limit of, say, twenty shocks per person. Then all subjects who refused to agree would receive a score of twenty. Here, again, the distribution would probably not be normal, for the two extreme scores, zero and twenty, would be those occurring most frequently.

When one encounters such data he must use "non-parametric" statistics, which do not depend on the assumption of normal distribution. Rho (ρ), the rank-order coefficient of correlation, is a popular non-parametric substitute for the Pearson r. It should be used with rank-order data or with data which has been found to be not normally distributed and has been transformed into rank-order form. Aside from describing differences in computational procedures, there is not much new to be said about the rank-order coefficient of correlation. Its numerical value may range from +1.00 to −1.00, its meaning is essentially the same as that of a Pearson r, it can be tested for significance, and its significance has essentially the same meaning as the significance of a Pearson r. The rank-order coefficient is not so efficient in detecting relationships between variables, and consequently requires the use of a few more subjects to achieve the same level of significance. As sample size increases, however, the value of a Pearson r is more and more nearly approached by a rank-order coefficient calculated from the same scores transformed into rank-order data. Sometimes one wishes an index of the strength of the relationship between one continuous variable, such as attitude change, and one dichotomous variable, such as sex. The point biserial coefficient of correlation is used in such a case. Again, this statistic yields values ranging from +1.00 to −1.00, it can be tested for significance, and its interpretations are similar to those of the Pearson r.

Sometimes an experimenter may wish to use a dichotomous measure. For example, he may only be able to get from his subjects an indication of whether they agree or disagree with a message, or he may observe whether they do or do not perform the behavior urged by the message. He may discover that his measure of attitude change yields scores that are not normally distributed, so he is forced to use it only as an indication of whether change did or did not occur. He wants to know whether different experimental treatments made any difference in subjects' attitudes or behavior change. One statistic he may use is chi-square (χ^2).

Consider again the example of the experimenter who hypothesizes that an introductory statement of major arguments enhances the effectiveness of a persuasive speech. Suppose, however, that instead of using a paper-and-pencil attitude test he now observes whether his subjects actually perform the behavior advocated in the speech. Now, instead of a test score, he has only the knowledge that each subject did or did not do what he was urged to do. The variable is dichotomous; it is neither normal nor even continuous.

The proper procedure here would be to classify subjects into four groups according to which of the two speeches they heard and according to whether they did or did not perform the desired behavior. Suppose 100 subjects were used. Of these, 50 heard the major arguments stated in the introduction and fifty did not. Of the 100 subjects, 60 performed the desired behavior and 40 did not. Figure 6 illustrates the number of subjects one would expect to fall into each of the four classes or cells if the type of speech made no difference.

	behavior performed		
	yes	no	
main arguments stated	30	20	50
main arguments not stated	30	20	50

type of introduction

Figure 6

Suppose, however, that the responses actually observed are those illustrated in Figure 7. Obviously the **observed** frequencies differ from the **expected** frequencies.

		behavior performed: yes	behavior performed: no	
type of introduction	main arguments stated	40	10	50
	main arguments not stated	20	30	50

Figure 7

The chi-square statistic is an index of the extent to which the observed frequencies depart from the expected frequencies. Once χ^2 is calculated, the experimenter refers to a table which shows the probabilities of various values of χ^2 occurring by chance, and determines whether the chance probability of a χ^2 as large as that obtained is less than .05. If it is, and if the frequencies deviate in the predicted direction, his hypothesis is confirmed. For those reading this book in lieu of a novel, the obtained χ^2 in this case is considerably greater than that needed for significance at the .05 level, and the experimenter lived happily ever after.

REFERENCES

Campbell, Donald T., and Donald W. Fiske. "Convergent and Discriminant Validation by the Multitrait-Multimethod Matrix," **Psychological Bulletin,** 56 (1959), 81–105.

Clevenger, Theodore, Jr. **Audience Analysis.** Indianapolis: Bobbs-Merrill, 1966, p. 43.

Goyer, Robert S. "A Test to Measure the Ability to Organize Ideas." Manuscript distributed by the Communication Research Center of the Department of Speech, Purdue University, September 1965.

Guilford, J. P. **Psychometric Methods.** New York: McGraw-Hill, 1954.

SIX

Measuring persuasive effects

In experiments in persuasion, the **criterion** measure, or the measure one is interested in being able to predict or alter, is usually something termed "attitude," although that seems to be on the verge of changing. In the first chapter the author argued that an attitude **is** a cluster of incidents of evaluative or approach-avoidance behavior, at least for scientific analysis and operational definition. That is, a number of instances in which an individual approaches an object or evaluates a concept favorably constitutes that individual's attitude toward the object or concept. Other writers have generally defined attitude as a tendency to evaluate an object or concept favorably or unfavorably. Whatever definition one chooses, it is important to settle on a means of measuring the behavior which the persuasive communication is designed to change.

The discussion in the first chapter, in which "attitude tests" and "overt behavior" were viewed as being fundamentally the same, to some extent begged the important question here. In "real-life" persuasion outside the experimental situation, there are certain types of behavior the speaker wishes to induce his audience to perform. He may want them to sign a petition, vote for a candidate, buy a product, donate money to a cause, or join a group. His interest in what they mark on a paper-and-pencil attitude test is usually underwhelming. Yet the experimenter, faced with the problem of comparing the effectiveness of alternative methods of persuading, often cannot duplicate the "real-life" situation well enough to make the experimental audiences believe they are responding with "real-life" behavior. Further, as has already been argued in the first chapter, if he could use an instance of unstructured overt behavior as his criterion measure, it would probably not be very reliable. Consequently the experimenter generally turns to paper-and-pencil attitude tests to measure the effectiveness of his experimental manipulations.

A brief and clear treatment of measurement and inference appears in Clevenger's volume in this series, to which I previously referred. I will assume that treatment is available to the reader, and will make this discussion somewhat more detailed and more specific to **attitude** measurement.

The traditional attitude tests such as those constructed by the methods of Thurstone and Chave (1929) and Likert (1932) contain statements such as "all American communists should be executed immediately and without trial" or "censorship can never make people moral." The individual being tested is instructed to respond to these statements on a Thurstone scale by checking those with which he agrees, or on a **Likert** scale by checking the extent to which he agrees or disagrees.

The basic assumption underlying the **Thurstone** approach is that statements about an attitude object or concept indicate varying degrees of favor or disfavor toward the attitude object on the part of the individual who makes or agrees with those statements. That is, the statements may be arranged on a psychological continuum bounded by extreme favor and extreme disfavor. Thurstone believed it is necessary, in order to construct an acceptable attitude test, to numerically describe the position of any single statement on that theoretical continuum. That is, he believed it necessary to submit the statements which are to compose the attitude test to a sample of the type of subjects with whom the test is to be used. Those subjects should then be asked to judge the degree of favorableness or unfavorableness which would be indicated by agreement with each statement. The assumption here is not that a given statement produces the same response on the part of every individual, or even that it always produces the same response on the part of one individual; the assumption is only that for each statement there is a **most frequent** response (see Edwards, 1957, p. 21).

The actual methods by which subjects are asked to make these judgments of the "favorability" of statements and the methods by which numbers are assigned may vary. The two most frequently used are the method of "paired comparisons" and the method of "equal-appearing intervals." In the "method of paired comparisons" the judges are asked to compare the attitude statements to each other in all possible pairs, and to decide which member of each pair indicates the greater degree of favor. This method, however, requires that the judges make a great many comparisons, and is not very useful when one wishes to construct an attitude test composed of very many items. Whereas a ten-item test will require only 45 judgments from each judge, a twenty-item test will require 190 judgments, and a forty-item test is almost prohibitive, requiring 780 judgments on the part of each judge.

Consequently, the "method of equal-appearing intervals" has been recommended by Thurstone and is more often used. Judges are told to sort cards containing the attitude statements into eleven piles, with the pile at one end containing those statements which seem most favorable, and the pile at the opposite end containing those statements which seem most unfavorable. This actually constitutes an eleven-point scale upon which the test statements are rated. The scale value for each attitude statement is the **median** of the distribution of ratings for that statement. Thurstone also recommends that statements for which the ratings vary widely should be dropped, assuming that the excessive spread of the ratings is caused by the ambiguity of the statement.

The attitude test itself is composed by choosing a number of statements which have been shown to be fairly equally spaced along the scale and to have no excessive variation in ratings. A subject is then asked to check those statements with which he agrees. His score on the attitude test is either the median or the mean of the scale values of the statements with which he agrees. Edwards states that "reliability coefficients typically reported for the correlation between two forms of the same equal-appearing interval scale are above .85."

At least three problems arise from constructing attitude tests by means of the Thurstone method of equal-appearing intervals: (1) There is no guarantee that the judges actually perceive the intervals as equal, and there is some evidence that they tend to judge the most extreme statements as less extreme than they are judged by the method of paired comparisons; there is some evidence that judgment of the extent to which a statement indicates favor or disfavor depends upon the attitude of the judge, and the method rests on the assumption that there is a psychological continuum bounded by agreement and disagreement, whereas there is some evidence that there are two continua, not necessarily collinear, lying on either side of the neutral point.

The Thurstone method obviously requires the use of a judging sample drawn from the population with whom the test is to be used, and requires quite a bit of calculation. Likert proposed that the experimenter take a number of attitude statements, simply judge whether they indicate favorable or unfavorable attitude toward the attitude object, and ask subjects to indicate whether they "agree strongly," "agree," "neither agree nor disagree," "disagree," or "strongly disagree." Strong agreement with a favorable statement is then scored "4" and strong disagreement "0"; strong agreement with an unfavorable statement is scored "0" and strong disagreement "4." The scores on individual items are then added to provide the measure of attitude toward the concept. This method, also called "the method of summated ratings," eliminates the need for a pre-sample to judge favorability of the attitude statements, and eliminates much of the drudgery of computation as well. Edwards reports a split-halves coefficient of reliability for a test constructed by the Likert method of .94, a coefficient of reliability between alternate forms of a test constructed by the Thurstone method of .88, and coefficients of correlation between the Likert test and each form of the Thurstone test of .72 and .92. These indicate that the Likert method produces tests at least as reliable as those produced by the Thurstone method, and indicate in addition that there is high agreement between tests produced by the two methods, which should be dissonance-reducing for those of us who do not have access to a large number of subjects, and operate a calculator only as a last resort.

A **"Guttman scale"** is a scale which has been subjected to "scalogram analysis" and found to be "unidimensional" or "cumulative" (see Guttman, 1950). This method of analysis is based on the assumption that it is desirable to have a test consisting of attitude statements which can be clearly ranked in order of the degree of favor they indicate. That is, the assumption is that one desires a test in which the items can be so ordered that if subject A agrees with attitude statement one he will agree with all the other statements as well; if he disagrees with statement four but agrees with statement five he will also disagree with statements one through three and will also agree with statements six through N. Another way of putting it is that, given that a subject has a score of twenty agreements on a thirty-item test, one knows which twenty statements the subject agreed with and which ten he disagreed with. If the test meets this criterion perfectly it is said to be perfectly "unidimensional," perfectly "cumulative," to have perfect "reproducibility," and to be a perfect "Guttman scale." Such a test is not likely, however; in reality measurement theorists speak of the "coefficient of reproducibility" of a given test, which "is a measure of the degree of accuracy with which statement responses can be reproduced from knowledge of the total scores alone" (Edwards, 1957, p. 188).

Besides giving one an index of reproducibility of a given test, scalogram analysis makes it possible to identify recurring patterns of response in addition to that the test is intended to measure. A test might, for example, be designed to measure attitude toward religion, but might contain two different types of test items: most measuring attitudes toward Protestantism but a few measuring attitudes toward Catholicism. The use of scalogram analysis would lead to the discovery of two recurrent response patterns in the data, and would suggest either the elimination of certain items or the construction of separate tests to measure the two independent attitudes. The discovery of a low coefficient of reproducibility is not enough in itself, however, to suggest the presence of a competing response pattern; the low reproducibility may be due instead to a great deal of random error.

A relatively recent approach to the construction of attitude tests, and one which differs considerably from those already mentioned, is the semantic differential technique of **Charles Osgood** (see Osgood, Suci, and Tannenbaum, 1957).

Osgood investigated the dimensions of "meaning" by asking subjects to rate words, object, or concepts on a series of seven-point scales bounded by bipolar adjective pairs. A typical scale consists of a line divided into seven parts, allowing the subject to place a check at the point on the line which seems to represent his response to the word or concept being rated. At one end of the line is printed an adjective such as "good," and at the opposite end of the line is printed an adjective which seems to be the exact opposite of the first, in this case the word "bad."

Osgood conceived of the "meaning" of a word as a point in "semantic space." That is, he believed that words are perceived and rated by subjects on various "dimensions," or to the extent that they possess different characteristics. Having obtained subjects' ratings of many different concepts on many different bipolar adjective scales, he conducted factor analyses to determine the "dimensions" or "factors" upon which the judgments were based. A "factor" or "dimension" consists of a number of scales which correlate highly with each other but do not show much correlation with the remaining scales. For example, a subject who, when rating the concept "psychology," places his mark at the "good" end of the "good-bad" scale is also very likely to mark the "fair" end of the "fair-unfair" scale and at the "valuable" end of the "valuable-worthless" scale. However, knowing how he has marked these three scales would not give one much basis for predicting how the subject would mark the "fast-slow" or "strong-weak" scales.

What Osgood found was that there generally seem to be three dimensions on which words are rated. These dimensions he labeled the "activity" dimension, represented by the "fast-slow" scale and others with which it correlates; the "potency" dimension, represented by the "strong-weak" scale and other scales with which it correlates; and the "evaluative" dimension, represented by scales such as "good-bad," "fair-unfair," and "valuable-worthless."

In a striking instance of serendipity, Osgood recognized the "evaluative" dimension as akin to the concept of "attitude." He argued that, if an attitude is defined as a predisposition to evaluative response, this evaluative dimension of meaning should constitute an excellent operational definition of attitude.

In attempting to validate this dimension as a measure of attitude, Osgood asked 50 subjects to rate "the Negro," "the church," and "capital punishment" on five evaluative scales (fair-unfair, valuable-worthless, pleasant-unpleasant, clean-dirty, and good-bad), and Thurstone scales designed specifically to measure attitudes toward each of these three concepts. Order of administration of the two tests was counterbalanced. Both tests were readministered two weeks later to test their reliabilities. The validity coefficients (correlations with the Thurstone measures) of the evaluative dimension scores computed from the initial test data were .82, .74, and .81 for the three concepts, respectively. The test-retest coefficients of reliability for the dimension scores were .87, .83, and .91, compared to reliability coefficients for the Thurstone items of .87, .81, and .78. The performance of the semantic differential scales is especially impressive in view of the fact that the same five scales were used for all three concepts, whereas the Thurstone items were designed for specific concepts, as the Thurstone technique requires.

Osgood also reports a case in which a 14-item Guttman-type test with a reproducibility coefficient of .92, designed to test attitudes of farmers toward "crop rotation," was administered to a group of subjects, 28 of whom later (and rather accidentally) completed three evaluative semantic differential scales, also with reference to the concept "crop rotation." The rank order coefficient of correlation between the evaluative dimension and the Guttman-type test in this case was determined to be .78.

A typical attitude test constructed using the semantic differential technique is reproduced in Figure 8.

> Please rate the concept "legalized wiretapping" on all of the scales that follow. Note that there are seven steps on each scale. A mark at one end of the scale means "extremely." A mark in the position second from the end means "quite." A check in the position third from the end means "slightly." A check in the middle position on any scale means that you are neutral or undecided or do not feel that the scale applies to the concept. Only one position should be checked on any scale, but please check all scales. Place checks on the lines, not on the dividers.

legalized wiretapping

intelligent	___:___:___:___:___:_____	stupid
beautiful	___:___:___:___:___:_____	ugly
valuable	___:___:___:___:___:_____	worthless
pleasurable	___:___:___:___:___:_____	painful
right	___:___:___:___:___:_____	wrong
good	___:___:___:___:___:_____	bad
annoying	___:___:___:___:___:_____	pleasing
attractive	___:___:___:___:___:_____	unattractive
impractical	___:___:___:___:___:_____	practical
useless	___:___:___:___:___:_____	useful

Figure 8

The discerning reader may have noticed that, while care was taken in earlier chapters to distinguish between "beliefs" and "attitudes," the measures described thus far have not provided any operational distinctions between the two. Fishbein was one of those mentioned who proposed a theoretical distinction between "beliefs" and "attitudes." He has also proposed separate procedures for measuring each of those concepts.

Fishbein has argued in lectures that those attitude tests which require the subject to respond to statements about an attitude object confound the subject's **beliefs** about the attributes possessed by an attitude object with his **attitudes** toward those attributes. For example, if one were attempting to measure a subject's attitude toward Jews with a test constructed by the Thurstone or Likert procedures, one might use a typical attitude statement such as "Jews are crafty businessmen." Fishbein's argument is that a subject's response to such an item confounds the extent to which he **believes** that Jews are crafty businessmen with his attitude toward "crafty businessmen." Thus the judging sample may have considered "crafty businessmen" to be bad, and may consequently have established agreement with that item to be an indication of an **unfavorable** attitude toward Jews. However, when the item is presented to an individual subject to test his attitude, that subject may feel that to be a crafty-businessman is a **good** thing, and may believe that Jews **are** crafty businessmen. In that case he would indicate **agreement** with the statement, but his agreement would indicate a favorable attitude toward Jews. Still, because the judging sample rated agreement as indicative of an unfavorable attitude, that is how it would be scored. A similar error would occur if the Likert method were used.

Actually, the problem probably is not as serious as it might appear at first glance. If the statement were subjected to the Thurstone procedure, the fact that it is ambiguous would probably result in a great deal of variation in the ratings of the judging sample, and Thurstone recommends elimination of these statements producing ratings of wide variation. In the Likert procedure, a perceptive experimenter would probably recognize the statement as ambiguous. In the Guttman procedure, the item would not "scale"; that is, it would probably not form part of a consistent response pattern and would probably be eliminated.

The more serious charge is that, by all three of these procedures, attitudes toward the attributes are held constant. That is, the procedures tend to select those statements which assert that the attitude object is related to attributes which are quite clearly good or bad. Then the score which a given subject receives is primarily a function of the extent to which he **believes** that the attitude object possesses the attribute (that Jews **are** crafty businessmen). For a purported measure of **attitudes** to rely primarily upon **belief** responses is a rather strange situation, to say the least.

Fishbein believes Osgood's semantic differential technique provides a measure of attitude which is less dependent upon beliefs. That may be true. To give the concept "Jew" a rating of "bad" on a "good-bad" scale is certainly less ambiguous than to agree that Jews are crafty businessmen. Still, one might view "good" and "bad" as two concepts and argue that, since they are almost completely unambiguous with regard to evaluation, response on a semantic differential scale depends **entirely** on the extent to which the subject **believes** that the attitude object possesses the attribute of "goodness." This opens the Osgood technique to the same criticism directed a moment ago at the Thurstone, Likert, and Guttman procedures. The argument also calls into question the whole distinction between beliefs and attitudes; at least it raises some doubt that attitudes can ever be tested **verbally** without relying on inferences drawn from beliefs.

The Bruner (see Bruner, Goodnow, and Austin, 1956) view that thought operates as a process of categorization lends a little more clarity to this tangle, although the tangle itself is never eliminated. "Beliefs," in this framework, are one's placements of objects and relationships into one of two categories: those which exist and those which do not exist. "Attitudes" are one's placements of objects (and probably relationships) into one of two categories: those which are good and those which are bad. Ultimately even this scheme breaks down, for one may be said to **believe** that an attitude object belongs in the "good" category. However, granting that "attitudes" and "beliefs" are **ultimately** indistinguishable, one can still define an "attitude" in Bruner's terms as the "belief" that a concept belongs either to the "good" or the "bad" category; to the category of things which are desirable and to be approached or to the category of things which are undesirable and to be avoided. Then beliefs having to do with placement of objects in other categories may be distinguished from this one, and can be distinguished from attitudes.

What does this do to the comparison of the Osgood technique with the Thurstone, Likert, and Guttman procedures? It seems to indicate that the Osgood technique produces a purer measure of attitude. To ask a subject to categorize a concept as good or bad, valuable or worthless, right or wrong, and attractive or unattractive seems very close to asking him whether he believes the concept falls in the category of things to be approached or the category of things to be avoided. That type of "belief," remember, is the only one which may also qualify as an "attitude." To ask a subject to categorize Jews as crafty businessmen or Communists as criminals seems further removed from asking him about this ultimate "belief-attitude." Consequently, by this definition at least, the Thurstone, Likert, and Guttman procedures depend more on a subject's beliefs than on his attitudes.

Fishbein (see **Fishbein** and **Raven,** 1962) has used the evaluative dimension of the semantic differential as his operational definition of attitude. As his operational definition of belief he uses other semantic differential scales bounded by such adjective pairs as "impossible-possible," "false-true," "existent-nonexistent," "probable-improbable," and "unlikely-likely." He found a test-retest coefficient of reliability of .90 for the attitude scales and .91 for the belief scales.

Using these two sets of scales one can measure a subject's **attitude** toward an "attitude object" or "object concept" such as "United States recognition of Communist China." He can also measure the extent to which the subject believes that "United States recognition of Communist China" is related to such "attributes" or "motivational concepts" as "increased United States prestige" and "increased probability of war." Finally, he can measure the subject's attitudes toward the motivational concepts themselves. From Fishbein's analysis described in the third chapter of this book—or from the author's own analysis described in the fourth chapter—one would predict that subjects' attitudes toward the attitude object or object concept should be a function of the sum of the products of the strength of each belief multiplied by the attitude toward the attribute or motivational concept.

There is experimental evidence that such a relationship exists. Biddle (1966), to whose study I have already referred, found a coefficient of correlation of .58 between his subjects' initial attitudes toward the attitude object (A_o in Fishbein's notation) and the sum of the products of the strength of each initial belief multiplied by the initial attitude toward the attribute ($\Sigma B_i a_i$ in Fishbein's notation). Following the experimental communication, the correlation between A_o and $\Sigma B_i a_i$ was found to be .65. Both these correlations were significant at the .01 level.

The problem of the low relationship between behavior on paper-and-pencil tests of attitude and more overt behavior in unstructured situations has already been considered. One final type of attitude test has been designed to measure what its proponent, **Triandus** (1964), calls "the behavioral component of attitudes." **Bogardus'** Social Distance Scale, proposed in 1928, was an early attempt to construct a paper-and-pencil test more indicative of overt behavior. The Bogardus scale asked subjects to indicate their willingness to participate in certain types of social behavior with the "stimulus person." It was designed to test the "behavioral component" of attitudes toward persons and toward social stereotypes, especially including ethnic and religious groups. Triandus objected to the Bogardus scale on the ground that it is not unidimensional. He attempted to construct what he called a "Behaviorial Differential," and subjected it to factor analysis to determine what dimensions subjects use to judge the acceptability of behavior toward other persons. He selected a list of about 700 "socially significant behaviors" from a random sampling of "behaviors" mentioned in American novels written after 1850. In a pretest he eliminated those behavioral items which did not discriminate well, those which produced too great a range in the resulting judgments, and those which seemed too similar. The final measure included 61 items of social behavior. The hypothetical "stimulus persons" differed in most combinations of race, sex, occupation, age, religion. Thirty-four "stimulus persons" were used. Thus the subjects were asked to indicate the likelihood of their participating in 61 different types of social behavior with 34 different hypothetical "stimulus persons." Triandus reports as a typical item:

A 50-year old, Negro, Roman Catholic, physician, male

1 2 3 4 5 6 7 8 9

would ___:___:___:___:___:___:___:___:___ would not

have a cocktail with this person

When the data was factor-analyzed, Triandus reports five factors generally appeared. The first factor seemed to indicate the extent to which the stimulus person, having been accorded formal social acceptance, would be subordinated or superordinated. The second factor indicated the extent to which the stimulus person would be considered a suitable marriage partner. Not surprisingly, even in this age of enlightenment, this second factor appeared consistently only when male subjects were judging female stimulus persons, and vice versa. The third factor "suggests same-sex friendship acceptance." The fourth factor was interpreted by Triandus as indicating the "social distance" a subject would like to maintain between himself and the stimulus person, and "seems to be reflecting mostly the rejection of Negroes." The fifth factor "is a pure subordination-superordination factor, suggesting interaction with supervisors and others of 'rank.' "

Triandus concludes that these results indicate that the "behavioral component" of attitudes is itself multidimensional. The obvious implication is that one wishing to measure "behavioral intentions" or the "behavioral component of attitudes" is not justified in adding scores on the individual scales of a test such as the Behavioral Differential on the assumption that they are all indicative of a tendency to maintain some sort of generalized social distance between the subject and the person judged. Instead, the indication seems to be that one type of behavior vis-à-vis a given social group does not necessarily predict another type of behavior vis-à-vis that group, even when both behaviors appear on the surface to be indicative of the same sort of approach or avoidance.

A more promising albeit more tedious approach to measurement of attitudes is suggested by Triandus' note that it would be feasible to perform a factor analysis for every individual subject to determine how that individual clusters his behaviors. If such a factor analysis were performed for every subject, one could determine which behaviors toward which types of stimulus persons tend to cluster or be mutually predictive **for each subject.** Further, more conventional attitude test items could be included.

As indicated in the opening chapter, it is my firm conviction that we will not be able to predict behavior very successfully until we abandon the unsophisticated and somewhat conceited notion that it is possible to decide on an a priori basis what categories of stimuli and behaviors are maintained by our subjects. We must, instead, rely on factor analysis to identify clusters of stimulus-behavior relationships. That is, we must begin an empirical search to discover which behaviors toward which stimuli tend to predict which other behaviors toward which other stimuli. We must face the possibility that these clusterings may be unique for every individual. Hopefully, however, we will find recurrent clusters so that we may generalize about limited groups of subjects, at least. Eventually we may build a catalog of generalized stimulus-behavior clusters. The stimulus-behavior cluster may become the modern successor to the primitive hypothetical construct of "attitude." The prospect appears tedious, but it may be a shorter route to the kind of predictability we are seeking than the rampant overgeneralizations which seem to be the present pattern.

REFERENCES

Biddle, Phillips R. "An Experimental Study of Ethos and Appeal for Overt Behavior in Persuasion." Unpublished doctoral dissertation, University of Illinois, 1966.

Bruner, Jerome S., Jacqueline J. Goodnow, and George A. Austin. **A Study of Thinking.** New York: Wiley, 1956.

Clevenger, Theodore, Jr. **Audience Analysis.** Indianapolis: Bobbs-Merrill, 1966, pp. 52–78.

Edwards, Allen L. **Techniques of Attitude Scale Construction.** New York: Appleton-Century-Crofts, 1957.

Fishbein, Martin. **Readings in Attitude Theory and Measurement.** New York: Wiley, 1967.

———, and B. H. Raven. "The AB Scales: An Operational Definition of Belief and Attitude," **Human Relations,** 15 (1962), 35–44.

Guttman, L. "The Basis for Scalogram Analysis," **Measurement and Prediction.** S. A. Stouffer, et al., eds. Princeton: Princeton University Press, 1950, pp. 60–90.

Likert, R. A. "A Technique for the Measurement of Attitudes," **Archives of Psychology,** No. 140 (1932).

Osgood, Charles E., George E. Suci, and Percy H. Tannenbaum, **The Measurement of Meaning.** Urbana: University of Illinois Press, 1957, especially chap. 5.

Thurstone, L. L., and E. J. Chave. **The Measurement of Attitude.** Chicago: University of Chicago Press, 1929.

Triandus, Harry C. "Exploratory Factor Analyses of the Behavior Component of Social Attitudes," **Journal of Abnormal and Social Psychology,** 68 (1964), 420–430.

Webb, E. J., D. T. Campbell, R. D. Schwartz, and L. Sechrest. **Unobtrusive Measures: Nonreactive Research in the Social Sciences.** Chicago: Rand McNally, 1966.

SEVEN

Audience characteristics

Let us now consider the various types of human character, in relation to the emotions and moral qualities, showing how they correspond to our various ages and fortunes.

ARISTOTLE, *Rhetoric*

As the reader is certain to note, it is difficult to draw any clear line between material which belongs in a chapter on audience analysis and that which belongs in a chapter having to do with the choices a persuader must make in preparing a persuasive message, for those choices depend upon the characteristics of the audience the persuader faces. The real difference between the two chapters is that in this one I will attempt to identify the audience characteristics which the persuader needs to consider, and in the next one I will suggest, when it seems appropriate, the ways in which he can adapt to those characteristics.

Stable audience characteristics

The characteristics I would like to consider in this section are those which remain relatively stable within an individual, and which are generally not related to any specific message topic. I will consider the effects of the listener's personality traits, sex, age, and intelligence, in that order.

Personality traits. In the book **Personality and Persuasibility** the Yale group defined general persuasibility as the characteristic of being susceptible to persuasion regardless of the speaker, topic, or message elements (see Janis and Field, 1959). Just as individuals differ in the extent to which they are persuaded by a given message, if a number of individuals could be exposed to all possible combinations of speakers, messages, and topics, it would be found that the average attitude change on the part of one individual would differ systemmatically and reliably from the average attitude change for other individuals. This residual variance, that part of the variance remaining after variances due to message differences, speaker differences, and topic differences have been subtracted from the total, is labeled "general persuasibility" by these writers. Janis and Field proposed that the characteristic be measured by exposing subjects to five different messages by five different speakers on one side of five different issues, measuring attitude change, exposing the subjects to five messages on the opposite sides of the issues, and measuring attitude change again. The amount of attitude change in response to all ten messages would then constitute the operational definition of general persuasibility. The measure abounds in face validity, for it is actually a small segment of the behavior it is purported to measure. When the test was somewhat modified by Cronkhite and Goetz (1965), who used different speeches and used semantic differential scales as the measure of attitude change, the odd-even coefficient of reliability, correlated for test length, was .87.

To this notion of conformity or general persuasibility, Willis and Hollander (1964) add not only a concept they term "independence," or the ability to respond relatively independently of persuasive attempts, but also something they call "anticonformity," the general tendency to respond in the direction opposite that advocated in a communication. They also suggest the possibility of a fourth mode of response, labeled "variability," the tendency to change one's mind from trial to trial, apparently regardless of communication. These concepts are interesting and deserve further research, but little can be said about them **without** further research.

Adorno, in his book **The Authoritarian Personality** (1950), described a personality trait, which he termed "authoritarianism," to be measured by a test called the "F-scale." One might generally describe the "authoritarian" person as one who is especially prone to use his attitudes and beliefs in the service of ego-defense, and especially likely to acquiesce to authority. The measure is relevant to persuasibility since a number of experimenters have reported that subjects who score high on the F-scale are more likely to conform (for example: Crutchfield, 1955; Wells, Weinert, and Rubel, 1956; Beloff, 1958; Nadler, 1959; Harvey, 1958, 1959; Harvey and Beverly, 1961; Harvey and Caldwell, 1959; Wright and Harvey, 1965). Millon and Simpkins (1957) qualified this somewhat, concluding that highly authoritarian individuals are more persuasible only when the persuader has high prestige. Other experimenters have failed to find any relation at all between authoritarianism and prestige (Hardy, 1957; Gorfein, 1961; Weiner and McGinnies, 1961). One is justified in questioning the reported relations, also, since the wording of F-scale items is such that subjects who have a tendency to acquiesce to positively-worded statements will receive a spuriously high score (Peabody, 1961). Beloff (1958) concluded that "acquiescence-inducing situations [the persuasive situation, for example] and the orthodox F-scale just measure the same thing." Other investigators, however, using a form of the F-scale which should eliminate the acquiescence effect, still found low but significant correlations with measures of conformity. Wright and Harvey (1965) suggest probably the best synthesis of research results in this area when they characterize highly authoritarian individuals as those who rely heavily on authority and show a greater tendency to protect their attitudes toward a limited number of "central" concepts at the expense of the larger number of peripheral ones.

Rokeach (1960) has argued that the F-scale measures only "right-wing" authoritarianism. He described and proposed a test to measure a trait he termed "dogmatism" or "closed-mindedness." The question now is how this trait, typical of extreme religious and political groups, relates to general persuasibility. Somewhat surprisingly, if one takes the term "open-mindedness" at face value, Rokeach states that the person with an open belief system is more likely to resist pressures from external sources. Thus it is the "closed-minded" or "dogmatic" person who should be most "persuasible," which seems almost a contradiction in terms. Yet the fact that such a relationship exists has been confirmed in studies by Norris (1965), Hunt and Miller (1965), and Cronkhite and Goetz (1965). Norman Miller (1965) has reported his dogmatic subjects were **less** persuasible, but that may have been due to an unfortunate flaw in his design. In order to disguise the purpose of the experiment, Miller told his subjects they were going to make a tape recorded speech in favor of their positions, and the experimental message (opposed to their views) was presented ostensibly to give them an idea of how they were to give the speech. Thus, when the subjects heard the speech opposing their views they were already committed to giving a speech favoring their views. The experiment by Hunt and Miller (1965) demonstrated that the effect of commitment is especially strong with dogmatic subjects. Consequently they may have been less easy to persuade **in this special case.** It may be that the theory of Wright and Harvey (1965) that authoritarian individuals change "peripheral" beliefs more easily and "central" beliefs less easily applies to dogmatic subjects as well.

It is not so easy to say just what the speaker can do with such information once he has it, however. First, it is not easy to identify a dogmatic individual, so the information that dogmatic individuals are easily persuasible and highly susceptible to authoritarian or prestige suggestion is not very useful unless one is speaking to the local Ku Klux Klan, John Birch Society, or Communist Party cell. Second, the knowledge that the audience is highly dogmatic and thus highly persuasible does not suggest ways in which a speaker should adapt to his audience, for general persuasibility has been defined as that part of the effect of persuasion which does not depend upon speaker, message, or topic. Third, the research may be no more than verification of a tautology. Unfortunately, all the items on the Rokeach Dogmatism Scale are also worded in such a way that agreement with the statement contributes to a high score, as was the case with the F-scale. Thus to the extent that **agreement with a statement** may be said to constitute "persuasibility," it is confounded with dogmatism. Fourth, research in the area is not far enough along to provide very complete explanations of **why** there is a relationship between "dogmatism" and "persuasibility." It is quite possible that the relationship may depend on other unidentified factors. The Cronkhite and Goetz study, for example, found that both "dogmatism" and "general persuasibility" are related to what they termed "attitude instability," the tendency of a subject's attitudes to fluctuate even in the absence of systemmatic attempts to persuade. This may bear a relationship to the "variability" mode of Willis and Hollander. This suggests that the speaker should not become greatly excited over the amount of attitude change he induces in a highly dogmatic group with a single speech, for those attitudes are likely to revert to their initial position or even more in the opposite direction, whereas a little attitude change on the part of an open-minded individual may be longer-lasting.

Another example is the experiment by Wagman (1955), who found some evidence that authoritarian personalities are more influenced by "authoritarian suggestion" than by "logical restructuring," while this is not necessarily true for nonauthoritarian personalities. Katz, Mc-Clintock, and Sarnoff (1957), as a third example, found that those who were moderately "ego-defensive" or authoritarian were especially responsive to messages which attempted to attack racial prejudice by giving "insight into the mechanisms of repression and projection." The inference is that it may sometimes be more useful to help ego-defensive subjects recognize the motives underlying their attitude and belief structures than to attack their beliefs with factual information. Such information seems much more useful than the mere knowledge that subjects who are "authoritarian" or "dogmatic" are generally more persuasible.

Another personality trait which has been given fairly thorough attention is self-esteem. The conclusion one would most likely reach from a survey of the literature is that persons high in self-esteem are generally difficult to persuade. Janis and Field (1959) found this to be true for high school boys, although not for girls; Abelson and Lesser (1959) found it true among first graders; and Linton and Graham (1959) confirmed it using older men as subjects. Janis (1955) reports one study, the results of which failed to achieve statistical significance, in which male college students were used as subjects, but even in this case the differences were in the right direction. Cox and Bauer (1964), using only women subjects, found an apparently curvilinear relationship between self-esteem and persuasibility.

Sometimes the personality trait of self-esteem has been practically equated with the personality trait of "aggressiveness," and the relationship does appear to be the same: More aggressive individuals are generally less persuasible. This has been confirmed, using various operational definitions of aggressiveness and various subject populations, by Abelson and Lesser (1959) and Janis and Rife (1959).

These studies were **descriptive,** however; there was no attempt to **manipulate** the subjects' aggressiveness, just as there was no attempt to manipulate their self-esteem. On the fairly well-founded assumption that a frustrated individual is aggressive (Dollard, *et al.*, 1939), Weiss and Fine (1956) experimentally manipulated aggressiveness by deliberately frustrating an experimental group of subjects. Frustrated subjects were more influenced by punitively-oriented communications than were nonfrustrated subjects. This, of course, runs counter to the general rule that aggressive subjects are less persuasible, and indicates that, whereas aggressive individuals may be less persuasible in general, they are unusually susceptible to messages which urge aggression. The fact that Weiss and Fine used **only** punitively-oriented communications prevents any conclusion about the **general** persuasibility of aggressive subjects. Experiments by Walters, Thomas, and Acker (1962), and Berkowitz and Rawlings (1963) certainly confirm the fact that subjects who are deliberately frustrated or shown scenes of violence in motion pictures become more aggressive, but they have little to say about the responses of such subjects to persuasion.

Carmichael and Cronkhite (1965) conducted an experiment designed to test responses of frustrated listeners to speeches that differed in language intensity. For the purpose of replication, however, they included two versions of a speech favoring the Peace Corps. Frustrated subjects were influenced significantly more by the **negative** speech than were nonfrustrated subjects. That pattern was reversed for the favorable speech: Nonfrustrated listeners were influenced more than frustrated listeners, although that specific difference was not significant. The pattern of this interaction, however, was significant at the .01 level. Unfortunately, the two speeches differed not only in that one called for unfavorable attitude change and the other called for favorable change: One also dealt with women's fashion changes while the other dealt with the Peace Corps; one speaker was male and the other was female; and one speaker was introduced as a home economist and the other as a prominent United States senator. Since they were used as replications, these differences were desirable from the point of view of the experimenters, but they do prevent the conclusion that the interaction pattern was attributable solely to the fact that one speech was "negative" and the other "affirmative."

One should note also that in both the Weiss and Fine and the Carmichael and Cronkhite experiments the communications were irrelevant to the source of the frustration. In the Weiss and Fine experiment the subjects were "frustrated" by being asked to solve complex problems in an inadequate amount of time, were told that the problems tested both their creativity and intellectual abilities, and were told they performed poorly. In the experiment by Carmichael and Cronkhite the subjects, enrolled in a required communication course, were told that their speeches, themes, and reading abilities were inferior, that they would be required to enroll in remedial courses in each of those areas and were given a load of extra assignments to complete. Yet the communications in the Weiss and Fine experiment dealt with juvenile delinquency and the behavior of our allies with regard to Communist China, while the speeches in the experiment by Carmichael and Cronkhite dealt with women's fashion changes and the Peace Corps.

Carmichael (1965) subsequently hypothesized that subjects who heard speeches denouncing the source of the frustration would be especially influenced. He used essentially the same means of frustration as in the Carmichael and Cronkhite experiment, but the speeches condemned either the required communication course or a required course in physical education. Frustrated subjects were more persuaded than nonfrustrated subjects regardless of the speech, but the effect was so overwhelming in the case of the speech condemning the required communication course that the interaction was significant. Incredibly, despite the fact that the speaker must have been agreeing with their point of view, frustrated subjects became less favorable toward him than did nonfrustrated subjects regardless of the speech, and again this effect was so overwhelming when the speaker condemned the required communication course that the interaction was significant.

Again, one cannot conclude much about the **general** persuasibility of frustrated subjects, because Carmichael included no communications urging **favorable** attitude change. There are at least two possible explanations for the fact that subjects induced to aggression by frustration have been **more** persuaded, while subjects determined to be more aggressive in the absence of frustration have been found to be generally **less** persuasible. (1) It may be that aggressiveness induced by frustration simply operates differently from aggressiveness as an observed personality trait. (2) It may be that aggressive subjects are generally less persuasible but are more persuaded by messages urging aggression.

The problem is further complicated by the fact that the "classic" Weiss and Fine experiment, as well as the experiments of Carmichael and Cronkhite and that of Carmichael, all confounded the variable of self-esteem with the variable of aggressiveness. Note that in each of these experiments the subjects' self-esteem was probably radically lowered. Carmichael reports, in fact, that his frustrated subjects scored significantly lower on a test of self-esteem and significantly higher on a test of aggressiveness. Since subjects having low self-esteem have been found to be generally more persuasible, one cannot be certain that the increased aggressiveness is responsible for the differences. Further, this is clearly a special kind of aggressiveness, since aggressiveness and self-esteem as personality traits have both been demonstrated to be predictive of **decreased** persuasibility.

The experiment needed here will simultaneously manipulate frustration-induced aggressiveness, induced self-esteem, relevance of the speech to the source of frustration, and punitiveness of the communications, while controlling the subject's personality traits of aggressiveness and self-esteem. It will be a complex experiment. Its problems serve as an illustration of the complex problems that arise in personality-oriented research.

Sex.   The evidence seems to indicate overwhelmingly that women are generally more persuasible than are men. The same relationship has been found by Knower (1936). Wegrocki (1934), Bowden, Caldwell, and West (1934), Willis (1940), Bateman and Remmers (1941), Haiman (1949), Paulson (1954), Pence and Scheidel (1956), King (1959), Janis and Field (1959), Furbay (1965), and Scheidel (1963), using various subject populations and topics. Cherrington and Miller (1933) are the only experimenters who have failed to find such a relationship, at least to the knowledge of the author.

A few qualifications of this general rule seem necessary, however. Cronkhite (1961), for example, found that men were more persuaded than were women by what he termed a "logical" speech, but that difference did not appear when an "emotional" speech was used. Tangentially supporting that finding, the "emotional" speech was more persuasive than was the "logical" speech among women, but the effects of the two speeches did not differ significantly among men. It is not clear (even to the experimenter) just how the two speeches differed, although college professors of speech, psychology, and sociology did rate them as significantly different on an "emotional-logical" scale.

The "logical" speech was composed of a chain of reasoning cast in syllogistic form, contained more evidence, and cited sources more carefully. The "emotional" speech used more intense and more personal language, and appealed to more and presumably stronger motives. It is difficult to be certain which of these differences was interacting with the sex of the subjects.

A more important qualification is that discovered by Knower (1935): that women do not seem to be more persuasible **when the speaker is a woman.**

Murphy, Murphy, and Newcomb (1937) argued some time ago that differences in persuasibility between the sexes must be "the result, not of biological but of cultural factors." Scheidel (1963) suggested that some of the difference may be due to the fact "that women appear generally to retain less from persuasive communications than do men" and to the fact that "both sexes draw generalizations from the case upon which they have been persuaded, but women, as compared with men, apply these generalizations more quickly to particular cases not considered in the persuasive appeal." Both of these suggestions seem to be supported by the data from Scheidel's experiment, but a third, while it seems reasonable, was not supported. This suggestion was that, since knowledge on a given topic seems to make a subject more resistant to persuasion on that topic, if one assumes that women are generally less knowledgeable about politics, then the fact that "the topics used for the persuasive speeches in most of the experiments have dealt with political questions" may explain why women have been found to be less persuasible. Obviously it would help the potential persuader to have a clearer idea of why women differ from men in their responses to persuasion, but it may be some time before a clearer explanation is available. One possibility which certainly should not be ignored is that men are made more aggressive by both cultural and biological influences. It is quite obvious that our culture trains men to be more dominant and aggressive, and there's some evidence that the male hormone produces dominance and aggressiveness. Since it is fairly well established that individuals who are aggressive are generally less persuasible, this aggressiveness probably also contributes to the tendency of males to resist persuasion.

Age. Another variable which presents similar problems is that of age. The general finding has been that the degree of success with which new tricks may be taught varies inversely with the age of the dog, as per folklore. Studies by Marple (1933) and by Janis and Rife (1959) seem to confirm the fact that older persons are less persuasible. The reasons for this negative relationship are probably at least as complex and as seldom studied as the reasons for the relationship between sex and persuasibility.

Intelligence.   The relationship between intelligence and persuasibility is not so clear. Wegrocki (1934) found that more intelligent persons were less persuasible, but he used very crude propaganda statements to induce change. Hovland, Lumsdaine, and Sheffield (1949) concluded that their intelligent army recruits (actually, those with more education) were more persuaded as a result of "logical" messages, whatever they may be. When Janis and Field (1959) used their measure of general persuasibility, it bore no detectable relationship to the intelligence of the listener. Cronkhite (1961) found no relationship between scholastic aptitude (SCAT) scores and attitude change as a result of either his "logical" or "emotional" speech. Among other problems of this study, however, was the fact that the range of subject intelligence was fairly well limited by the fact that all subjects were college students. Pence and Scheidel (1956) looked for but found no significant relationship between critical thinking ability and persuasibility. Thus there appears to be no evidence for any relationship between intelligence and general persuasibility. There is a little evidence, however, that intelligent individuals may be less persuaded by crude propaganda and that individuals of higher educational level may be more persuaded by "logical" argument.

This research which has attempted to determine relationships between various audience characteristics and general persuasibility seems to be of limited use to the speaker. One of the problems is that it is difficult for a speaker to find out about the personality characteristics and intelligence of his listeners unless the audience is so small he can talk to or test each one personally, or he is speaking to a large and well defined population which has been carefully tested in advance. Another problem is that it is not very useful to know merely that a given type of audience is difficult to persuade. One usually has little choice about the composition of his audience. He may know that if he is trying to persuade an all-male audience he will have a more difficult time, but he can hardly use that information to make his job easier. He might conceivably manipulate "personality" characteristics such as self-esteem and aggressiveness, but there is really not any wealth of evidence to show that the personality differences "cause" differences in persuasibility. The research which is really needed would show **how** audience characteristics relate to persuasibility and how they interact with message variables. Such information will be much more useful to the speaker.

Prior attitudes and beliefs

Next I would like to consider some research evidence which may give us some insight into the question of why an individual's attitude and belief structure may sometimes be so difficult to change. After considering all the factors operating to maintain a stable structure, which will be my first order of business in this section, one begins to wonder how persuasion ever succeeds. Add to this the second consideration of this section, the means by which individuals attempt to avoid being persuaded, and the image of the persuader as a suave and efficient manipulator of audience attitude begins to fade to be replaced by the image of a desperate man pushing one button after another, hoping desperately that something will work.

Causes of resistance. Listeners may have **extreme** attitudes, may become deeply **involved** in their attitudes and beliefs, and may feel there is too much **disparity** between their own attitudes and beliefs and those the persuader is asking them to accept. They may feel **committed** to their attitudes and beliefs. They may feel loyalty to the **opinions of others.**

Extremity, involvement, and disparity. One of the best-established findings of social psychology is that individuals who have well-established attitudes and beliefs act so as to maintain them; the more extreme the attitudes, the more difficult they are to change. Basic studies such as those by Levine and Murphy (1941), Edwards (1941), Cooper and Jahoda (1947), and Hasdorf and Cantril (1954) showed that individuals with extreme attitudes toward Communism, the New Deal, racial prejudice, and even the outcome of a specific intercollegiate athletic contest perceived messages and information so as to support their own attitudes. I will have more to say later about the things individuals do to resist attitude change; I present these findings now only as an indication that individuals having extreme attitudes **do** resist attitude change.

The first major attempt to state the relationship between the extremity of an individual's attitude and his response to a message advocating its change was expressed by Hovland, Harvey, and Sherif (1957) and presented in more detail by Hovland and Sherif in 1961. The most refined presentation of the theory and the research supporting it is to be found in the book by Sherif, Sherif, and Nebergall (1965). Basically, the findings reported in all these sources seem to indicate that **individuals will reject communications which urge too much attitude change** and **the amount of disparity they will tolerate is less when their own attitudes are more extreme.** It is not yet clear from the literature whether the persuader will get more attitude change when he asks for more, but a constantly decreasing percentage of what he asks for, or whether there will come a point at which the listeners will reject his position so strongly that they will not change at all or change in the opposite direction. The evidence seems to indicate that, with listeners whose attitudes are close to neutral, the persuader should ask for a great deal of attitude change because, although he will get a smaller **proportion** of what he asks for, he will get a greater absolute **amount.** On the other hand, with listeners having more extreme attitudes, the persuader must be careful not to ask for too much attitude change lest the listeners respond by changing attitude in the opposite direction. For reports, summaries, and bibliographies of research on this question see Goldberg (1954), Hovland, Harvey, and Sherif (1957), Hovland and Pritzker (1957), Fisher and Lubin (1958), Cohen (1959), Zimbardo (1960), and Freedman (1964).

Sherif, Sherif, and Nebergall (1965) argue that each individual has a "latitude of acceptance" on both sides of his own attitude position, and he will accept communications within that region. Further out in both directions he has "latitudes of rejection," and any communication advocating that he change attitude into those regions will either fail to cause him to change attitude at all or cause him to change attitude in the opposite direction. Finally, somewhere between those two types of regions, the authors mention "latitudes of noncommitment."

This analysis suggests an interesting possibility. Suppose a speaker is asked to participate in a debate, and has some freedom to decide who his opponent will be. He might be well-advised to choose as an opponent that individual who will take a very extreme position opposite his, in the hope that the radical opponent will be greeted with rejection, and then for his own part the speaker should urge a moderate degree of attitude change. This might be called the effect of the "Devil's advocate," who takes an extreme position opposite what he really believes in the hope of getting his listeners to reject his assumed position and move in the direction of his true position.

Another possibility is for the persuader to urge his listeners to change attitudes in increments. Instead of asking at the beginning of the message for all the attitude change he really wants them to make, he might ask for several smaller amounts of change, either in separate parts of the message or in separate messages (see Ward, 1964).

One of the problems which arises in reading the research on the effects of the extremity of a listener's attitudes and his involvement in them is that some of the writers use the term "ego-involvement" to mean "attitude extremity." I would rather use the term "involvement" to refer to the state in which the listener perceives the object concept to be linked to many strong motivational concepts, so that his attitude toward the object concept depends upon his attitudes toward these other concepts, and is consequently likely to be quite stable. Attitudes so anchored are also likely to be more extreme, but not **necessarily,** so that it is confounding to use "attitude extremity" and "involvement" as if they are synonymous. The research evidence seems to indicate that, as expected, attitudes in which the listener is deeply involved are more difficult to change. Eagly and Manis (1966), for example, used two messages, one arguing for stricter school rules for boys and the other arguing for stricter control over girls' fashion choices. Thus one was "involving" in the present sense for boys only and the other for girls only. The more involving message in each case produced greater derogation of both the communication and the communicator. Ward (1965) also attempted to manipulate listener involvement quite similarly, and found that the more highly involved listeners perceived attitude statements opposed to their own attitudes as being more disparate than did listeners who were not so involved. This "displacement" or "misperception" of messages seems to be one common means of avoiding attitude change, and will be discussed in more detail very shortly.

Another interesting finding, but one not totally unexpected, is that a persuader who is liked and considered credible by a listener can extend the listener's latitude of acceptance; that is, he can urge greater attitude change on the part of the listener without having either himself or his message rejected than can a disliked speaker of low credibility (see Aronson, Turner, and Carlsmith, 1963; Berkowitz and Goranson, 1964).

Commitment. If the persuader knows the extent to which his listeners have **committed** themselves to their present beliefs and attitudes, he will be better able to decide whether it is worthwhile to attempt to persuade them and better able to decide how much attitude change he should urge. He will also want to know the extent to which they have deliberately committed themselves to listen to his arguments. Since little research has been done regarding the effect of "commitment to listen," I will consider that question at the end of this section, considering first the effect of the listeners' commitment to his initial attitudes and beliefs.

If the listener has deliberately **chosen** to make a **public** statement of his attitudes and beliefs, if that public statement has been unexpectedly **rewarded,** and if the commitment is **salient,** his attitudes and beliefs will be more difficult to change.

I will proceed on the assumption that a commitment, by definition, must be "public" to some extent. I suppose it might be interesting to find out whether a subject who writes an opinion and then throws away the paper is less easily persuaded than one who does not write his opinion at all, but the knowledge would not be very useful. A commitment in this view, in order to be a commitment, must be a revelation of the individual's opinion (attitude or belief) to at least one other person.

The first question to be answered, then, is the question of whether the least-public sort of commitment causes resistance to subsequent opinion change. There is a limited amount of research evidence indicating that it does, despite the contention of Hovland, Janis, and Kelley (1953) that it does not. Some experiments have shown that subjects asked to make ambiguous judgments of visual phenomena tend to resist influence if they have previously committed themselves to a given range of judgments (Fisher, Rubenstein, and Freeman, 1956). Gerard (1964) has also found that subjects who commit themselves to resist the influence of others, or to yield to it, tended to maintain that course of action more in a "face-to-face" than in an "anonymous" condition. The effect of minimally public commitment has not been observed in the persuasive situation as far as I know. Of course, it is rather difficult to conduct an experiment in which subjects really believe their commitment will remain totally anonymous.

Does it make a difference if listeners perceive their commitments as more public? There is a little evidence that it does. Pelz (1955) found that more students volunteered for psychology experiments when they were asked to commit themselves publicly, but a smaller percentage of those in the public commitment group actually showed up for the experiment. Schachter and Hall (1952) found no significant effect of "publicness" of commitment. Hovland, Campbell, and Brock (1957) had their subjects listen to a persuasive message on one side of an issue, write a paragraph telling their own opinions, and then listen to a message on the opposite side. Subjects who signed the paragraphs stating their opinions and expecting them to be published changed less in response to the second message than did subjects who thought their opinions were to be anonymous. Sears, Freedman, and O'Connor (1964) report that public commitment caused greater "polarization" of audience attitudes only when the subjects anticipated hearing a subsequent **debate,** but not when they merely anticipated hearing two speeches related only in that they were on opposite sides of the same issue.

The technique of saying, "Now I know you all agree . . . ," is one often used by speakers. It represents a form of what Rosenbaum and Zimmerman (1959) and Rosenbaum and Franc (1960) have called "external commitment," and it seems to work. These experimenters proceeded by telling certain of their subjects, "You have been selected because you oppose integration," for example, regardless of their actual attitudes. When "external commitment" was congruent with actual opinions, the subjects changed attitudes less than a control group; when the "external commitment" was incongruent with actual opinions, Rosenbaum and Franc found that it facilitated attitude change in response to a subsequent communication. In a sense, this might be considered a variation of "public commitment."

One of the most public types of commitment is the giving of a speech before an audience. Much of the research on commitment is research on the question of the effect produced upon the attitudes of an individual who gives a speech in which he states that he believes in a given position. Usually the experimenters have studied the situation in which the individual publicly advocates a position contrary to his own opinion, but many of the findings seem generalizable. Such research is usually listed as the literature of "role-playing" or "self-persuasion."

Myers, in 1921, discovered that soldiers whose attitude toward Army life was negative changed attitude favorably after delivering favorable classroom speeches. Janis and King (1954) found that subjects who, with the aid of a prepared outline, played the role of sincere advocates of a given point of view were actually more influenced by the communication than were those who only read the outline and listened to the speech. The same experimenters (King and Janis, 1956) then discovered that subjects who improvised much of their speeches were more influenced than those who read aloud from a prepared text. Scott (1957, 1959a, 1959b) had subjects debate on the sides of questions opposite their beliefs and assigned fictitious "wins" at random. He discovered that the winners showed the greatest attitude change. Bostrum, Vlandis, and Rosenbaum (1961) found that subjects who received randomly assigned grades of "A" on classroom themes opposing their "real" opinions changed opinion more than did subjects assigned "D" or no grade. The basic effect of having subjects engage in behavior contrary to their opinions has been confirmed in innumerable experiments. This research is summarized by Cohen (1960) and in the book by Brehm and Cohen (1962).

Beyond the basic effect, there are a number of other interesting findings. Warning subjects that expressing opinions contrary to their own may cause them to change their opinions does not seem to reduce the effect, for example (see McGinnies, Donelson, and Haaf, 1964). As might be expected, the speaker changes attitudes most if his listeners are either neutral or favorable toward the **expressed** opinions, if he is made aware of their reactions by discussion afterward. A variety of personality traits, including especially "dogmatism" and "fantasy ability," have been found to be related to attitude change in this situation (see Hunt and Miller, 1965, Elms, 1966, and Harvey and Beverly, 1961).

The experiments cited thus far do not deal very directly with the question of **why** the effect occurs. Jones (1966) has presented evidence that, if subjects are given little choice about expressing the incongruent opinions but are given considerable justification for doing so, merely **preparing** for a speech is adequate to cause change. This seems to indicate that the speaker probably does not "persuade himself" in the sense that he **listens** to himself, but Bem (1966) interprets some of his results as indicating at least "that an individual's beliefs and attitudes are often based on observations of his own overt behavior. . . ."

Two other explanations are presently competing for acceptance in the psychological literature. The one preferred by Janis and King is derived from learning theory and holds that role-playing is simply practice in the behavior of expressing a specific opinion; if the behavior is rewarded or reinforced it will continue, and if unrewarded it will be abandoned. The other, derived from that dissonance theory, is the cognition that one holds a given opinion is dissonant with the cognition that he is expressing a contrary opinion; the individual changes the opinion in order to reduce the dissonance. Both explanations have a great deal of supporting research evidence. The dissonance explanation is not applicable to the situation in which the individual expresses opinions **consonant** with those he actually holds; that is, it does not serve as an explanation of the anchoring effect of public commitment to a prior private opinion.

There is certainly plenty of evidence that the expression of specific attitudes can be encouraged by reward or reinforcement, that attitude change results, and that it persists (Kelman, 1953; Hildum and Brown, 1956; McGuire, 1957; Scott, 1957, 1959a, 1959b; Ekman, 1958; Staats and Staats, 1958; Rhine and Silun, 1958; Staats, Staats, and Heard, 1960; Maccoby, Maccoby, Romney, and Adams, 1961; Das and Nanda, 1963; Weiss, Rawson, and Pasamanick, 1963; Sarbin and Allen, 1964). Insko (1965) even found that, when subjects were interviewed by telephone and positively or negatively reinforced with "good" or "bad" for agreement or disagreement with a series of opinion statements, the effect on attitude could still be observed a week later. An often-cited study by Verplanck (1955) revealed much earlier that even the number of opinion statements occurring in conversation could be controlled by reinforcement.

In some circumstances, however, one would predict from the dissonance theory approach that subjects given greater reward for making a public statement contrary to their beliefs will change attitude less as a result of that "commitment" (see Brehm, 1960). If the "justification" for taking the discrepant stand is greater, the dissonance and consequent attitude change should be less. Festinger and Carlsmith (1959) paid subjects for telling others that a boring task was interesting. Generally, the more the subjects were paid, the less they changed their attitudes toward the task. Cohen (1962) conducted an experiment in which Yale students were approached in their rooms and asked to write essays favoring certain actions of the New Haven police. The more they were paid for writing the essay, the less attitude change occurred as a result of writing it. Somewhat similar results have been reported by Cohen, Brehm, and Fleming (1958) and by Rabbie, Brehm, and Cohen (1959).

A storm of controversy has arisen over the question raised by this type of experiment. Rosenberg (1965), in an article titled "When Dissonance Fails . . ." (clever rhetoricians, these psychologists), reports an experiment in which he asked Ohio State students to write essays in favor of banning Ohio State from playing in the Rose Bowl. In order to eliminate subjects' fear that the experimenter would consider them paid liars and rationalizers, he used one experimenter as the "compliance-inducer" and another as post-tester. He also changed the amounts of payments to fifty cents, one dollar, and five dollars. His results were opposite those of Festinger and Carlsmith and of Cohen: the more subjects were paid, the more they changed attitudes as a result of writing the essays.

Nuttin (1964, 1966), in a paper titled "Dissonant Evidence about Dissonance Theory," replicated the experiments of both Rosenberg and Cohen. He got Cohen's results, the opposite of Rosenberg's, but failed in his attempt to replicate the findings of Festinger and Carlsmith. Carlsmith, Collins, and Helmreich (1966) also replicated the Festinger and Carlsmith experiment, but added a condition in which some subjects wrote a purportedly anonymous essay. They found in the face-to-face condition that subjects who were paid most changed least, but the opposite was true with anonymous essay writing. They concluded that merely writing arguments in favor of a position, **without commitment,** does not arouse dissonance.

Janis and Gilmore (1965) asked subjects to write an essay arguing that all college students should be required to take an extra year of mathematics and physics. They paid rewards of either one dollar or twenty dollars. The amount of reward made no difference, and subjects, when interviewed, reported that the twenty dollar reward seemed "inappropriate" and they were "surprised" at its size. Elms and Janis (1965) asked subjects to write anonymous essays advocating sending qualified students to study in Russia for four years. Some subjects were told it was the United States State Department paying their rewards, while others were told they were being paid by a research firm hired by the Soviet Embassy. Under "unfavorable" sponsorship, the amount of money paid made no difference, but when the sponsor was purported to be the United States State Department, subjects who were paid more changed attitude more. Wallace (1966) interprets the results of an experiment he conducted as indicating that the dissonance analysis applies only when the subject believes someone else considers him "insincere," thus creating dissonance.

One important distinction to be made is that in **all** the studies in which subjects changed attitudes less when paid more, they knew **before the act of commitment** that they were to be paid and how much they were to be paid. Freedman (1963) has demonstrated that greater "justification" presented **after** subjects take action discrepant with their opinions does **not** produce less attitude change as in the Festinger and Carlsmith experiment. Further, the dissonance analysis applies only when the subject publicly commits himself to a position which does not represent his **actual** opinion, which is a kind of "commitment" which the persuader will seldom encounter. Even when these two conditions are met, there are a number of important qualifications which seem to be necessary in order for the dissonance analysis to apply. Consequently it seems fairly safe to say that the subject who publicly commits himself to the opinion he actually holds and is unexpectedly rewarded for it will be more adamant in his subsequent adherence to that opinion.

The reader may wonder why I have specified that the subject must be **unexpectedly** rewarded in order for commitment to increase the stability of his opinion. That such a qualification is necessary seems to be indicated by the results of an experiment by Kiesler and Sakumura (1966). These experimenters paid subjects one dollar or five dollars for reading aloud a communication concerning voting by eighteen-year-olds which was "consistent with their prior beliefs." Later all subjects received a strong countercommunication [read silently] on the same topic. The hypothesis was confirmed: Subjects receiving the greater payment for performing the consonant act later showed greater attitude change in the direction advocated by the countercommunication. The explanation offered by Kiesler and Sakumura is that "the greater inducement offered a subject for performing an act consistent with his beliefs, the less committed he is to that act, and the less the resistance to subsequent countercommunications."

On the other hand, it may be that subjects who are **punished** for publicly committing themselves to their opinions also become more adamant about those opinions. Festinger (1961) has written, ". . . rats and people come to love the things for which they have suffered," and studies by Aronson and Mills (1959) and by Festinger, Rieken, and Schachter (1956), among others, seem to bear him out. Marlowe, Frager, and Nuttall (1965) have applied this idea to the commitment question specifically. Their subjects were asked to express their opinions about Negroes and were then told that, since their opinions were "not the right ones" for the experimenters' purposes, they would not be allowed to participate in an experiment which would have paid either a dollar and a half or twenty dollars. Subjects who thought they had lost twenty dollars were significantly more willing to commit themselves to actions congruent with their opinions than were those subjects who thought they had lost less. This relationship did not hold true when the loss of money was not presented as being the **result** of having the "wrong" opinions. This finding suggests a strange picture; I may have to re-phrase the statement to say that subjects who are **punished or unexpectedly rewarded** for publicly committing themselves to their opinions are subsequently less likely to change those opinions.

One final qualification seems necessary: The subject must perceive that he has deliberately **chosen** to commit himself to his opinion rather than having been coerced into the commitment. That qualification seems strongly indicated by the findings of Brehm (1959), Brehm and Cohen (1959), Brock (1962), and Freedman and Steinbruner (1964).

One might argue that it doesn't really matter whether an individual is rewarded or punished for his commitment, since the commitment seems to make his attitude more stable either way. Note, however, that the experimental evidence does seem to suggest that the commitment is more effective if it is **either** rewarded or punished than if it is simply not reinforced at all (**neither** rewarded nor punished), and the range within which the individual perceives himself as being neither rewarded nor punished may be rather wide.

Now the discussion of commitment has thus far centered on the **commitment to one's own opinions,** which seems to act **against** the desires of the persuader. Let us not forget, on the other hand, that the listener, by the act of exposing himself to the persuasive communication, has committed himself in another way, this time to the benefit of the persuader: **he has committed himself to listen.** Thus, to the extent that he has deliberately **chosen** to listen and to the extent that he is punished or unexpectedly rewarded for that action, his attitudes may be expected to change so as to become more nearly consonant with the action. McGuire and Millman (1965) have reported evidence which seems to indicate that a listener may begin to change his opinions once he has committed himself to listen to a speech which is opposed to them, and a study by Brooks and Scheidel (1967) suggests the same thing.

The question of the effect of reward and punishment for the commitment to listen has not been answered by experimental evidence, so far as I know. If the listening experience is interesting and rewarding, one would predict greater attitude change if one were operating on the basis of reinforcement theory. However, operating on the basis of dissonance theory one would predict that if a listener has deliberately chosen to listen to a speech contrary to his own opinions, and if the listening experience is dull and unrewarding, the commitment to listen will be dissonant with the unrewarding experience, and the listener should change his opinions in order to reduce that dissonance. This suggests a good experiment for some enterprising student.

The opinions of others. Listeners also use the opinions of friends and others they may believe to be authorities as anchoring points for their own opinions. Classic studies have shown that this is true not only when subjects are making ambiguous and subjective judgments (Sherif, 1935, 1936, 1937), but also when the judgments to be made are not at all ambiguous and might be expected to be totally objective (Asch, 1952; Crutchfield, 1955). It has been demonstrated that listeners will even go along with the judgment of a group when the group makes decisions contrary to norms it has previously established. If a persuader is perceived by his listeners as being "outside" a group important to them, both persuader and message will be rejected (Iwao, 1963).

This tendency of listeners to conform to the opinions of groups to which they belong or would like to belong has been given a great deal of study under such headings as "conformity," "small-group communication," "group dynamics," "person-perception," "interpersonal attraction," and the like. I have chosen to discuss much of the literature which has to do with the kind of person who is influential in molding another individual's opinions in a section of the next chapter dealing with the persuasive characteristics of the communicator and the sources he cites. That decision was an arbitrary one, however; certainly the characteristics which make a persuader persuasive are also those which cause the listener's acquaintances to be influential in maintaining his existing opinions. For more complete coverage of the influence of others' opinions, the reader might read that section along with this one.

The alert reader will also notice that "conformity," the tendency to acquiesce to the opinions of a group, sounds a great deal like "persuasibility," the general tendency to acquiesce to the opinions of another. The really interesting part of this confusion is that, to the extent that an individual "conforms" to the opinions of groups he values, he should be less "persuasible" in response to a persuasive message. Yet the traits appear very similar. Clearly there is much analysis and research to be done before we know the relationship between the two.

Theory and research having to do with group interaction is a field of study in itself. The reader who is especially interested in that field should refer to another book in this series (Phillips, 1966) and to the selected bibliography it contains.

I would like to consider specifically the effect group opinions have upon listeners in the persuasive situation. Such groups have been classified as "membership groups" and "reference groups," with the assumption that there is a great deal of overlap between the two categories. A membership group is a group of which the listener is a member; a reference group is one which has influence upon his opinions. Note that reference groups can be positive or negative; they can influence the listener's opinion in that he will tend to **agree** or **disagree** with them. A positive reference group is likely to be an effective anchor for an individual's opinions to the extent that he (1) likes the members of the group, (2) respects their opinions or depends upon them for social support, (3) values his membership in the group, (4) has a low power position within the group, (5) perceives the group as united in opinion, (6) feels close to and is committed to continue working with the group, (7) perceives the group as salient and relevant to the persuasive situation, and (8) perceives the stimuli to be judged as ambiguous and the judgment subjective.

Hare (1962) lists fifteen studies showing that groups to which an individual is most attracted exert the most influence on him. That question is hardly open to dispute. Back (1951), for example, paired subjects so they were "congenial," told them they had been so paired, and found those who were more "congenial" showed more agreement in the task he assigned them to perform. Sampson and Insko (1964) found that their subjects not only changed their judgments so as to increase their similarity to the judgments of another person who was well liked, but also changed them so as to **decrease** their similarity to those of another person who was **disliked**. There have been numerous studies of the causes of interpersonal compatibility, and these are surveyed in some detail in the section dealing with source effects. In addition to the causes surveyed, it appears there is at least one cause which operates especially strongly in a group situation: If the individual perceives the group as liking him, he is more likely to be influenced by that group. Wyer (1966), for example, found that when incentive to perform well was **high,** subjects conformed to group judgments unless they were not accepted by the group and disliked its members. On the other hand, when incentive to perform well was low, subjects refused to conform to group judgments only when they liked the group but were rejected by its members. Thus being liked by a group which an individual likes does seem to serve as an incentive to conform to group judgments, when performance incentive is otherwise low.

The evidence seems to indicate quite clearly that an individual uses the opinions of others as evidence about "reality," as if he is not quite certain of his own judgments and needs to have them verified. This is true to some extent when the judgments are factual in nature, and more so when they are judgments which involve values. Festinger (1954) postulates a drive or need for self-evaluation or measurement, which is especially high when the judgment involves abilities, attitudes, and beliefs which cannot be compared to any objective physical referent.

The individual is especially likely to rely on group judgments if his experience with that group has indicated that their judgments are accurate (see Hollander, Julian, and Haaland, 1965). Given group support, the individual is willing to make decisions which might be considered more "risky" than those he would be willing to make on his own (Bem, Wallach, and Kogan, 1965; Wallach and Kogan, 1959, 1961, 1965; Wallach, Kogan, and Bem, 1962, 1964). Interestingly, membership in a group may lead the individual to come to rely more heavily on the judgments of that group than upon those of other groups, even when the objective evidence does not indicate that the judgment of his own group is superior (Blake and Mouton, 1962; Strickland, Jones, and Smith, 1960).

A third cause of an individual's acceptance of the judgments of a group may be that he values and wishes to maintain his membership in that group or his role in relation to its members. Back (1951) found more agreement among group members when they were told they had been paired on the basis of high prestige. Charters and Newcomb (1952) found that Catholic subjects who attended religious services only infrequently (and whom they assume valued their membership less) were more influenced by a non-Catholic communication. As Cartwright and Zander (1960) put it:

> In many instances a group may be attractive to a person primarily because it is a means to reaching some goal which exists outside the group. Membership is a path to something desirable in the environment. An important reason for joining a sorority on a university campus, for example, is the prestige that the girls obtain in the college community by belonging to that group, according to findings reported by Willerman and Swanson [1953]. Similarly, Rose [1952] states that the major benefit that the members say they derive from belonging to a large union "local" is that it obtains higher wages and job security for them. In both of these instances, the member values the group because it helps achieve a goal which exists outside the group [p. 75].

Obviously, the effect of such a group on a member's opinions depends upon the extent to which he perceives that the group expects opinion conformity as a requirement for continual membership. A religious group may require conformity of opinions regarding religion, and a political group may require only conformity of political opinions.

Further, a number of studies, principally by Hollander and his associates, have demonstrated that an individual who has a high power position in a group is likely to have and to perceive himself as having greater freedom to deviate from group opinions (see, for example: Hovland, Janis, and Kelley, 1953; Hollander, 1958, 1964). These findings seem similar to those having to do with the individual's perception of the extent to which he is liked by the group, which have been mentioned earlier.

A number of studies have demonstrated that the "majority opinion" is at least effective in determining an individual's opinions (Moore, 1921; Marple, 1933; Burtt and Falkenburg, 1941), and at least two studies have found that the extent to which "majority opinion" approaches unanimity makes a great deal of difference. Asch (1951, 1956) and Kiesler, Zanna and DeSalvo (1966) found that an individual did not yield to group judgments nearly as often if he had even **one** other member to agree with him, and Pelz (1955) found that **perceived** group consensus (although not **actual** consensus) was an important factor in determining an individual's behavior. Somewhat surprisingly, an increase in the actual size of the group does not seem to produce corresponding increases in the extent to which a member will yield to group opinion (Asch, 1952; Goldberg, 1954), and may even **decrease** yielding (Frye, Spruill, and Stritch, 1964). It does seem reasonable to assume, however, that when the listener has several reference and/or membership groups whose opinions are relevant, the size of any one of those groups in **relation to the others** should be one of the factors which determines the extent to which he is likely to acquiesce to the opinion of that group.

The individual will be more likely to be influenced by a group with which he has been closely associated for some time and with which he expects to continue to be closely associated. Allport (1962) has referred to "structural assurances" which "are of two types. They are the indications that the structure **will be likely to continue its operation** . . . and the indications given the individual that **he is accepted** in the structure and that he will probably be able in the future to **hold his place in it.**" Gerard and Rotter (1961) report that an individual who expects to continue with a group is more likely to conform to the judgments of that group. This must be qualified somewhat, however, for Zeff and Iverson (1966) have found that the individual who is threatened with being "demoted" to a group of lower status is most likely to conform, at least if he believes the members of his present group to be comparable and congenial. The interested reader might also refer to the more complex findings of Kiesler and Corbin (1965), Hall and Williams (1966), Cohen (1958), and Kelley (1951).

The listener will be more influenced by the opinions of those groups which are especially **salient** at any given time. That is, he will be influenced by a group to the extent that he is aware of his relationship to that group and aware of the relevance of the group's opinions to opinions the persuader is asking him to accept. Charters and Newcomb (1952) found that Catholic subjects who were reminded of their Catholicism gave more typically "Catholic" response on a questionnaire. The effect was not significant with Jews and Protestants, however, so one must maintain some reservations.

I have mentioned several times that individuals are more likely to conform to group judgments when the stimuli to be judged are ambiguous or the judgment subjective. This has been reported by Sherif (1936), Asch (1952), and Crutchfield (1955). This seems to suggest, among other things, that reference groups are more likely to serve as anchors for an individual's **attitudes** than for his **beliefs** (as I have defined those terms). Since beliefs are generally more objective in that they have to do with relationships among concepts, they may be less ambiguous than attitudes, which only **depend upon** beliefs. An experiment seems in order to test this question.

One implication of this and the mass of group research which has not been surveyed seems clear: The persuader should be aware of the membership and reference groups of his listener and should use those groups to cause attitude change. The persuader is, in a sense, a deviant member of the audience group, and may expect to be rejected if he persists in bucking group opinion (Schachter, 1951). He is to some extent an "out-group" communicator (see Iwao, 1963), in that he may not be perceived initially as a member of the audience group, so he must work to cause the audience to perceive him as a member. He is also outside of some of the other groups to which his listeners may belong. Consequently his major tasks with regard to reference groups will be: (1) to call attention to all the membership and reference groups he and his listeners have in common; (2) to minimize the importance of all the membership and reference groups they do not have in common; (3) to maximize the importance of all the listener's reference and membership groups which have opinions consonant with those he is trying to get the listener to accept; (4) to aid the listener in perceiving that these group opinions are consonant with those of the persuader; (5) to minimize the importance of all the listener's reference and membership groups which have opinions opposed to those of the persuader; (6) to show the listener whenever possible that the persuader's opinions are not opposed to those of groups important to him; (7) to point to new and attractive groups which have opinions consonant with those of the persuader; and (8) to point to unattractive groups which have opinions opposed to those of the persuader. In maximizing and minimizing the importance of the groups to the listener, the persuader should keep in mind the variables just surveyed which seem to determine the extent to which a group will serve as a reference group for a listener.

Means of resistance. Now assuming that listeners are difficult to persuade if they hold extreme attitudes which have been publicly stated and which have been supported by the opinions of others, how do such listeners avoid changing their attitudes in response to a strong persuasive message? Among other things, they may misperceive and forget it, they may deprecate its arguments, they may seek information to refute it, they may devaluate its importance, they may differentiate its attitude object, or they may deprecate the speaker. The latter of these possibilities is covered in the next chapter under the section headed "Source Effects." Fortunately for the speaker, while it seems possible for the listener to use all of these means of resistance simultaneously, the evidence thus far indicates that most listeners choose to use one to the exclusion of the others (Steiner and Rogers, 1963; Pervin and Yatko, 1965).

Avoiding dissonant information. More than a dozen important writers in the field of persuasion and attitude change have assumed that individuals will avoid information inconsistent with their opinions. A number of studies have been interpreted as lending support to that assumption. The study by Brodbeck (1956) is one of those most often cited. Subjects in that experiment heard propaganda which either supported or contradicted their opinions on wiretapping. Subjects who heard the propaganda contradicting their own opinions and who changed those opinions were asked whether they would prefer to hear pro or con speakers. Brodbeck reported there was a tendency for subjects to choose discussion likely to support their initial opinions. As Steiner (1962) has pointed out, however, the tendency was not significant at the .05 level, and even if it had been it would not have indicated **rejection** of dissonant information. Mills, Aronson, and Robinson (1959) asked subjects to choose either an objective or an essay examination, and then found that they chose to read articles which favored the type of test they had chosen, although they did not seem to prefer articles dealing with the faults of the type of test they did not choose. Rosen (1961) essentially replicated the study by Mills, Aronson, and Robinson, but his results seem to lead to the conclusion that subjects prefer either favorable or unfavorable information about a chosen alternative to any kind of information about an unchosen alternative. Thus these studies, while often cited as evidence for the proposition that subjects avoid information inconsistent with their own opinions, actually failed to support that proposition, as did experiments by Festinger and Thibaut (1951), Gerard (1953), Ehrlich (1957), Adams (1961), and Feather (1962, 1963). One study, by Mills (1965a), does lend some support. Subjects were asked to choose one of a number of products which they had previously ranked in order of

desirability. The subjects were subsequently more interested in reading advertisements for the products they chose and less interested
in reading advertisements for the products they rejected than would
have been predicted on the basis of desirability rankings alone. Two
other studies, by Festinger (1957, pp. 162–176) and by Cohen, Brehm,
and Latané (1959) also seem to support the hypothesis that subjects
avoid dissonant information.

Just in case the initial prediction was incorrect, Festinger (1964a)
has come up with an explanation of why subjects may sometimes seek
out information contrary to their own opinions. He argues that dissonance is aroused by a subject's knowledge of the existence of contrary information or opinions. He may reduce such dissonance by
confronting the opinion and refuting it, or he may ignore the opinion
and use some alternative means of dissonance reduction. If he is
confident of his own position, he will confront the opposing opinion
or information; otherwise he will ignore or avoid it. Experiments by
Canon (1964), Mills (1965b), and by Mills and Ross (1964) lend some
support to this explanation.

Misperceiving dissonant information.   Listeners probably misperceive and forget dissonant information more quickly. So far, however,
it has been very difficult to determine how much of the observed effect
is due to selective perception and how much is due to selective recall,
since both are generally measured by retention tests.

Often-cited studies by Levine and Murphy (1943), Edwards (1941),
Kendall and Wolfe (1949), and Hasdorf and Cantril (1954) seem to lead
to the conclusion that subjects will perceive and remember information in such a way as to minimize its contradiction of their own attitudes and beliefs. A study by Taft (1954) would lead to some modification of that conclusion, however. In this case, Negro subjects re-
called more information favorable to Negroes and more information
unfavorable to Negroes, but the recall of Negro and white subjects
did not differ significantly for neutral information. Jones and Kohler
(1958) report their subjects remembered strong arguments favoring
their own positions and weak arguments opposing them. Jones and
Aneshansel (1956) found their subjects remembered opposing arguments as well as their own **when they expected a subsequent debate.**
The persuader, then, must face the fact that his audience is likely to
misperceive or misremember information contradicting its own opinions, unless (1) the listeners are mildly ego-involved and thus in-

terested, (2) they believe the information may be easily refuted, or (3) the information appears **useful** to them. A good speaker addressing a hostile audience might be well-advised to suggest to his listeners that they may expect to encounter others of his own persuasion, and that they will be better prepared if they know the arguments to expect.

Deprecating opposing arguments. Listeners may judge opposing arguments to be less plausible than they are, or may judge arguments they favor to be more plausible than they actually are. This failure of objective reasoning has been demonstrated repeatedly, in studies by Lefford (1946), Thistlethwaite (1950), Feather (1964), and Waly and Cook (1965). The studies by McGuire (1960) and Schunk (1967), mentioned in an earlier chapter, demonstrated that a subject's acceptance of a conclusion is more likely to be determined by his judgment of the **desirability** of that conclusion than it is by the subject's belief in the premises to which the conclusion is logically related.

Seeking supportive information. People who hear a message contradicting their own opinions often seek information to refute the message and support their original opinions. Festinger (1964b) has offered this as an explanation of the tendency of listeners to indicate that they have changed opinions in the direction of the message and then shift back later, not only to their original opinions, but to more extreme positions in the direction opposite that advocated. To prevent this, the persuader should try to anticipate the kinds of social and informational support his listeners will be able to find and refute that support in advance.

Devaluating importance of the issue. Festinger (1957) suggested that subjects may reduce dissonance by coming to view the cognitions involved as less important. That subjects do come to see their **choices** as less important after they have made irrevocable decisions has been amply demonstrated (Brehm and Cohen, 1960), and there is some evidence that the same thing occurs after a listener encounters a dissonance-producing message (Cronkhite, 1966). It is difficult to say just how this information is to be used by the persuader. If he wants his audience to perform some fairly easy behavior, such as giving verbal assent to his proposition, he may be willing to let them consider the proposition to be less important; he may even encourage them to see it as such. ("Your signature on this document is just a formality, sir.") On the other hand, if the persuader expects his listeners to take some difficult action, he is going to have to persuade them that his proposition is not only true but also important.

Differentiating. In the third chapter I mentioned the possibility that a listener who has an unfavorable attitude toward some global concept C but hears favorable information about that concept may come to differentiate concept C into concept C_1, toward which he remains unfavorable, and C_2, toward which he becomes favorable. This was one of the means which Cooper and Jahoda (1947) report were used by their subjects to avoid attitude change. Actually, the research in this area makes one begin to wonder just what "attitude change" **is;** what Brown (1962) has called "differentiation" may be the basic process underlying what has been termed "attitude change." As Asch (1940) says, there may be "a change in the object of judgment, rather than in the judgment of the object." Consider again the example used in the third chapter. A white southerner is tested and found to have a negative attitude toward the term "Negro," which he applies to a unified stereotyped concept of dark-skinned persons who are dirty, lazy, and mentally inferior. He is then exposed to a persuasive message which convinces him that some Negroes are bright, industrious, and neat. After the message, he is again asked to indicate his attitude toward "Negro," but "Negro" is no longer a unified concept for him. He produces some sort of "average" which, being more favorable than the pretest score, shows up as favorable attitude change, but conceals the fact that the individual's conceptual framework has changed instead. It is ironic that social psychologists, who are among the most vocal opponents of stereotyping, depend upon it so heavily in measurement. A study by Lewis (1941) demonstrates that this "differentiation" phenomenon does occur in some cases, at least. The persuader may take advantage of this means of dissonance-reduction: He may encourage his listeners to shift their focus from a global object of judgment to a more specific one, and may get the desired attitude change without ever confronting his listeners with the unpleasant thought that they have "changed their minds."

REFERENCES

Abelson, R. P., and G. S. Lesser. "The Developmental Theory of Persuasibility," **Personality and Persuasibility.** Carl S. Hovland and Irving L. Janis,
eds. New Haven: Yale University Press, 1959, pp. 141–166.

Adams, J. S. "Reduction of Cognitive Dissonance by Seeking Consonant Information," **Journal of Abnormal and Social Psychology,** 62 (1961), 74–78.

Adorno, T. W., Else Frenkel-Brunswik, D. J. Levinson, and R. N. Sanford. **The
Authoritarian Personality.** New York: Harper, 1950.

Allport, Floyd H. "A Structuronomic Conception of Behavior, Individual and
Collective: I. Structural Theory and the Master Problem of Social
Psychology," **Journal of Abnormal and Social Psychology,** 64 (1962), 3–30.

Aronson, Elliot, and Judson Mills. "The Effect of Severity of Initiation on
Liking for a Group," **Journal of Abnormal and Social Psychology,** 59 (1959),
177–181.

Aronson, J. Turner, and J. Carlsmith. "Communicator Credibility and Communication Discrepancy as Determinants of Opinion Change," **Journal of
Abnormal and Social Psychology,** 67 (1963), 31–36.

Asch, Solomon E. "Studies in the Principles of Judgments and Attitudes: II.
Determination of Judgments by Group and Ego Standards," **Journal of
Social Psychology,** 12 (1940), 433–465.

———. "Effects of Group Pressure upon the Modification and Distortion of
Judgments," **Groups, Leadership, and Men.** H. Guetzkow, ed. Pittsburgh:
Carnegie Press, 1951, pp. 177–190.

———. **Social Psychology.** New York: Prentice-Hall, 1952, chap. 16.

———. "Studies of Independence and Conformity: A Minority of One Against
a Unanimous Majority," **Psychological Monographs,** 70 (1956), Issue 416.

Back, Kurt W. "The Exertion of Influence through Social Communication,"
Journal of Abnormal and Social Psychology, 46 (1951), 9–23.

Bateman, R. M. and H. H. Remmers. "A Study of the Shifting Attitude of High
School Students when Subjected to Favorable and Unfavorable Propaganda," **Journal of Social Psychology,** 13 (1941), 395–406.

Beloff, H. "Two Forms of Social Conformity: Acquiescence and Convention-
ality," **Journal of Abnormal and Social Psychology,** 56 (1958), 99–104.

Bem, Daryl J. "Inducing Belief in False Confessions," **Journal of Personality
and Social Psychology,** 3 (1966), 707–710.

———, Michael L. Wallach, and Nathan Kogan. "Group Decision-Making Under Risk of Aversive Consequences," **Journal of Personality and Social
Psychology,** 1 (1965), 453–460.

Berkowitz, Leonard, and Richard E. Goranson. "Motivational and Judgmental

Determinants of Social Perception," **Journal of Abnormal and Social Psychology,** 69 (1964), 296–302.

Berkowitz and Edna Rawlings. "Effects of Film Violence on Inhibitions Against Subsequent Aggression," **Journal of Abnormal and Social Psychology,** 66 (1963), 405–412.

Blake, Robert R. and Jane S. Mouton. "Overevaluation of Own Group's Product in Intergroup Competition," **Journal of Abnormal and Social Psychology,** 64 (1962), 237–238.

Bostrum, Robert N., John W. Vlandis, and Milton E. Rosenbaum. "Grades as Reinforcing Contingencies and Attitude Change," **Journal of Educational Psychology,** 52 (1961), 112–115.

Bowden, A. W., F. F. Caldwell, and G. A. West. " 'Halo' Prestige," **Journal of Abnormal and Social Psychology,** 26 (1934), 400–406.

Brehm, J. W. "Increasing Cognitive Dissonance by a *Fait Accompli*," **Journal of Abnormal and Social Psychology,** 58 (1959), 379–382.

————. "A Dissonance Analysis of Attitude-Discrepant Behavior." **Attitude Organization and Change.** Milton J. Rosenberg and Carl I. Hovland, eds. New Haven: Yale University Press, 1960, pp. 164–197.

————, and Arthur R. Cohen. "Choice and Chance Relative Deprivation as Determinants of Cognitive Dissonance." **Journal of Abnormal and Social Psychology,** 58 (1959), 383–387.

————. **Explorations in Cognitive Dissonance.** New York: Wiley, 1962.

Brock, Timothy C. "Cognitive Restructuring and Attitude Change," **Journal of Abnormal and Social Psychology,** 64 (1962), 264–271.

Brodbeck, May. "The Role of Small Groups in Mediating the Effects of Propaganda," **Journal of Abnormal and Social Psychology,** 52 (1956), 166–170.

Brooks, Robert D., and Thomas M. Scheidel. "Speech as Process: A Case Study," **Speech Monographs,** 35 (1968), 1-7.

Brown, Roger. **Social Psychology.** New York: Free Press, 1965, chap. 11.

Burtt, Harold and Don Falkenburg. "The Influence of Majority and Expert Opinion on Religious Attitudes," **Journal of Social Psychology,** 14 (1941), 269–278.

Canon, L. K. "Self-Confidence and Selective Exposure to Information," **Conflict, Decision, and Dissonance.** Leon Festinger, ed. Stanford: Stanford University Press, 1964.

Carlsmith, J. Merrill, Barry E. Collins, and Robert L. Helmreich. "Studies in Forced Compliance: I. The Effect of Pressure for Compliance on Attitude Change Produced by Face-to-Face Role Playing and Anonymous Essay Writing," **Journal of Personality and Social Psychology,** 4, (1966), 1–13.

Carmichael, Carl W. "Attitude Change as a Function of the Relevance of Communications and Their Sources to Frustrating Experiences." Unpublished doctoral dissertation, University of Iowa, 1965.

————, and Gary Cronkhite. "Frustration and Language Intensity," **Speech Monographs,** 32 (1965), 107–111.

Cartwright, Dorwin, and Alvin Zander. **Group Dynamics: Research and Theory.** Evanston: Row, Peterson, 1960.

Charters, W. W., and Theodore M. Newcomb. "Some Attitudinal Effects of Experimentally Increased Salience of a Membership Group," **Readings in Social Psychology.** Eleanor E. Maccoby, Theodore M. Newcomb, and Eugene L. Hartley, eds. New York: Holt, Rinehart and Winston, 1958, pp. 276–281.

Cherrington, B. M., and L. W. Miller. "Changes in Attitude as the Result of a Lecture and Reading Similar Material," **Journal of Social Psychology,** 4 (1933), 479–484.

Cohen, Arthur R. "Upward Communication in Experimentally Created Hierarchies," **Human Relations,** 11 (1958), 41–53.

————. "Communication Discrepancy and Attitude Change," **Journal of Personality,** 27 (1959), 386–396.

————. Attitudinal Consequences of Induced Discrepancies Between Cognitions and Behavior," **Public Opinion Quarterly,** 24 (1960), 297–318.

————. "An Experiment of Small Rewards for Discrepant Compliance and Attitude Change," **Explorations in Cognitive Dissonance,** J. Brehm and Arthur R. Cohen, eds. New York: Wiley, 1962, pp. 73–78.

————, J. Brehm, and W. Fleming. "Attitude Change and Justification for Compliance," **Journal of Abnormal and Social Psychology,** 56 (1958), 276–278.

Cohen, J. W. Brehm, and B. Latane. "Choice of Strategy and Voluntary Exposure to Information Under Public and Private Conditions," **Journal of Personality,** 27 (1959), 63–73.

Cooper, E. and M. Jahoda. "The Evasion of Propaganda: How Prejudiced People Respond to Anti-Prejudice Propaganda," **Journal of Psychology,** 23 (1947), 15–25.

Cox, Donald, and Raymond A. Bauer. "Self-confidence and Persuasibility in Women," **Public Opinion Quarterly,** 28 (1964), 453–466.

Cronkhite, Gary. "The Relation of Scholastic Aptitude to Logical Argument and Emotional Appeal." Unpublished master's thesis, Illinois State University, 1961.

————. "Autonomic Correlates of Dissonance and Attitude Change," **Speech Monographs,** 33 (1966), 392–399.

————, and Emily Goetz. "Dogmatism, Persuasibility, and Attitude Instability." Paper presented at the convention of Speech Association of America, New York City, December 1965.

Crutchfield, R. S. "Conformity and Character," **American Psychologist,** 10 (1955), 191–198.

Das, J. P. and P. C. Nanda. "Mediated Transfer of Attitudes," **Journal of Abnormal and Social Psychology,** 66 (1963), 12–16.

Dollard, John, Leonard W. Doob, Neal E. Miller, O. H. Mowrer, and Robert R. Sears. **Frustration and Aggression.** New Haven: Yale University Press, 1939.

Eagly, Alice H., and Melvin Manis. "Evaluation of Message and Communicator as a Function of Involvement," **Journal of Personality and Social Psychology,** 3 (1966), 483–485.

Edwards, A. L. "Political Frames of Reference as a Factor Influencing Recognition," **Journal of Abnormal and Social Psychology,** 36 (1941), 34–50.

Ehrlich, Danuta, et al. "Postdecision Exposure to Relevant Information," **Journal of Abnormal and Social Psychology,** 54 (1957), 98–102.

Ekman, P. "A Comparison of Verbal and Nonverbal Behavior as Reinforcing Stimuli of Opinion Responses." Unpublished doctoral dissertation, Adelphi College, 1958.

Elms, Alan C. "Influence of Fantasy Ability on Attitude Change through Role Playing," **Journal of Personality and Social Psychology,** 4 (1966), 36–43.

———, and Irving L. Janis. "Counter-Norm Attitudes Induced by Consonant versus Dissonant Conditions of Role-Playing," **Journal of Experimental Research in Personality,** 1 (1965), 50–60.

Feather, N. T. "Cigarette Smoking and Lung Cancer: A Study of Cognitive Dissonance," **Australian Journal of Psychology,** 14 (1962), 55–64.

———. "Cognitive Dissonance, Sensitivity, and Evaluation," **Journal of Abnormal and Social Psychology,** 66 (1963), 157–163.

———. "Acceptance and Rejection of Arguments in Relation to Attitude Strength, Critical Ability, and Intolerance of Inconsistency," **Journal of Abnormal and Social Psychology,** 69 (1964), 127–136.

Festinger, Leon. "A Theory of Social Comparison Processes," **Human Relations,** 7 (1954), 117–140.

———. **A Theory of Cognitive Dissonance.** Stanford: Stanford University Press, 1957.

———. "The Psychological Effects of Insufficient Rewards," **American Psychologist,** 16 (1961), 1–11.

———, ed. **Conflict, Decision, and Dissonance.** Stanford: Stanford University Press, 1964a.

———. "Behavioral Support for Opinion Change," **Public Opinion Quarterly,** 28 (1964b), 404–417.

———, and J. Carlsmith. "Cognitive Consequences of Forced Compliance," **Journal of Abnormal and Social Psychology,** 58 (1959), 203–210.

Festinger, H. Rieken, and Stanley Schachter. **When Prophecy Fails.** Minneapolis: University of Minnesota Press, 1956.

Festinger and J. Thibaut. "Interpersonal Communication in Small Groups," **Journal of Abnormal and Social Psychology,** 46 (1951), 92–99.

Fisher, S., and A. Lubin. "Distance as a Determinant of Influence in a Two-Person Serial Interaction Situation," **Journal of Abnormal and Social Psychology,** 56 (1958), 230–238.

Fisher, I. Rubenstein, and R. Freeman. "Intertrial Effects of Immediate Self-Committal in a Continuous Social Influence Situation," **Journal of Abnormal and Social Psychology,** 52 (1956), 325–329.

Freedman, Jonathan L. "Attitudinal Effects of Inadequate Justification," **Journal of Personality,** 31 (1963), 371–385.

———. "Involvement, Discrepancy, and Change," **Journal of Abnormal and Social Psychology,** 68 (1964), 290–295.

Freedman and John D. Steinbruner. "Perceived Choice and Resistance to Persuasion," **Journal of Abnormal and Social Psychology,** 68 (1964), 678–681.

Frye, Roland L., Jean Spryill, and Thomas M. Stritch. "Effect of Group Size on Public and Private Coalescence, Efficiency, and Change," **Journal of Social Psychology,** 62 (1964), 131–139.

Furbay, Albert. "The Influence of Scattered versus Compact Seating on Audience Response," **Speech Monographs,** 32 (1965), 144–148.

Gerard, H. B. "The Effect of Different Dimensions of Disagreement on the Communication Process in Small Groups." **Human Relations,** 6 (1953), 249–271.

———. "Conformity and Commitment to the Group," **Journal of Abnormal and Social Psychology,** 68 (1964), 209–211.

———, and G. S. Rotter. "Time Perspective, Consistency of Attitude, and Social Influence," **Journal of Abnormal and Social Psychology,** 62 (1961), 565–572.

Goldberg, Solomon C. "The Situational Determinants of Conformity to Social Norms," **Journal of Abnormal and Social Psychology,** 49 (1954), 325–329.

Gorfein, D. "Conformity Behavior and the 'Authoritarian Personality,'" **Journal of Social Psychology,** 53 (1961), 121–125.

Haiman, Franklyn S. "An Experimental Study of the Effects of Ethos in Public Speaking," **Speech Monographs,** 16 (1949), 190–202.

Hall, Jay, and Martha S. Williams. "A Comparison of Decision-Making Performances in Established and Ad Hoc Groups," **Journal of Personality and Social Psychology,** 3 (1966), 214–222.

Hardy, K. R. "Determinants of Conformity and Attitude Change," **Journal of Abnormal and Social Psychology,** 54 (1957), 289–294.

Hare, A. P. **Handbook of Small Group Research.** New York: Free Press of Glencoe, 1962.

Harvey, O. J. "Reactions to Unfavorable Evaluations of Self by Others,"

Technical Report No. 8, 1958. Vanderbilt University, Contract NONR 249 (02), Office of Naval Research.

————. "Personality Correlates of Concept Functioning and Change Across Situations," Technical Report No. 3, 1959. University of Colorado, Contract NONR 1147(07), Office of Naval Research.

————, and G. D. Beverly. "Some Personality Correlates of Concept Change through Role-Playing," **Journal of Abnormal and Social Psychology,** 58 (1961), 125–130.

Harvey and D. F. Caldwell. "Assimilation and Contrast in Response to Environmental Variation," **Journal of Personality,** 27 (1959), 125–135.

Hastorf, A., and H. Cantril. "They Saw a Game: A Case Study," **Journal of Abnormal and Social Psychology,** 49 (1954), 129–134.

Hildum, D. C., and R. W. Brown. "Verbal Reinforcement and Interviewer Bias," **Journal of Abnormal and Social Psychology,** 53 (1956), 108–111.

Hollander, E. P. "Conformity, Status, and Idiosyncrasy Credit," **Psychological Review,** 65 (1958), 117–127.

————. **Leaders, Groups, and Influence.** New York: Oxford, 1964.

————, James W. Julian, and Gordon A. Haaland. "Conformity, Process and Prior Group Support," **Journal of Personality and Social Psychology,** 2 (1965), 852–858.

Hovland, Carl I., E. H. Campbell, and T. Brock. "The Effects of 'Commitment' on Opinion Change Following Communication," **The Order of Presentation in Persuasion,** Carl I. Hovland, ed. New Haven: Yale University Press, 1957, pp. 23–32.

Hovland, O. J. Harvey, and Muzafer Sherif. "Assimilation and Contrast Effects in Reactions to Communication and Attitude Change," **Journal of Abnormal and Social Psychology,** 55 (1957), 244–252.

Hovland, Irving L. Janis, and H. H. Kelly. **Communication and Persuasion.** New Haven: Yale University Press, 1953.

Hovland, A. A. Lumsdaine, and F. D. Sheffield. "The Effects of Presenting 'One Side' versus 'Both Sides' in Changing Opinions on a Controversial Subject," **Experiments on Mass Communication,** Vol. 3 of **Studies in Social Psychology in World War II.** Princeton: Princeton University Press, 1949, pp. 201–227.

Hovland and H. A. Pritzker. "Extent of Opinion Change as a Function of Change Advocated," **Journal of Abnormal and Social Psychology,** 54 (1957), 257–261.

Hovland and Muzafer Sherif. **Social Judgment.** New Haven: Yale University Press, 1961.

Hunt, Martin, and Gerald R. Miller. "Open- and Closed-Mindedness, Belief-Discrepant Communication Behavior, and Tolerance for Dissonance." Paper presented at the convention of the Speech Association of America, New York City, December 1965.

Insko, Chester A. "Verbal Reinforcement of Attitude," **Journal of Personality and Social Psychology,** 2 (1965), 621–623.

Iwao, Sumiko. "Internal versus External Criticism of Group Standards," **Sociometry,** 26 (1963), 419.

Janis, Irving L. "Anxiety Indices Related to Susceptibility to Persuasion," **Journal of Abnormal and Social Psychology,** 51 (1955), 663–667.

Janis and Peter B. Field. "A Behavioral Assessment of Persuasibility," **Personality and Persuasibility,** Carl I. Hovland and Irving L. Janis., eds. New Haven: Yale University Press, 1959, pp. 29–54.

Janis and J. B. Gilmore. "The Influence of Incentive Conditions on the Success of Role Playing in Modifying Attitudes," **Journal of Personality and Social Psychology,** 1 (1965), 17–27.

Janis and Bert T. King. "The Influence of Role Playing on Opinion Change," **Journal of Abnormal and Social Psychology,** 49 (1954), 211–218.

Janis and D. Rife. "Persuasibility and Emotional Disorder," **Personality and Persuasibility,** Carl I. Hovland and Irving L. Janis, eds. New Haven: Yale University Press, 1959, pp. 121–137.

Johnson, Homer H., James M. Torcivia, and Mary Ann Poprick. "Effects of Source Credibility on the Relationship Between Authoritarianism and Attitude Change," **Journal of Personality and Social Psychology,** 9 (1968), 179–183.

Jones, E. E., and J. Aneshansel. "The Learning and Utilization of Contra-Valuent Material," **Journal of Abnormal and Social Psychology,** 53 (1956), 27–33.

Jones and R. Kohler. "The Effects of Plausibility on the Learning of Controversial Statements," **Journal of Abnormal and Social Psychology,** 57 (1958), 315–320.

Jones, Stanley E. "Attitude Changes of Public Speakers During the Investigative and Expressive Stages of Advocacy," **Speech Monographs,** 33 (1966), 137–146.

Katz, Daniel, Charles McClintock, and Irving Sarnoff. "The Measurement of Ego Defense as Related to Attitude Change," **Journal of Personality,** 25 (1957), 465–474.

Kelley, H. H. "Communication in Experimentally Created Hierarchies," **Human Relations,** 4 (1951), 39–56.

Kelman, H. C. "Attitude Change as a Function of Response Restriction," **Human Relations,** 6 (1953), 185–214.

Kendall, P., and K. M. Wolfe. "The Analysis of Deviant Cases in Communications Research," **Communications Research, 1948–1949,** P. F. Lazarsfeld and F. N. Stanton, eds. New York: Harper, 1949, pp. 152–170.

Kiesler, Charles A., and Lee H. Corbin. "Commitment, Attraction, and Conformity," **Journal of Personality and Social Psychology,** 2 (1965), 890–895.

Kiesler and Joseph Sakumura. "A Test of a Model for Commitment," **Journal of Personality and Social Psychology,** 3 (1966), 349–353.

Kiesler, Mark Zanna, and James DeSalvo. "Deviation and Conformity: Opinion Change as a Function of Commitment, Attraction, and Presence of a Deviate," **Journal of Personality and Social Psychology,** 5 (1966), 458–467.

King, Bert T. "Relationships Between Susceptibility to Opinion Change and Child-Rearing Practices," **Personality and Persuasibility,** Carl I. Hovland and Irving L. Janis, eds. New Haven: Yale University Press, 1959.

King, and Irving L. Janis. "Comparison of the Effectiveness of Improvised versus Non-Improvised Role-Playing in Producing Opinion Changes," **Human Relations,** 9 (1956), 177–178.

Knower, Franklin H. "Experimental Studies of Changes in Attitudes: I. A Study of the Effect of Oral Argument on Changes of Attitude," **Journal of Social Psychology,** 6 (1935), 315–344.

————. "Experimental Studies of Changes in Attitude: II. A Study of the Effect of Printed Argument on Changes in Attitude," **Journal of Abnormal and Social Psychology,** 30 (1936), 522–532.

Lefford, A. "The Influence of Emotional Subject Matter on Logical Reasoning," **Journal of General Psychology,** 34 (1946), 127–151.

Levine, J. M., and G. Murphy. "The Learning and Forgetting of Controversial Material," **Journal of Abnormal and Social Psychology,** 38 (1943), 507–517.

Lewis, Helen B. "Studies in the Principles of Judgments and Attitudes: IV. The Operation of Prestige Suggestion," **Journal of Abnormal and Social Psychology,** 45 (1941), 229–256.

Linder, D. E., J. Cooper, and E. E. Jones. "Decision Freedom as a Determinant of the Role of Incentive Magnitude in Attitude Change," **Journal of Personality and Social Psychology,** 6 (1967), 245–254.

Linton, H., and E. Graham. "Personality Correlates of Persuasibility," **Personality and Persuasibility,** Carl I. Hovland and Irving L. Janis, eds. New Haven: Yale University Press, 1959, pp. 69–101.

Maccoby, Eleanor E., Nathan Maccoby, A. K. Romney, and J. S. Adams. "Social Reinforcement in Attitude Change," **Journal of Abnormal and Social Psychology,** 63 (1961), 109–115.

McGinnies, Elliott, Elaine Donelson, and Robert Haaf. "Level of Initial Attitude, Active Rehearsal, and Instructional Set as Factors in Attitude Change," **Journal of Abnormal and Social Psychology,** 69 (1964), 437–440.

McGuire, William J. "Order of Presentation as a Factor in 'Conditioning' Persuasiveness," **The Order of Presentation in Persuasion,** Carl I. Hovland, et al., eds. New Haven: Yale University Press, 1957, pp. 98–114.

————. "A Syllogistic Analysis of Cognitive Relationships," **Attitude Organization and Change,** M. J. Rosenberg, et al., eds. New Haven: Yale University Press, 1960, pp. 65–111.

McGuire and Susan Millman. "Anticipatory Belief Lowering Following Forewarning of a Persuasive Attack," **Journal of Personality and Social Psychology,** 2 (1965), 471–479.

Marlowe, David, Robert Frager, and Ronald Nuttall. "Commitment to Action Taking as a Consequence of Cognitive Dissonance," **Journal of Personality and Social Psychology,** 2 (1965), 864–868.

Marple, Clare. "The Comparative Susceptibility of Three Age Levels to the Suggestion of Group versus Expert Opinion," **Journal of Social Psychology,** 4 (1933), 176–186.

Miller, Norman. "Involvement and Dogmatism as Inhibitors of Attitude Change," **Journal of Experimental Social Psychology,** 1 (1965), 121–132.

Millon, T., and L. D. Simkins. "Suggestibility of Authoritarians and Equalitarians to Prestige Influence," **American Psychologist,** 12 (1957), 404.

Mills, Judson. "Avoidance of Dissonant Information," **Journal of Personality and Social Psychology,** 2 (1965a), 589–593.

––––––. "Effect of Certainty About a Decision Upon Postdecision Exposure to Consonant and Dissonant Information," **Journal of Personality and Social Psychology,** 2 (1965b), 749–752.

––––––, Elliot Aronson, and H. Robinson. "Selectivity in Exposure to Information," **Journal of Abnormal and Social Psychology,** 59 (1959), 250–253.

Mills, and Abraham Ross. "Effects of Commitment and Certainty Upon Interest in Supporting Information," **Journal of Abnormal and Social Psychology,** 68 (1964), 552–555.

Moore, Henry. "The Comparative Influence of Majority and Expert Opinion," **American Journal of Psychology,** 32 (1921), 16–20.

Murphy, Gardner, L. B. Murphy, and T. M. Newcomb. **Experimental Social Psychology,** rev. ed. New York: Harper and Row, 1937.

Myers, Gary C. "Control of Conduct by Suggestion: An Experiment in Americanization," **Journal of Applied Psychology,** 5 (1921), 26–31.

Nadler, E. B. "Yielding, Authoritarianism, and Authoritarian Ideology Regarding Groups," **Journal of Abnormal and Social Psychology,** 58 (1959), 408–410.

Norris, Eleanor L. "Attitude Change as a Function of Open- or Closed-Mindedness," **Journalism Quarterly,** 42 (1965), 571–575.

Nuttin, J. M., Jr. "Dissonant Evidence About Dissonance Theory." Paper read at Second Conference of Experimental Social Psychologists in Europe, held in Frascati, Italy, 1964. See next entry.

––––––. "Attitude Change After Rewarded Dissonant and Consonant 'Forced Compliance,'" **International Journal of Psychology,** 1 (1966), 39–57.

Paulson, Stanley F. "The Effects of the Prestige of the Speaker and Acknowledgment of Opposing Arguments on Audience Retention and Shift of Opinion," **Speech Monographs,** 21 (1954), 267–271.

Peabody, Dean. "Attitude Content and Agreement Set in Scales of Authoritarianism, Dogmatism, Anti-Semitism, and Economic Conservatism," **Journal of Abnormal and Social Psychology,** 63 (1961), 2–9.

Pelz, Edith Bennett. "Discussion, Decision, Commitment, and Consensus in 'Group Decision,'" **Human Relations,** 7 (1955), 251–274.

Pence, O. M., and Thomas M. Scheidel. "The Effects of Critical Thinking Ability and Certain Other Variables on Persuasibility." Paper read at the convention of the Speech Association of America," Chicago, December 1956.

Pervin, Lawrence A., and Raymond T. Yatko. "Cigarette Smoking and Alternative Methods of Reducing Dissonance," **Journal of Personality and Social Psychology,** 2 (1965), 30–36.

Phillips, Gerald M. **Communication and the Small Group.** Indianapolis: Bobbs-Merrill, 1966.

Rabbie, J., J. Brehm, and Arthur R. Cohen. "Verbalization and Reactions to Cognitive Dissonance," **Journal of Personality,** 27 (1959), 407–417.

Rhine, R. T., and Betsy A. Silun. "Acquisition and Change of a Concept Attitude as a Function of Consistency of Reinforcement," **Journal of Experimental Psychology,** 55 (1958), 524–529.

Rokeach, Milton. **The Open and Closed Mind.** New York: Basic Books, 1960.

Rose, A. **Union Solidarity.** Minneapolis: University of Minnesota Press, 1952.

Rosen, S. "Postdecision Affinity for Incompatible Information," **Journal of Abnormal and Social Psychology,** 63 (1961), 188–190.

Rosenbaum, Milton E., and D. E. Franc. "Opinion Change as a Function of External Commitment and Amount of Discrepancy from the Opinion of Another," **Journal of Abnormal and Social Psychology,** 61 (1960), 15–20.

Rosenbaum, and I. M. Zimmerman. "The Effect of External Commitment on Response to an Attempt to Change Opinions," **Public Opinion Quarterly,** 23 (1959), 247–254.

Rosenberg, Milton J. "When Dissonance Fails: On Eliminating Evaluation Apprehension from Attitude Measurement," **Journal of Personality and Social Psychology,** 1 (1965), 28–42.

Sampson, Edward E., and Chester A. Insko. "Cognitive Consistency and Performance in the Autokinetic Situation," **Journal of Abnormal and Social Psychology,** 58 (1964), 184–192.

Sarbin, Theodore R., and Vernon L. Allen. "Role Enactment, Audience Feedback, and Attitude Change," **Sociometry,** 27 (1964), 183–193.

Schachter, Stanley. "Deviation, Rejection, and Communication," **Journal of Abnormal and Social Psychology,** 46 (1951), 190–207.

———, and R. Hall. "Group-Derived Restraints and Audience Persuasion." **Human Relations,** 5 (1952), 397–406.

Scheidel, Thomas M. "Sex and Persuasibility," **Speech Monographs,** 30 (1963), 353–358.

Schunk, John. "Probability and Desirability Determinants of Relationships Among Beliefs in Rhetorical Propositions." Unpublished doctoral dissertation, University of Illinois, 1967.

Scott, W. A. "Attitude Change through Reward of Verbal Behavior," **Journal of Abnormal and Social Psychology,** 55 (1957), 72–75.

———. "Cognitive Consistency, Response Reinforcement, and Attitude Change," Sociometry, 22 (1959a), 219–229.

———. "Attitude Change by Response Reinforcement: Replication and Extension," **Sociometry,** 22 (1959b), 328–335.

Sears, D. O., J. L. Freedman, and E. F. O'Connor. "The Effects of Anticipated Debate and Commitment on the Polarization of Audience Opinion," **Public Opinion Quarterly,** 28 (1964), 615–627.

Sherif, Muzafer. "A Study of Some Social Factors in Perception," **Archives of Psychology,** 27 (1935), 187.

———. **The Psychology of Social Norms.** New York: Harper, 1936.

———. "An Experimental Approach to the Study of Attitudes," **Sociometry,** 1 (1937), 90–98.

———. Carolyn Sherif, and Roger Nebergall. **Attitude and Attitude Change.** Philadelphia: Saunders, 1965.

Staats, A. W., and Carolyn Staats. "Attitudes Established by Classical Conditioning," **Journal of Abnormal and Social Psychology,** 57 (1958), 37–40.

Staats, Staats, and W. Heard. "Attitude Development and Ratio of Reinforcement," **Sociometry,** 23 (1960), 338–350.

Steiner, Ivan D. "Receptivity to Supportive versus Nonsupportive Communications," **Journal of Abnormal and Social Psychology,** 65 (1962), 266–267.

———, and E. D. Rogers. "Alternative Responses to Dissonance," **Journal of Abnormal and Social Psychology,** 66 (1963), 128–136.

Stricker, George. "Scape-Goating: An Experimental Investigation," **Journal of Abnormal and Social Psychology,** 67 (1963), 125–131.

Strickland, L. H., E. E. Jones, and W. P. Smith. "Effects of Group Support on the Evaluation of an Antagonist," **Journal of Abnormal and Social Psychology,** 61 (1960), 73–81.

Thistlethwaite, D. "Attitude and Structure as Factors in the Distortion of Reasoning," **Journal of Abnormal and Social Psychology,** 45 (1950), 442–458.

Verplanck, W. S. "The Control of the Content of Conversation: Reinforcement of Statements of Opinion," **Journal of Abnormal and Social Psychology,** 51 (1955), 668–676.

Wagman, Morton. "Attitude Change and Authoritarian Personality," **Journal of Psychology,** 40 (1955), 3–24.

Wallace, John. "Role Reward and Dissonance Reduction," **Journal of Personality and Social Psychology,** 3 (1966), 305–312.

Wallach, Michael A., and Nathan Kogan, "Sex Differences and Judgment Processes," **Journal of Personality,** 27 (1959), 555–564.

————. "Aspects of Judgment and Decision-Making: Interrelationships and Changes with Age," **Behavioral Science,** 6 (1961), 23–36.

————. "The Roles of Information, Discussion, and Consensus in Group Risk Taking," **Journal of Experimental Social Psychology,** 1 (1965), 1–19.

————, and D. J. Bem. "Group Influence on Individual Risk Taking," **Journal of Abnormal and Social Psychology,** 65 (1962), 75–86.

————. "Diffusion of Responsibility and Level of Risk Taking in Groups," **Journal of Abnormal and Social Psychology,** 68 (1964), 263–274.

Walters, R. H., E. L. Thomas, and C. W. Acker. "Enhancement of Punitive Behavior by Audio-Visual Displays," **Science,** 136 (1962), 872, 873.

Waly, Patricia, and Stuart W. Cook. "Effect of Attitude on Judgments of Plausibility," **Journal of Personality and Social Psychology,** 2 (1965), 745–749.

Ward, William D. "Opinion Change as Related to Sequence of Degrees of Change Suggested," **Psychological Reports,** 14 (1964), 93–94.

Ward, Charles D. "Ego Involvement and the Absolute Judgment of Attitude Statements," **Journal of Personality and Social Psychology** 2, (1965), 202–208.

Wegrocki, H. J. "The Effect of Prestige Suggestibility on Emotional Attitude," **Journal of Social Psychology** 5, (1934), 384–394.

Weiner, H., and E. McGinnies. "Authoritarianism, Conformity, and Confidence in a Perceptual Judgment Situation," **Journal of Social Psychology,** 55 (1961), 77–84.

Weiss, R. F., H. E. Rawson, and B. Pasamanick. "Argument Strength, Delay of Argument, and Anxiety in the 'Conditioning' and 'Selective Learning' of Attitudes," **Journal of Abnormal and Social Psychology,** 67 (1963), 157–165.

Weiss, Walter, and Bernard J. Fine. "The Effect of Induced Aggressiveness on Opinion Change," **Journal of Abnormal and Social Psychology,** 52 (1956), 109–114.

Wells, W. D., G. Weinert, and M. Rubel. "Conformity Pressure and Authoritarian Personality," **Journal of Psychology,** 42 (1956), 133–136.

Willerman, B., and L. Swanson. "Group Prestige in Voluntary Organizations," **Human Relations,** 6 (1953), 57–77.

Willis, E. E. "The Relative Effectiveness of Three Forms of Radio Presentation in Influencing Attitudes," **Speech Monographs,** 7 (1940), 45.

Willis, R. H. and E. P. Hollander. "An Experimental Study of Three Response Modes in Social Influence Situations," **Journal of Abnormal and Social Psychology,** 69 (1964), 150–156. See also supplementary note following the article, p. 157.

Wright, Jack M., and O. J. Harvey. "Attitude Change as a Function of Authoritarianism and Punitiveness," **Journal of Personality and Social Psychology,** 1 (1965), 177–181.

Wyer, Robert S., Jr. "Effects of Incentive to Perform Well, Group Attraction, and Group Acceptance on Conformity in a Judgmental Task," **Journal of Personality and Social Psychology,** 4 (1966), 21–26.

Zeff, Leon H., and Marvin A. Iverson. "Opinion Conformity in Groups Under Status Threat," **Journal of Personality and Social Psychology,** 3 (1966), 383–389.

Zimbardo, P. G. "Involvement and Communication Discrepancy as Determinants of Opinion Conformity," **Journal of Abnormal and Social Psychology,** 60 (1960), 68–94.

EIGHT

The persuader's choices

Obviously much of the material surveyed in the preceding chapter has some clear implications for the choices to be made by a prospective persuader. However, in this chapter I would like to deal more directly with three questions: (1) What choices must be made by the person who seeks to persuade a listener? (2) What are the available alternatives in each case? (3) Under what circumstances should each alternative be chosen? For the sake of organizational clarity, these questions will be considered with respect to choices in seven areas:

1. selecting sources to be used in a message
2. selecting the motivational concepts
3. demonstrating the relationships
4. organizing material within a communication
5. deciding upon a time of presentation
6. selecting the language to be used
7. selecting a style of delivery if the message is to be presented orally

Effects of sources

This section will deal with the effects of sources in general. The information, however, may be applied in several ways. Quite often it is possible to select one speaker or writer from a number of candidates who might present a persuasive message. Even when there is no choice in this respect, the persuader usually has a choice at least about the way in which he is to be introduced and, failing that, he certainly has a choice as to the type of image he will create **within** the message. Finally, most persuaders choose to cite other sources expressing opinions or attesting to facts. Thus, whole the persuader in some cases may have no choice about the reputation he has acquired, he may choose another to speak for him, he may choose to present himself or have himself introduced in a variety of ways, and he has a great deal of choice as to the other sources he cites.

Much of the research dealing with the effects of sources has been summarized by Anderson and Clevenger in a rather comprehensive article published in the June 1963 issue of **Speech Monographs.** The reader who is especially interested in this topic should refer to the article, as I will not review the older research in as much detail. In addition, much of the material which might be dealt with in a section such as this is covered elsewhere in the book. For example, the congruity hypothesis of Osgood and Tannenbaum, which is certainly a theory regarding the effects of sources, was described in the third chapter along with a number of other theories at least partially relevant here. Some of the interactions of "prestige suggestion" with personality types were mentioned in the seventh chapter, and the interaction of sources with evidence, organization, timing of messages, language, and delivery will be surveyed later in this final chapter. Thus my primary concern in the present section is to identify the characteristics which listeners may perceive speakers to have, and to discuss to some extent the direct effects of such characteristics.

Dimensions of "ethos." "Ethos" is the term rhetoricians have used as a linguistic wastebasket for any discernible source characteristic for better (or worse) than two thousand years. Aristotle recognized the fact that ethos is not a unidimensional concept, but he lacked the statistical tools to do anything more than say so. Berlo and Lemert performed factor analyses of subjects' ratings of sources on semantic differential scales. They have reported (Berlo, 1961; Lemert, 1963) finding four factors consistently enough to mention, which factors were labeled "trustworthiness," "competence," "dynamism," and "sociability." The fourth factor, "sociability," was rather weak and did not appear in every study or with every type of source. Andersen (1961) reports a similar analysis in which he found only two dimensions: "evaluation" and "dynamism." Finally, McCroskey (1966) found two factors which he labels "character" and "authoritativeness," and believes they correspond to the "trustworthiness" and "competence" factors of Berlo and Lemert. He explains his failure to find a "dynamism" dimension as due to the fact that he used "no items . . . directed toward this factor," which seems to make sense.

A more extensive study of the dimensionality of interpersonal judgments seems to be that done by Norman (1963). The judgments which provided the data were not judgments of a **speaker** in this case, but the factors found have been demonstrated to hold up in a variety of situations. The factors identified by Norman were labeled "agreeableness," "extroversion," "emotional stability," "conscientiousness," and "culture." The correspondence between Norman's structure and that of Berlo and Lemert is like an Amazon, rough but conceivable. "Agreeableness" appears to correspond roughly with "trustworthiness"; "extroversion" and "emotional stability" may be parts of "dynamism," although "extroversion" includes some of the "sociability" scales as well; and "conscientiousness" and "culture" may be the components of "competence," although some of the scales in the "conscientiousness" cluster might be expected to contribute to "trustworthiness."

Another dimension on which listeners probably judge speakers is that of **similarity to themselves.** The subjects in the factor-analytic studies just cited were not given opportunities to make such judgments; hence no such factor appeared. It is surprising that so little has been done to test the question of whether the speaker should attempt to identify with his listeners. The work of Byrne (1961, 1962, 1964, 1966) has made it clear that "interpersonal attraction" is greater when the **attitudes** of two persons are similar. There is also some evidence that there is greater interpersonal attraction between persons similar in personality and other respects as well, but the evidence is far from conclusive. I will add "identification" or "similarity" to the list of dimensions upon which a source is probably judged, but it is important to remember that "identification" has not been empirically demonstrated to be independent of the others in the list.

Effects of the dimensions.   It would be very neat to examine each of these factors or dimensions in turn to determine the relationships which they bear to persuasion. That seems to be a rather unlikely project at this point, however. Those who have done research in the area of source effects have seldom distinguished among the various dimensions of "ethos." Most of them have also used paper-and-pencil tests of attitude for the criterion measure. The study that is needed here is one that systemmatically varies each of these dimensions to determine what kinds of speakers are capable of inducing what kinds of behavior. It may be that the kind of speaker who will be most successful in getting listeners to change their marks on paper will not be the most successful in getting them to join a protest march.

Further, it was hypothesized in the fourth chapter that the persuasive force of the speaker may operate in two ways. First, the speaker may be an attractive motivational concept in himself, so that his being associated with the proposal (or object concept) makes it more attractive. Second, the speaker may testify to the relationship between the proposal and some desired goal. It is very likely that some speaker characteristics assume greater importance to the extent that the speaker himself is operating as a motivational concept, whereas other speaker characteristics assume greater importance to the extent that the speaker is testifying to a relationship. Two experiments have been conducted which make similar distinctions. Kerrick (1958) found that sources "relevant" to the desired action produced greater attitude change than did "irrelevant" sources. Aronson and Golden (1962) conducted an experiment in which each group heard either a Negro or a white speaker (irrelevant credibility) introduced as either educated or uneducated (relevant credibility). Both relevant and irrelevant credibility were found to be effective in producing attitude change. In both these cases it was the decision of the experimenters as to what was to distinguish "relevant" from "irrelevant" sources and characteristics. The empirical test of the hypothesis will be the demonstration that attitude change is more accurately predicted when the speaker is treated **both** as a belief-inducer **and** as a motivational concept in the algebraic model outlined in the fourth chapter.

In the meantime, a great deal of evidence has accumulated regarding the effectiveness of ethos, although most of it is confused by failure to measure the separate dimensions of the concept. It seems safe to conclude that a speaker who is "agreeable" in Norman's terms, "trustworthy" in Berlo's sense, "safe" in Lemert's, or possessed of good "character" as McCroskey puts it is likely to be more persuasive. Further, if he has "culture" and "conscientiousness" (Norman), "competence" (Berlo), "qualification" (Lemert), or "authoritativeness" (McCroskey), he will enhance that persuasiveness. Andersen's "evaluative" factor seems to encompass both of these. Andersen and Clevenger (1963) survey much of the older literature in which "ethos" or "credibility" was treated as unidimensional. Most of these researchers seem to have been manipulating both "trustworthiness" and "competence" simultaneously, so that they were confounded. The experiments by Hovland and Weiss (1951), Kelman and Hovland (1953), and Hovland and Mandell (1952) were important exceptions. Cohen (1964) concluded from these and other studies that "the greater the trustworthiness or expertness, the greater the change toward the position advocated by the communicator." While his conclusion seems justified, more research is needed to determine the relative importance of trustworthiness and expertness in different situations.

The writer knows of no evidence to indicate that the "extroversion," "emotional stability," or "dynamism" of the speaker affects his persuasiveness in any way. The lack of evidence may be due to the lack of research, however.

Finally, there is a little evidence that "identification," or speaker-listener similarity, has some effect on attitude change, but the relationship is probably a confusing one. First, as previously noted, greater "identification" or "similarity" often is accompanied by greater attraction. This would suggest that the listener ought to be more persuaded by speakers similar to himself. However, if the speaker with whom the listener identifies most closely is persuasive only because the listener **likes** that speaker better, the concept of identification doesn't have much utility of its own; one might as well measure "liking" or "attraction" directly. If a relationship exists, it may be complicated by listener self-esteem. For example, listeners who identify with a high-prestige source must be high in self-esteem, and thus difficult to persuade (see Cronkhite, 1964). Further, the individual low in self-esteem would be expected to identify most closely with speakers he holds in low esteem; would he, then, also be more persuaded by such speakers? I suspect the answers are going to be quite complex.

Despite all the work in this area, a great deal remains to be done. What is needed is a systemmatic program of research designed to answer two questions: (1) What **source characteristics** produce what difference in what **listener perceptions of the source,** and (2) What listener perceptions of the source produce what differences in **audience response?**

The listener perceptions of the source—the factors of ethos—have already been surveyed and found to include "trustworthiness," "dynamism," "competence," "sociability," "evaluation," "agreeableness," "extroversion," "emotional stability," "conscientiousness," "culture," "objectivity," and probably "identification," depending on who did the study, what kind of subjects he used, what kinds of topics he used, what kinds of speakers he used, what kinds of test items he used, and what kinds of factor analysis he used. The list could be made even longer if one were to consider the numerous factor analyses of speech rating scales to be relevant to this question. Someone with a good mind for analysis should try to make sense of this area before it reaches maximum entropy.

Once there is some clear conception of the ways in which listeners perceive speakers, it should be possible to focus on the two questions mentioned. We will, however, be faced with the task of organizing the **source characteristics** into some conceptual scheme before we can manipulate them and observe differences in listener perceptions. Barry Fulton (1967) has proposed such a scheme. He suggests classifying source characteristics as "exogenous" or "endogenous," and again as "implicit" or "explicit," producing the following 2 x 2 table:

	implicit	explicit
exogenous	education occupation intelligence	size shape facial features
endogenous	intent organization evidence	language: fluency, grammar delivery: extrovert-introvert

There are, of course, many more items to be classified in each category. Those given are only illustrative.

With detailed analyses of source characteristics and audience perceptions of sources, we can turn to the second question of how these two types of variables interact to produce differences in audience response to a communication. The sort of study needed will be of the type Sereno and Hawkins (1967) have already attempted, in which the source characteristic of fluency was manipulated, while listener perceptions of the speaker were measured along with attitude change and retention.

One final practical suggestion: the speaker should be very careful about the way he chooses to increase his "ethos." An experiment by Biddle (1966) has demonstrated that certain efforts of a speaker to improve his own "ethos" by what he says in a speech may be successful **if he has been introduced favorably,** but not if he has had no introduction. Extrapolation of the data suggests the hypothesis that attempts to improve his "ethos" might even hurt his image if he has received an **unfavorable** introduction. The whole question depends, no doubt, on how subtle the speaker can be. A man such as Henry Grady, using imaginative techniques, may be able to improve his image regardless of the circumstances in which he speaks.

Motivational concepts

A theoretical discussion of motivational concepts occupied much of the fourth chapter of this book, and that discussion will not be repeated. Briefly, it was suggested that the speaker may choose both **negative** and **positive** motivational concepts; that is, he may argue that his proposal will help the listener achieve valued goals and maintain consistent values as well as help him avoid undesirable consequences and violation of values.

Goals and values. Minnick (1957) has compiled lists of goals and values of contemporary Americans which the persuader would do well to study. As Redding (1966) has suggested, such lists may serve as topical systems to remind the persuader of appeals which he might otherwise overlook. The present writer strongly recommends the use of such lists, with a few reservations. First, many of the values listed are those of Americans several decades ago, being distilled from sociological surveys conducted as far back as the 'thirties. It is true that American goals and values tend to remain stable, but they do change, and that change may be accelerated by instantaneous mass communication. The persuader should consult the most recent survey available. Second, the values listed are very general, as they must be if they are to be applicable regardless of unique characteristics of specific situations and specific listeners. Still, such generality seriously limits the utility of such lists. For example, it is easy to find examples of contradictory values in the same list. To some extent, that may merely reflect the fact that Americans hold inconsistent values, and perhaps it need not concern us. On the other hand, I suspect it is also a symptom of overgeneralization: **some** Americans hold **some** of these values in **some** situations. The lists may be useful if the speaker knows only that he is to face an audience of "contemporary Americans." However, if he knows anything else about his listeners or the circumstances under which they will be listening, then other lists, including those he may compile from his own experience, may be more useful. Third, the lists are most useful as mnemonic devices to help the speaker remember appeals he might otherwise forget. It has been eloquently argued that one good appeal is all that is needed to move an audience, and the speaker may be wasting time running through check-lists when he could better concentrate on constructing a strong argument *ex visceribus causa,* out of the particulars of his own case.

The greatest utility of the lists, I suspect, is that they represent **issues** upon which listeners have different opinions. For example, instead of saying "Americans think economic conditions cannot be effectively controlled by economists," it might be useful to specify the **type** of listener who is likely to have such an opinion, and the time at which such an opinion is likely to be most salient. Another useful approach might be to list the "god-terms" of specific groups in American society. At any rate, there is room for a great deal of very practical research to determine goals and values of specific types of listeners under certain circumstances. Until such research becomes more popular, the persuader will have to rely on his own informal observation and such surveys as he may be able to conduct.

The most useful approach a speaker can take is to find out **why** his listeners hold their opinions. He must learn to be sensitive to the functions served by the attitudes and beliefs of his listeners. The job of changing opinions is well under way when the reasons for those opinions are known. The goals and values that are relevant usually become obvious once the attitude and belief structure is understood. Such sensitivity may or may not be developed by studying lists of goals and values of contemporary Americans.

Fear appeals. There has been a mass of research in recent years dealing with the role of "fear appeals" in persuasion. For the most part this research seems to have been based on appeals to self-preservation or avoidance of pain. Some of that literature has been summarized by Miller (1963) and by Miller and Hewgill (1965). The initial study in this area was conducted by Janis and Feshbach (1953).

Their somewhat unexpected finding was that although a strong "fear appeal" produced high anxiety on the part of listeners, those listeners exposed to a **minimal** fear appeal showed greater conformity to the behavior suggested in the speech. This effect could not be explained by "defensive avoidance" during the speech, for subjects who listened to the strong fear appeal retained as much factual content as did those who listened to the minimal fear appeal.

Janis and Feshbach suggest, however, that "defensive avoidance" may have operated **after** the speech; that is, those subjects who heard the strong fear appeal may have forgotten it or come to view it as less important, thus leading to fewer reports of behavioral conformity at the time of the delayed post-test. Fishbein has suggested in class lectures what may be a more perceptive explanation. He notes that subjects hearing the strong fear appeal were shown pictures of really repulsive —and rare—dental diseases. They were told, in effect, that poor dental hygiene leads to such diseases. Fishbein suggests they may have concluded that since they had no such diseases, they must not have poor dental hygiene, and therefore had little need to change their behavior. Subjects who heard the minimal fear appeal, however, were told that failure to care for their teeth properly would lead to dental cavities, which most of them had probably experienced. Poor dental hygiene leads to cavities; I have cavities; *ergo,* I must have poor dental hygiene, and should follow the recommendations of the lecture.

Acceptance of such an explanation would not make the findings less important, but would have different implications for the persuader. Speakers are often tempted to picture the tragic consequences which will befall those who fail to conform to the speaker's recommendations. The stronger the threat, however, the more likely is the listener to comfort himself with the thought that "it won't happen to me." If the consequences pictured are unusual, it is much easier for the listener to use that avenue of avoidance; he can say "It hasn't happened to me, and it hasn't happened to anyone I know." He may then conclude either that the speaker is wrong or that the speaker is talking to someone else.

Peggy Duncan (1966) has suggested another possibility. She points out that the subjects were high school students, and might be expected to fear social disapproval as much as anything else. One would hardly expect high school students to rush out of the auditorium after such a lecture, whip out their toothbrushes, and begin to brush in unison. It is much more likely that the strong fear appeal was an object of laughter and possibly even ridicule; adolescents (and adults) commonly meet threat in that way. Stated quite simply, anyone who took the strong fear appeal seriously may have been threatened with social disapproval. Such an explanation does not necessarily compete with Fishbein's; the one may even enhance the other.

Carmichael and Cronkhite (1965) have suggested a third explanation. They note that some current theorists in the field of motivation hold that organisms act so as to maintain a level of arousal consistent with the time of day and the task at hand. This suggests that the subjects may have rejected a stimulus which was unpleasant because it tended to induce an inappropriately high level of arousal. These "activation theorists" have also reported studies demonstrating a consistent inverted-U relationship between arousal and performance. That is, task performance generally improves with increasing arousal up to a point, after which new increments in arousal lead to poorer performance. This point of diminishing returns occurs sooner if the task is a complex one. Thus it may be that the strong fear appeal pushed the level of arousal too high for efficient performance of the task at hand. It is especially interesting in this regard to note that a later replication of this study (Janis and Feshbach, 1954) found the effect most pronounced with listeners who were chronically anxious. The studies done thus far, however, have usually manipulated the subjects' arousal either by means of the messages themselves or by means of external circumstances. All the differing characteristics of the messages or the circumstances have been confounded with the subjects' arousal. A hitherto unpublished study by Helmreich has demonstrated that the relationship between the anxiety and the message can be a confounding element in experiments of this sort. One possibility is to administer different dosages of amphetamine and chlorpromazine to listeners to see if arousal thus manipulated bears the hypothesized curvilinear relationship to attitude change.

It is important to point out that a good many experiments conducted since 1953 have either failed to replicate the findings of Janis and Feshbach, or have found strong fear appeals producing greater attitude change. One of the problems, of course, is that there is no very good way to measure the "strength" of a given fear appeal, especially if one is based on the threat of dental disease and another on the threat of cancer. One could measure the physiological level of arousal produced by each type of message, but that would answer a somewhat different question. Still, it is surprising that research of this sort has made no use of physiological measurement.

Bearing in mind the fact that messages cannot be equated for "strength" of fear appeal, it might still be useful to consider some of the circumstances under which the Janis and Feshbach findings have been contradicted or modified.

Goldstein's (1959) experiment was one of the few which seem to confirm the findings of Janis and Feshbach, although the significance of the difference is not clearly reported. Janis and Terwilliger (1962), using smoking and lung cancer messages, failed to find significant differences in attitude change, although subjects under high threat made more statements explicitly rejecting the message when given an opportunity to do so. Moltz and Thistlethwaite (1955) report no significant differences in attitude change using dental hygiene messages again, but neither did they find any significant differences in immediate postcommunication measures of "dental anxiety"; that is, the message differences apparently failed to "take."

It is astonishing that such paltry evidence has produced such a flurry of speculation and such a furor of research. A whole generation of persuaders has been reared in the belief that fear appeals which are too strong may produce less attitude change, when the evidence seems to indicate that such a thing rarely occurs, and may be explained in other terms when it does occur. Janis himself has hypothesized that reduction of a **strong** drive has greater effect upon acceptance of recommendations than does reassurance following mild warnings (see Janis, 1962; Janis and Leventhal, in press). His hypothesis seems to be confirmed by the studies of Berkowitz and Cottingham (1960); Niles (1964); Wolfe and Governale (1964); Leventhal and Niles (1964); Leventhal and Niles (1965); Leventhal, Singer, and Jones (1965); Singer (1965); Leventhal and Singer (1966); Leventhal and Watts (1966); and Kraus, El-Assal, and DeFleur (1966).

Berkowitz and Cottingham (1960), for example, found interaction among subject interest in the topic, relevance of the topic to the subject, and level of fear appeal. Simple effects which were significant indicated greater attitude change with the strong fear appeal. The most interesting finding, however, was that among subjects for whom the topic was interesting, those who heard the strong fear appeal changed more when the material was less relevant to them. Niles (1964) used the topic of lung cancer, and reports that more subjects among those who heard the strong fear appeal indicated intentions to act than did those who heard a less powerful communication. Leventhal and Niles (1964) report the same finding, with one important qualification: Chest X-ray equipment was immediately available. Leventhal, Singer, and Jones (1965) found subjects exposed to a high fear appeal urging them to have tetanus shots indicated greater intention to get them, although there was no significant difference in the number who **actually followed through.** Leventhal and Singer (1966), using the topic of dental hygiene, found that the high fear appeal produced more statements of **intention** to act. Leventhal and Watts (1966) found that low and medium fear appeals were more effective in convincing smokers to have immediate chest X-rays, and this was especially true among heavy smokers. However, **five months later** there was a significantly greater decrease in smoking among subjects who had heard the strong fear appeal as compared to subjects who had heard the moderate and mild appeals. It seems important to point out that getting a chest X-ray actually poses a further immediate threat to a heavy smoker. Coming at a time when he was already threatened, it is not especially amazing that he avoided the X-ray. He did not avoid taking less threatening action, however. Finally, Kraus, El-Assal, and DeFleur (1966) conducted a survey of subjects who had read "high fear appeal" warnings in newspapers urging special methods of viewing an eclipse of the sun. Despite the use of phrases such as "complete blindness," "burning the eyes out," and "severe eye damage," the messages produced considerable compliance and little hostility: 23 of the sample of 41 used one of the recommended methods. There was no "low fear appeal" group for comparison, however, which certainly limits the usefulness of the study.

Leventhal, Singer, and Jones (1965) attempted to summarize the findings at that time with the statement: "The findings suggest that when environmental conditions or the subject's dispositional characteristics make action seem highly possible and effective, fear will promote action and attitude change." The summary may be brought up to date by adding the qualification that fear appeals seem to work best when the topic is of less immediate concern to the listener or when the recommended action does not pose a further threat to him.

It seems worthwhile, however, to mention something about "the subject's dispositional characteristics." Studies by Goldstein (1959),

Leventhal and Perloe (1962), Dabbs (1964), and Niles (1964) all suggest that the effect of fear appeals depends also upon the level of self-esteem or "coping-avoiding" behavior of the listener. The theory, generally substantiated by the research mentioned, is that "copers" and those high in self-esteem confronted with a high fear appeal accompanied by a specific plan of action will take the action suggested; "avoiders" and those low in self-esteem will respond to the high fear appeal by some mechanism of defense avoidance. Speisman (1964) demonstrated that such mechanisms are effective means of reducing anxiety due to a communication. His subjects watched a film titled "Subincision," which showed crude operations performed on the genitalia of adolescent boys in a primitive puberty rite. Subjects who heard an accompanying sound track designed to encourage defensive adjustments such as "denial" and "intellectualization" produced significantly lower skin conductance than did subjects who heard no sound track or a "traumatic" sound track.

Another important "dispositional characteristic" of listeners may be cognitive complexity or discriminative ability. Janis and Milholland (1954) report that learning in response to a high threat appeal did not differ significantly from learning from a low threat appeal, which confirmed a finding of the original experiment by Janis and Feshbach (1953). However, Uhlmann and Saltz (1965) report that listeners most capable of making complex discriminations in the presence of distracting stimulation were better able to recall anxiety- and nonanxiety-connected discourse on both immediate and delayed post-tests. There was no decrement in recall during the three-hour delay period. Low differentiators, however, forgot a significant amount of the **anxiety** material but no significant amount of nonanxiety material.

Finally, Robbins (1962) reports that fear-arousing communications produce **instigation to aggression** as well as anxiety; thus high fear appeals may be especially useful when the speaker is urging some form of aggression.

The speaker, then, is well advised to present a specific plan of action and to demonstrate its feasibility and effectiveness **whenever** he uses a strong fear appeal. He may confidently use the strong fear appeal followed by a specific program of action when he is dealing with listeners who have a history of coping effectively with their problems, and when the action he urges is aggressive in nature, not too difficult, and is not likely to pose a further threat. The appeal should be realistic enough that the listener cannot easily take refuge in the thought that it is not likely to concern him, and should especially avoid an excess of horror which might be ludicrous instead of terrifying.

Non-fear appeals. While the research investigating the use of fear appeals has not proceeded in a totally orderly and efficient manner, we do know a great deal more than we did fifteen years ago. It is unfortunate that so much effort has been concentrated on fear appeals and so little on other types of appeals. It should be possible to investigate the use of appeals to sympathy, the expectation of reciprocity, avoidance of guilt, achievement of reward, self-determination, competition, and ego-satisfaction, as well as a host of others. In fact, such investigations should be easier to conduct, as experimenters profit from the experience gained in the raid on fear appeals. Consider some of the interesting possibilities.

There is, for example, a considerable bibliography of studies dealing with cooperative and competitive behavior, but not enough of that literature deals with the use of **communication** in inducing such behavior. No research of which I am aware has been designed to determine how one may base an appeal on cooperation or on competition, or when one should use such appeals.

Rapoport (1964), for example, reports that members of mutually dependent pairs tend to imitate each others' responses; that is, they tend to develop **either** cooperative **or** competitive responses rather than one member of the pair being competitive and the other cooperative. Further, subjects involved in a game of mutual dependency generally tend to exploit their opponents less when they anticipate future interaction with that opponent, according to a study by Marlowe, Gergen, and Doob (1966). A series of studies (Berkowitz and Daniels, 1963, 1964; Daniels and Berkowitz, 1963; Berkowitz, Klanderman, and Harris, 1964) have demonstrated that subjects who perceive another person to be totally dependent upon them will give the other person more help than if he were only partially dependent. Schopler and Bateson (1965) contend this is true for females but not for males. Another series of studies (Davis and Jones, 1960; Glass, 1964; Lerner, 1965a, 1965b; Lerner and Simmons, 1966) indicates that subjects who observe another person ostensibly receiving painful shocks for failure in a learning task reject and devalue that other person more when they believe they will see him suffer more at a later time and when they can do nothing to help. Even when subjects believe that other persons are being punished or rewarded by chance, the individual who is rewarded is judged to have performed better than the individual who is punished. Most of all, if the subject believes he himself is responsible for the suffering of another person, that other person will be rejected. That is, there seems to be a blind faith that fate is just; people get what they deserve, and that is especially true if the listener feels somewhat responsible.

This is only a small sample of the interesting findings to be gleaned from the **Journal of Personality and Social Psychology** and from the **Journal of Conflict Resolution.** What is surprising is the fact that we know so little about the role of these motives in persuasion. Certainly it is possible to fashion persuasive appeals to each of these motives, just as we fashion fear appeals, and it should be possible to do with each of these motives what has been done in research on fear appeals.

Demonstrating the relationship

Many writers of textbooks in persuasion and argumentation speak glibly of **"reasoning"** and **"evidence"** as if they think they know what those terms mean. Some of them may. If one defines "reasoning" as any case in which an individual infers the truth or falsity of one assertion or state of affairs given the truth or falsity of another, and if one defines "evidence" as any assertion given in support of another, then one has two definitions which are at least usable; that is, one can then distinguish "reasoning" and "evidence" from "non-reasoning" and "non-evidence." Such definitions are not likely to satisfy most people in the field, however, unless one goes further to define "correct reasoning" and "sound evidence." One possibility is to specify the rules by which reasoning is to be conducted so as to be "correct," as the rules for syllogistic reasoning have been specified, for example. The problem inherent in this approach is that, while one may establish formal validity in a hypothetical universe in which all the necessary conditions are satisfied, the system breaks down if used as a vehicle for practical reasoning. The classical syllogism demands universal premises, for one thing, and is thus useful in a probabilistic universe only to the extent that the demand for universality can be violated. Even if it could be adapted to operate in a universe of probabilities, it does not appear that the syllogism is a very successful model of the operation of the human mind, if it was ever intended to be that, nor does it appear that it is a very efficient tool for human reasoning, if it was ever intended to be that. If one views McGuire's (1960) work as a test of the probabilistic syllogism as a **model** of human cognitive processes, then the model accounted for less than 25 percent of the variance; if it is to be viewed as a test of the probabilistic syllogism as a **tool** of human cognitive processes, then the tool was used with less than 25 percent accuracy. Neither interpretation is very impressive.

Attempts to define "sound" evidence have also fallen short of universal success. Most such definitions ultimately depend upon the judgment of some individual who is or is not convinced by the evidence and/or reasoning at hand. Even if that individual who serves as judge is the mythical "reasonable man" who appears so frequently in the literature of argumentation (although seldom in real life), his judgments are unlikely to be accepted as *vox dei* by anyone other than a few disciples.

McCroskey (1968, 1969) points out that studies by Cathcart (1953) and Bettinghaus (1953) revealed significant differences in favor of citing the sources for assertions in a persuasive message. On the other hand, Gilkinson, Paulson, and Sikkink (1954) and Ostermeier (1967), testing similar hypotheses, report no significant differences. Anderson (1958) found no significant differences when he varied the number of "authoritative" quotations and the extent of commentary on the qualifications of the authorities. Costley (1958) found no significant difference when he varied the type and amount of statistical evidence in a persuasive message. Wagner (1958) found no significant differences in attitude change when he varied the number of tape-recorded statements, "authoritative quotations," and pictures presented in conjunction with a persuasive appeal. Finally, Dresser (1962) found no significant differences in attitude change when he attributed assertions to satisfactory or questionable authorities, or when he included irrelevant or internally inconsistent assertions.

McCroskey's general thesis is that the "perceived ethos" of the source of the message interacts with the quality of the evidence presented in such a way that evidence of high quality increases the effectiveness of the message for a low-ethos source when attitude change is measured immediately after the message, and increases the effectiveness of the message for both high and low-ethos sources when delayed attitude change is measured. The quality of the evidence is hypothesized to make no difference in immediate attitude change for a high-ethos source. Further, McCroskey hypothesized that the use of evidence in a persuasive message tends to increase the perceived ethos of the source of the message.

McCroskey used as his definition of "evidence" in his series of studies "factual statements originating from a source other than the speaker, objects not created by the speaker, and opinions of persons other than the speaker which are offered in support of the speaker's claims." The results of the series of experiments may be said to have generally supported McCroskey's predictions, with some important qualifications. The first qualification is that the ethos of the **experimenter** must be neutral (i.e., not too high) in order for the effects to appear. Second, the effects appeared **with some topics** but not with others, for reasons which were sometimes made clear by other studies, but some of which were unexplained. Third, the speaker's **delivery** must be good (or at least passable) in order for the effects to appear. Fourth, there may be some difference between what the experimenter intended as "good" evidence and what the listener perceives as "good" evidence. In the studies reported, it does appear that listeners, and especially college audiences, do perceive unbiased and reluctant evidence to be better than biased evidence as the experimenter expected, but the evidence may also need to be "new" to the listener in order for him to perceive it as "good."

With these qualifications, McCroskey's predictions appear to have received some support, and may be considered at least a tentative basis for a theory of evidence. The interested reader would be well-advised to read McCroskey's reports more thoroughly, and to pay special attention to the model of a persuasive unit which he presents as a conclusion in the source cited.

Still, some problems remain. One of these is the fact that **the role of evidence as defined by McCroskey** (and by most of the others cited) **is actually an interaction between the ethos of the speaker and the ethos of the authorities he cites.** A low-ethos speaker is well-advised to cite the testimony of others, assuming those others have greater ethos than his own. The high-ethos speaker, on the other hand, may only hurt himself by citing the testimony of others, since those others are likely to have lower ethos than his own. I suspect further research may reveal that evidence may act to produce attitude change in ways other than increasing or decreasing the ethos of the speaker, although increments and decrements in speaker ethos may still be an incidental effect. Consider, for example, the situation in which a low-ethos speaker cites a high-ethos authority testifying to some fact irrelevant to the speaker's proposition. The prediction based on McCroskey's studies would be that citation of such an assertion will be effective, but I would like to reserve judgment on that point until someone attacks the question more directly. As another example, consider the situation in which a low-ethos speaker cites a high-ethos authority, but the testimony of the authority is internally contradictory or contrary to facts of which the audience is aware. I continue to entertain what I think is a reasonable doubt that the speaker will have helped himself. McCroskey has made a considerable contribution to our understanding of the ways evidence operates to produce attitude change, but there is still some doubt that the ethos of the authority is the only determinant of the effectiveness of a given item of evidence.

A second problem is the fact that most of these studies confound "reasoning" and "evidence." It may be that there is no need to separate the two. On the other hand, we may find it useful to make a distinction between the citation of assertions and the means by which speakers cause listeners to draw inferences from those assertions.

The findings of McGuire (1960) and Schunk (1967), that individuals make inferences which conform to some extent to the rules of probability, have already been mentioned. Gilson and Abelson (1965) have argued that there has been an overemphasis in the psychological literature of the role played by motivation in determining the acceptance or rejection of assertions. They insist we must begin to pay more attention to what they call the "reality component." They also point out that "the literature on concept formation turns out to be surprisingly irrelevant to our present purposes. Studies of concept learning generally involve the **recruitment of a hypothesis** to account for the **given evidence,** whereas we are concerned here with the **recruitment of evidence** to test **a given statement.**"

In the study they conducted as a step toward remedying the bias they decry, they used two types of what they term "evidence," which seem more reasonable when viewed as types of inference. They speak of "subject-specific" and "object-specific" evidence. Their basic prototype of the evidential assertion is a statement of the type "subjects verb objects," or "A's have X." When the listener is asked to infer a generalization from a series of such assertions in which the subject remains constant, as in the series "A's have X, A's have Y, A's have Z, B's don't have X, B's don't have Y, B's don't have Z," the series is said to be **"subject-specific"** since the generalization relates attributes to a specific subject. When the object of the series remains constant and the generalization relates subjects to a specific attribute-object, as in the series "A's have X, B's have X, C's have X, A's don't have Y, B's don't have Y, C's don't have Y," the series is said to be **"object-specific."** The study demonstrated that listeners tend to generalize more when they hear an object-specific series of assertions than when they hear a subject-specific series, but they generalize **most** when the two types of assertions are mixed. Gilson and Abelson also found that assertions which used "manifest" verbs such as "have" produce greater generalization than do assertions using "subjective" verbs such as "like."

The experiment by Gilson and Abelson is obviously less compelling than their appeal for research of this type, but it does demonstrate that there is a need for research to determine the conditions under which listeners are willing to make certain types of inferences. A number of other researchers have approached similar questions.

Woodworth and Schlosberg (1954, p. 843), for example, report that subjects are better able to draw inferences from "linear syllogisms" ($A>B$, $B>C$, $\therefore \cdots$) than from nonlinear syllogisms ($A>B$, $C<B$, $\therefore \cdots$). De Soto (1960) found that subjects are good at giving things **linear** orderings, but poor at ordering them in other ways, and found in a second study (De Soto, 1961) that subjects are poor at giving items more than one ordering. De Soto, London, and Handel (1965) found that subjects are better at learning evaluative orderings proceeding from better to worse than from worse to better, that they tend to "end-anchor" orderings so that combinations in which one of the extremes appears first are more easily remembered, they learn downward orderings and syllogisms more easily than upward orderings, and they encounter more difficulty in learning orderings which are not easily conceptualized in space (lighter-darker, for example).

Dawes (1964) reports that it is more common for audiences to make inferential errors classified as "overgeneralization" (belief that a disjunctive relationship is nested) than for subjects to make errors of "pseudo-discrimination" (belief that a nested relationship is disjunctive), and that errors of overgeneralization engender greater confidence. (For simplicity, errors of overgeneralization appear to be instances of overenthusiastic **synthesis,** and errors of pseudodiscrimination appear to be instances of overenthusiastic **analysis).** Walster (1966) found that subjects tend to believe persons are more responsible for the consequences of their actions when those consequences are more serious, and Feather (1959) has tested the effect of anxiety level upon the subjective judgment of probability.

At the moment there is not enough of this sort of research for one to come to any general conclusions. The findings do seem to indicate that listeners are more easily induced to make inferences of some types under some conditions. The study of formal logical systems is not likely to reveal to the speaker the mechanics of human inference, whereas empirical research may eventually do so. On the other hand, the research on the use of evidence, surveyed earlier, while certainly of considerable use to the persuader, does not shed much light on the reasoning process. I believe this area, largely unexplored, can be a fruitful field for future research.

Message organization

The line between this section and the next is necessarily as vague as the line between any single message and the next, for this section purports to describe the effects of various patterns of organization within a single message, while the next section is intended to describe the effects of various sequences and timings of a series of messages. If one considers the smallest unit of meaning to constitute a message, then any speech or article is a **series** of messages; conversely a long series of communications (a debate, for example) may be viewed as constituting a **single** message. Finding myself in an unavoidable dilemma, I would like to invoke the artful dodge (i.e., cop-out) of letting the contents of this section constitute the operational definition of what I mean by the organization of elements within a single message.

Does organization matter? A number of researchers centered upon this rather gross question by rearranging more or less at random various elements of persuasive messages. Smith (1951) found that when he rearranged two or more major units of speeches (introduction, transitions, conclusions) the listeners changed attitude significantly less than when the elements were presented in the intended order.

Beighley (1952) rearranged at random the paragraphs of two speeches and found no significant differences in listener **comprehension.** Thompson (1960) rearranged at random the sentences either within each of eight major points in a speech or within the introduction, body and conclusion. He found significant differences in **retention** on an immediate post test, but no significant differences in immediate attitude change. Darnell (1963) also found that sentence rearrangement produces significant differences in message **retention.** Finally, Sharp and McClung (1966) found that random rearrangement of the sentences within a speech produces a significant deficit in audience **attitude toward the speaker.**

Thus, while the question is still open, the speaker seems well advised against randomly reordering the material within his speech. That conclusion will surprise only those who have read or heard of a few early studies which failed to detect differences in attitude change due to random reordering. As long as one remembers that failure to find significant differences does not **prove** the null hypothesis, there is no problem. Personally, I have heard some speeches which were so bad that random rearrangement of the individual **words** would have produced no significant differences in attitude change, and have seen some attitude tests so bad that they could not have detected such differences if they had occurred.

Introductions. To say without reservation that introductions, transitions, and conclusions do or do not produce greater attitude change would be absurd. Such organizational units may do a number of things, and the things they do are likely to be effective at times and ineffective at others. Consider introductions, for example. One type of introduction is that designed to tell the listener how the message is organized and what he is to look for in the speech. Teachers of speech and English have told countless generations of students that such an introduction is necessary. Suppose, however, that the speaker tells the listener what to listen for, and the listener listens for it, but doesn't like what he hears. In that case, the persuader would have been better off to forget the introduction. Similarly, a speaker may clearly state his thesis and major arguments at the outset of his speech, just as he has been told to do, and find that his hostile audience refuses to listen to the rest of his speech. Henry Grady, for example, after waiting for General Sherman to finish his speech, and after waiting for the audience to stop singing "Marching Through Georgia," might have clearly stated his thesis that the northerners must forget the Civil War and help rebuild the South. He might have done that, but he would probably have ended up spending his next paycheck from the Atlanta **Constitution** on tar solvent. Instead, he chose a second type of introduction designed to emphasize the interests he and his listeners had in common, and to make his listeners like him. He happened to succeed. If he had failed, our conclusions about such introductions might have been different.

However, some generalizations may be possible. Carter (1955), Hovland, Lumsdaine, and Sheffield (1949), Wittich and Fowlkes (1946), and May and Lumsdaine (1958) have all found significant improvement in retention when some sort of introduction was used to focus audience attention on certain parts of the message. This, of course, does not necessarily mean that audience attitude change will be greater, unless the arguments upon which audience attention is focused are particularly persuasive.

A number of studies, on the other hand, indicate that it may be unwise to forewarn an audience which one intends to persuade. Allyn and Festinger (1961) found that subjects who were forewarned about the content of a communication arguing against a position they held strongly, rejected the speaker more and changed attitudes less than did those who were not forewarned. Thus, it appears one is especially ill-advised to state one's thesis and major arguments if the audience is known to be hostile. That conclusion, however, must be qualified; if the speaker is liked by the audience and if the listeners believe the speaker likes them, it may be more effective to state the thesis openly. Mills and Aronson (1965) found that subjects changed attitudes more if a well-liked communicator openly admitted his intent to persuade them than if he did not admit his intent, but they changed **less** when a disliked communicator announced his intent than when he did not. Mills (1966) found the same pattern to hold when the listeners were made to believe that the speaker did or did not like them. Experiments by Walster and Festinger (1961) and by Brock and Becker (1965) also indicate that a speaker might do well to hide his intent even when speaking to an audience somewhat favorable to his point of view. These experimenters found that when listeners were highly **involved** with the topic and when they were favorable toward the speaker's point of view, they were more influenced when they thought they were accidentally overhearing the message than when they knew it was intended for them. This was not true when the listeners were unfavorable or uninvolved.

Two other studies suggest possible reasons for this phenomenon. Hollander (1958), for one, found that a group member may successfully nonconform after some record of conformity; as Hollander puts it, his conformity seems to earn him "idiosyncrasy credits" which he may cash in by later nonconformity. This seems closely related to the notion that a speaker should begin by emphasizing the extent of his agreement with his audience, saving revelation of the disagreement for later. Weiss, Rawson, and Pasamanick (1963) found that subjects learned to choose the one of two separate and unrelated opinions which was presented with less delay between the opinion and the arguments which supported it. Thus it may be that listeners have less time to compose counterarguments if the speaker's position is followed immediately by support. This latter study, of course, does not necessarily dictate that the opinion should not be stated first, only that it be quickly followed by support.

Conclusions. It appears that the findings regarding the use of conclusions are less equivocal than those regarding the use of introductions. Conclusions may be of many types, of course, but two important types are the summary conclusion and the appeal for action. The explicit summary conclusion might be expected to increase the listener's understanding and retention of the arguments in a message, thus increasing his attitude change. However, a conclusion which is too explicit might conceivably create a negative response from the listener, especially if he felt the persuader was biased, or if the conclusion called for more attitude change or for more overt action than the listener was willing to give.

Testing this question, Hovland and Mandel (1952) found that college subjects changed attitude more in response to a speech in which explicit conclusions were drawn, regardless of whether the speaker was biased or impartial. Hovland and Pritzker (1957) found conclusions that appealed for a great deal of change produced more change than those that advocated less change, but the actual change was a smaller proportion of that advocated. Biddle (1966) found that the addition of an appeal for specific action added as the conclusion of a persuasive speech produced greater attitude change and a more favorable subsequent rating of the speaker as well. It is not merely that an appeal for action is superior to no appeal, for Leventhal and Singer (1966) found that such appeals were more effective **when placed in the conclusion** than elsewhere in the speech.

It appears, then, that most audiences respond most favorably to a message in which the persuader does not state his purpose in the introduction, but rather uses that introduction to emphasize areas of agreement between himself and his audience—and then uses the conclusion to make an appeal for specific action.

Best foot forward? A number of experimenters have attempted to determine where in a message the strongest arguments should be placed. Studies of serial learning indicate that subjects learn best the material that is placed either first or last in a series. Crafts (1932) and Tannenbaum (1954) have confirmed this finding in the area of communication, reporting that items mentioned either early or late in a message are better remembered than those mentioned nearer the middle of a message. Jersild (1929) and Doob (1953) report that material presented early in messages was remembered better than material mentioned later. Adams (1920) and Sponberg (1946) concluded that **retention** is better if more attention-arresting material or stronger arguments are placed first rather than last.

Studies of **retention,** however, are not directly relevant to persuasion. One might assume that the most effective speech will be that in which the strongest arguments are placed where they will be best remembered, but this is only an assumption. There are other considerations in a persuasive message. One which might be especially important is that the persuader wants the listener to believe he is a credible and trustworthy source and that his arguments are sound. One might expect the impression which the listener forms from the opening arguments in a message to affect the listener's evaluation of subsequent arguments. Experiments in the area of personality impression-formation indicate that listeners do form first impressions which affect their subsequent judgments, unless they are warned against such first impressions.

However, the findings regarding attitude change have not been consistent. Cromwell (1950), for example, found greater attitude change when strong arguments were presented last, while Sponberg (1946) found greater attitude change when strong arguments were presented first. Gilkinson, Paulson, and Sikkink (1954), replicating Sponberg's experiment, found it was more effective to present the strong arguments last on the only topic on which they found a significant effect. Gulley and Berlo (1956) and Sikkink (1956) found no significant differences between the two orders of presentation.

The only conclusion to be made at this time seems to be that **the strongest arguments should be placed first or last** rather than in the middle of the message.

There seem to be any number of possible reasons for the conflicting results in this area. First is the difficulty of specifying what constitutes a "strong" argument. An argument may be "strong" in several senses: it may be radical, in that it urges a great deal of change; it may appeal to a strong motive; it may use a great deal of evidence; it may be attributed to a highly credible source; it may be highly "rational"; it may use strong language; it may simply be longer; and/or it may have been pretested and found to be more effective in changing attitudes than were the other arguments. Results may be different depending upon the way in which argument strength is defined.

Second, a listener whose interest in a given topic is low may be induced to pay more attention if an interesting argument is presented first, but the listener whose interest is already high may respond better to the climactic order.

Third, a listener who strongly disagrees with the speaker's proposition and/or has a great deal of information on the opposite side of the question, may have to hear a strong argument first before he will listen to the rest of the speech. If he encounters a weak argument first he may easily refute it, conclude that the remaining arguments will be similarly weak, and stop listening.

Finally, the time at which attitudes are tested may be an important factor. If they are tested immediately after the speech, the testing comes much closer to the final argument than to the initial argument. A delayed post-test might show results much different from those on an immediate post-test.

Problem or solution first?   Another question confronting the persuader as he organizes his message is the question of whether to describe first the problem for which he then proposes a solution, or to describe the solution first and then explain the reasons for its acceptance. The major experiment in this area is that of Cohen (1957), who found that it is more effective to present the problem first, followed by the solution. He found this to be true on both immediate and delayed post-tests of attitude. However, he found that the difference in effectiveness became even more critical on the delayed post-test for subjects low in "need for cognition," that is, for subjects who show little need to impose their own organization upon messages they hear. Leventhal and Singer (1966) found no significant effects due to different placements of fear arousal and recommendations for action. Newton (1966), noting Cohen's suggestion that listeners who heard the solution first were confused as to its purpose, hypothesized that the presentation of a brief introduction explaining the purpose of the speech might make the solution-problem order more effective. He found no significant effects of order upon attitude change, but found significantly greater retention for the problem-solution order when the introduction was included. At this point, the safest procedure for the persuader appears to be to put the problem before the solution.

Attack now or later?   The question of the effect of refutation belongs more properly in the next section, but the persuader must decide when organizing his speech where to place the refutation in relation to his constructive arguments. One might expect, if the listener already knows a host of opposing arguments (as, for example, when he has just heard a speech on the opposite side of the proposition), that those arguments will have to be refuted before he will listen to the constructive arguments of the persuader. On the other hand, if the listener has not been previously prejudiced by an opposing speech but is likely to hear such a speech later, one might expect the persuader to be more effective if he mentions counter arguments only near the end of his speech, and refutes them at that point. However, the only published experiment I have found in this area is that by Thistlethwaite, Kamenetsky, and Schmidt (1956), who found no significant differences attributable to the placement of refutation. Their subjects were all opposed to the point of view advocated in the message.

When to cite the source?   One final consideration concerns primarily the situation in which the persuasive message is drawn almost entirely from a source other than the persuader or the situation in which the persuader can be anonymous throughout the message. The question then is when to tell the listeners the identity and/or qualifications of the source.

Tannenbaum, Macauly, and Norris (1966) found that derogation of a source **before** that source presented a persuasive message reduced attitude change, but derogation of the source after the message had no effect. Husek (1965) found that even when the source has low credibility, attributing the message to the source **after** the communication is still better than not mentioning him at all, but mentioning him **before** the communication is **worse** than not mentioning him at all. Greenberg and Miller (1966) did the most complete experiment in this area, in that they used sources of both low and high credibility. Delayed identification of the highly credible source was no more effective than delayed identification of the source of low credibility. In fact, **prior** identification of the highly credible source was no more effective than delayed identification of the low-ethos source. However, the group which heard the low-credibility source identified **before** they read the message changed attitude less than those in the other conditions.

The conclusion seems to be that the persuader can avoid the negative effect of mentioning a disliked source by mentioning him only **after** the audience has heard what he has to say.

Interaction of messages

Obviously a persuasive message is not a one-shot affair fired by a speaker at an audience within a vacuum. Altogether too little attention has been given to the effects of one message on another. I would like to consider three types of message interaction: (1) interaction of a series of messages directed at the same audience; (2) interaction of a number of messages produced by the same source; and (3) interaction of messages produced by a source-receiver and a receiver-source.

Message-message interaction. The early studies of message interaction were done primarily by a group of scholars at Yale and are reported in the book **The Order of Presentation in Persuasion** edited by Carl I. Hovland and published in 1957. These early studies seem to have been of two types. One type was that in which the researchers attempted to determine whether the first or the second of two opposing messages is the more likely to be accepted by a listener. This type of study has generally been discussed under the rubric "primacy-recency," but that term has also been used to cover a multitude of other sins, so I have avoided using it. The second type of early study was that in which the researchers attempted to determine whether a "two-sided" or "one-sided" message is more effective in reducing the impact of subsequent counter-propaganda.

The message in which opposing arguments are at least mentioned (and possibly refuted) seems to be most effective in all cases except one: It may be less effective initially if the listener has less than an eighth-grade education **and** already favors the position advocated in the communication. Even then, however, the two-sided communication may be more effective in reducing the effect of subsequent counter-propaganda, which is our concern in this section. An additional caution: If the opposing arguments are so compelling that they are stronger when merely mentioned than one's own arguments are when fully developed, then it is obvious they should not be mentioned. The best advice to the persuader in such a case is that he should probably change his own attitude.

The findings of the first type of study are more equivocal. The extent to which a listener is likely to be affected by the first of two opposing communications seems to depend upon the extent to which he commits himself to a point of view after the first communication and before the second. If he commits himself strongly and publicly to the point of view expressed in the first communication, he is less likely to change attitude when he hears the second.

There seem to be two important variables evident in these early studies: To the extent that the listener is aware that he may encounter subsequent propaganda, and to the extent that he commits himself after hearing the first message, he will be less likely to be swayed by subsequent opposing arguments. This seems to be evident from the research before 1957.

Further, it seems to me some of the research surveyed in the previous section have implications for this question. I would like to advance hypotheses which seem to make some sense out of the research in the area. First, if the listener is not particularly aware of opposing arguments at the outset of the first speech, he will be most persuaded if he is not told of those opposing arguments until *after* he has heard the first speech; that is, not until the conclusion. Second, if the persuader expects the listener to encounter subsequent counter-propaganda, it will probably be most effective to get the listener to commit himself strongly at the conclusion of the first speech, *then* warn him that he may hear opposing arguments, and refute those arguments. Third, if the listener who is initially unaware of counter-arguments is told in the **introduction** of the first speech that there is a second side to the question, he will change attitude less as a result of the first speech and will be less willing to commit himself at the conclusion of that speech. Fourth, if the listener is already aware of opposing arguments before hearing the "first" message (which probably means it is not **really** the first message he has heard on the topic), it will probably be most effective for the persuader to mention opposing arguments at the outset of the speech, refute them, then present his own arguments and get as much commitment as possible from the listener.

Some considerably more sophisticated research has been done since 1957. The fact that listeners who are forewarned of a persuasive message will be less influenced by that message has been confirmed by more than a score of studies. More important are the ways in which that general finding has been qualified and elaborated, primarily by McGuire.

McGuire and Papageorgis (1961) tried putting either refutation of counter-arguments against "cultural truisms" or direct support of those truisms into the first message. They found the refutation of counter-arguments no more effective than direct support if the sub-jects encountered the counter-arguments immediately after the ini-tial message, but refutation was superior if the counter-arguments came two days later. This tends to confirm McGuire's theory that the forewarning provided by refutation causes the subject to construct "belief defenses" of his own during the time which intervenes be-tween the two messages. The same experiment revealed that reading an essay (passive condition) produces greater resistance to subse-quent counter-propaganda than does writing an essay (active condi-tion). This, of course, may be due to the fact that the essays read were simply more persuasive than those the subjects wrote themselves.

Papageorgis and McGuire (1961) also discovered a refutational first message caused greater resistance to subsequent counter-propaganda than did a supportive first message, and found further that the resist-ance produced by prior refutation generalizes to counter-arguments not even mentioned in the first message. In fact, refutation of the specific arguments which appeared in the subsequent counter-propa-ganda was no more effective than refutation of different counter-arguments, but both refutational messages were superior to the sup-portive message. McGuire (1961a) also found that the refutation of arguments which did not appear in the subsequent counter-propa-ganda was no less effective than prior refutation of the counter-arguments which actually appeared, but a prior message which included both supportive and refutational defense was superior to either type of refutational defense or supportive defense alone.

McGuire (1961b) reports that a combination of active (written) and passive (read) defenses was superior to either defense when presented alone, in the condition in which the specific arguments refuted were those actually mentioned in subsequent counter-propaganda. But these differences did not appear when the counter-arguments refuted were different from those later encountered. McGuire (1962a) found that passive defenses were more effective than active defenses, and the superiority of passive defenses was greatest for the refutation-same condition, less for the supportive condition, and least for the refutation-different condition. However, all types of passive defenses showed decreased effectiveness when the counter-argument was delayed, while all the active defenses showed increased effectiveness over time.

The question of when the counterattack comes seems to be an important one. I have already mentioned one study in which no differences appeared between effectiveness of supportive and refutational defenses when the counterattack came immediately, but the refutational defenses were superior when the attack was delayed. This must be qualified by the finding of Anderson and McGuire (1965) that supportive defenses were less effective than either type of refutational defense, even when the attack immediately followed the defense. McGuire and Papageorgis (1962) found that the refutation-same condition produced greater resistance to immediate counterattack than did the refutation-different condition, but McGuire (1962b) found that the effectiveness of refutation of the specific counter-arguments mentioned later **decayed more rapidly** than did the effectiveness of refutation of different counter-arguments. In fact, the immunity to attack by **novel** counter-arguments **increases** over a period of seven days. In addition, the same study found again that immunity produced by refutational defenses decayed less rapidly than that produced by supportive defenses.

It appears then, that one may make some additional conclusions from these studies by McGuire which were not evident from the earlier studies. Not only is forewarning an effective means of reducing the effects of subsequent counter-propaganda, but refutation of counter-arguments in the initial message appears to be more effective than argument merely supportive of the initial position—and superiority of refutation becomes more evident if the counter-argument is delayed. One need not even attack the specific counter-arguments he antici-pates; in fact, attacking specific counter-arguments becomes less effective if the counterattack is delayed, while attacking counter-ar-guments not anticipated becomes more effective with delayed counterattack. Finally, presenting one's own refutation appears to be more effective than inducing the listener to prepare his own refuta-tion, although that superiority may disappear if the counterattack is delayed.

There is some evidence that merely forewarning listeners of im-minent counter-propaganda may reduce the effect of that counter-propaganda (Freedman and Sears, 1965). On the other hand, McGuire and Millman (1965) found that listeners may tend to change their be-liefs in the direction of the counterattack even before the counter-attack comes when they are merely forewarned. Of course, immuni-zation always produces a little of the disease it is designed to guard against. This preparatory attitude change seems to be an indication that listeners use the intervening time to reduce the disparity be-tween their own beliefs and the anticipated counterattack. Manis and Blake (1963) report that they also reduce the disparity by perceiving the counterattack to be less radical **when they have been forewarned about it.** However, this effect was found by Manis (1965) to occur only when the counterattack was delayed; when the counterattack came immediately the subjects who had been forewarned perceived it as **more** radical than when they were not forewarned.

If the reader has by now lost track of the myriad qualifications and elaborations of the general theory, he may cling to this fairly sub-stantial straw: It seems fairly clear that prior refutation reduces the effect of subsequent propaganda more effectively than prior con-structive argument, even when the counter-arguments refuted are not those the listeners subsequently encounter.

Finally, there is fairly good evidence that the refutation is more effective if it **precedes** the counter-propaganda: Kiesler and Kiesler (1964) report that the material used in forewarning had **no** effect when presented after the counterattack, and Tannenbaum, Macaulay, and Norris (1966) found that attempts to restore beliefs had less effect than forewarning.

Source-mediated interaction.   The congruity hypothesis of Osgood and Tannenbaum has been described in Chapter Three as a general theory of attitude change designed to predict the behavior of a listener who hears a liked or disliked source make a favorable or unfavorable statement about a liked or disliked concept. As noted at the beginning of this section on message interaction, however, a single persuasive message does not occur in a vacuum: The listener may have heard other sources make statements about the same concept, or may have heard the same source make statements about other concepts. Audience response to a single persuasive message, then, is likely to be determined in part by responses to previous messages. Further, since those responses may be mediated by the message **sources** as well as the message **topics,** two messages may interact even though their topics and content are irrelevant to one another.

There is a paucity of research in this area. Two experiments by Tannenbaum have demonstrated, however, that the phenomenon of source-mediated message interaction does occur. The first of these was conducted by Tannenbaum and Gengel (1966). In this experiment, three men made favorable, unfavorable, or neutral statements about the concept of "teaching machines." Later, subjects encountered a communication from the United States Office of Education which either favored or opposed teaching machines. The results certainly support the notion that messages interact, although they do not totally support the predictions drawn from the congruity hypothesis. Subjects who changed attitude favorably as a result of the second communication also changed attitudes favorably toward all three of the initial sources; but they changed attitudes most favorably toward the person who had initially favored teaching machines, less favorably toward the person who had been neutral, and least favorably toward the person who had opposed "teaching machines." Subjects who changed unfavorably as a result of the second communication also become somewhat less favorable toward the person who had initially favored teaching machines, became more favorable toward the person who had been neutral, and became most favorable toward the person who initially opposed teaching machines and was thus in agreement with their new attitudes.

This first experiment was actually a study of what might be termed "topic-mediated source interaction," but it set the stage for the second study, which is more relevant to our present purposes. Tannenbaum (1966) exposed subjects to messages which linked a source favorably to two concepts, unfavorably to the two concepts, or favorably to one concept and unfavorably to the other. Subjects then encountered a message favorable or unfavorable to one of the concepts, teaching machines. This time Tannenbaum found that subjects who became more favorable toward teaching machines also became more favorable toward the initial source if he had been linked favorably to that concept, and became less favorable toward the source if he had been linked unfavorably to the concept. Further, he found that subjects who became less favorable toward teaching machines also became less favorable toward the source if he had been positively linked to the concept and more favorable toward the source if he had been negatively linked to the concept. Thus this experiment confirmed the predictions from the congruity hypothesis much more clearly than did the Tannenbaum and Gengel study.

However, this study went beyond that by Tannenbaum and Gengel to determine whether generalization would occur not only from the second message back to the first source, but also from that source to another concept to which that source had been previously linked. Remember that the source had also been linked positively or negatively to a second concept, that of Spence's learning theory. Tannenbaum reports that his predictions about attitude change toward this second concept were also confirmed. If the attitude change that transferred back to the initial source was favorable, attitude change toward the second concept was also favorable if the linkage had been favorable, and it was unfavorable if the linkage had been unfavorable. If the attitude change which transferred back to the initial source was unfavorable, attitude change toward the second concept was favorable if the linkage had been unfavorable, and it was unfavorable if the linkage had been favorable. It appears, then, that: (1) attitudes toward source and concept linked by an assertion tend to transfer to each other in a congruent fashion; (2) subsequent attitude change toward the concept will transfer back to the source in a congruent fashion; (3) the attitude that has transferred back to the source will transfer congruently to other concepts to which that source may be linked.

Message-feedback interaction. The primary thesis of Raymond A. Bauer (1964) in his paper "The Obstinate Audience" seems to be that quite often the feedback **is** the message. Too often the hopeful persuader or student of persuasion forgets that the "message" is the message only because he has arbitrarily specified it as such. The objective observer may be unable to tell the feedback from the message without a program. The persuader should not set about to persuade without accepting the probability that he himself will be to some extent persuaded. The preceding chapter contained a brief review of the literature relating to the phenomenon of "self-persuasion," but it should be clear that the material reviewed there would be quite relevant here. The persuader speaking before a hostile audience is likely to advocate a position which is somewhat of a compromise between his own views and those of the audience. If the audience response is favorable, the persuader may end up being the persuadee. If the audience response is **discriminating**—that is, most favorable to those arguments least representative of the persuader's position and least favorable to those arguments most representative of his position—the effect may be even more pronounced. And if the persuader faces a number of hostile audiences, the cumulative effect may well be greater attitude change on his part than on the part of any one of his listeners.

In addition to the material cited in the previous chapters, there have been very few studies designed to determine directly the effect of the "feedback" upon the "message." Zimmerman and Bauer (1966) found that people who anticipated giving a speech remembered more of the material they thought the audience would dislike. Bauer and Bauer (1960) have questioned the simplicity of the assumption that trends in the mass media persuade mass audiences and thus cause social trends; they suggest and cite research to support the possibility that content of the mass media is to a considerable extent determined by what people will accept. One might go even further and suggest that the mass audience would be even more successful in "persuading" the mass media if it were not for the fact that those in control of the media have been so thoroughly hoodwinked by the myth of their own power that they spend too much time talking and not enough time listening.

Much of the research in this area was reviewed and discussed in a symposium in 1964, attended by Raymond Bauer, Herbert Krugman, Elihu Katz, and Nathan Maccoby, among others, and reported in Payne (1965). Unfortunately, most of the research findings to date have been serendipitous; the researchers have been studying an unrelated question and have produced results which they could explain only as a function of "audience" effect upon the "persuader." Consequently, there is more "implication" and "inference" in the findings than is desirable.

The study needed in this area is the sort that compares attitude change of persuaders speaking to hostile audiences with that of persuaders speaking to partisan audiences. If the effect of the audience is actually as great as the incidental findings indicate, it may be worthwhile to begin a serious program of research to determine the ways in which audiences exert influence upon the speaker and the ways in which speakers respond to such influence.

Effects of language

The intended scope of this section is quite narrow in relation to the area which could be covered. First, the **speculation** has been endless regarding the role of language in persuasion. Some of that material was covered in the earlier chapter which surveyed rhetorical theories of persuasion. The purpose of the present section, however, is to survey the **experimental** findings relevant to language effects.

A second area which will not be covered is the large body of research dealing with the ways in which individuals acquire and use language. The persuader might be interested in such questions, but the practical implications of such research for the persuader's choice of language are rather few at present. The interested reader might consult a book such as that by Miron and Jacobovitz (1967).

Language clarity.   A third area, studies of the effects of language **clarity,** would be more relevant to persuasion if it were not for the fact that researchers in this area have been almost universally concerned with **retention** rather than **attitude change.** It is interesting to speculate that language clarity, which has been demonstrated to be related to message retention, may thus affect attitude change. However, some research is needed to demonstrate that increased understanding due to increased language clarity does increase attitude change. The reader may have noticed a number of studies already reviewed which have reported no differences in attitude change even though retention differences were reported—and he may have noticed studies reporting no differences in retention even though differences in attitude change were reported. Such findings might lead one to suspect that there is no simple relationship between retention of arguments and attitude change. It may be that deliberate ambiguity is an effective persuasion device under certain circumstances. Certainly some research is needed to test that possibility. Such research would use language clarity as an independent variable, attitude change as the dependent variable, and retention as an intervening variable.

One of the difficulties with such research is that the direction of causality will be difficult to determine: Differences in retention may produce differences in attitude change, but differences in attitude change may also produce differences in retention, as listeners misunderstand and/or forget material not consonant with their developing attitudes. A really intricate experimental design using analysis of covariance with more than one covariate might be capable of clarifying these relationships.

A second difficulty is that most researchers use separate analyses of variance for their retention and attitude change measures, making it impossible to compare the two effects directly. This is understandable: It would be trivial to discover that there is a difference between retention and attitude change in response to a given message, since the two are measured on different scales. However, if the two measures were treated as an additional dimension of an analysis of variance, the discovery that this "measure" dimension was involved in an **interaction** with the dimension of language clarity would not be trivial; one could then conclude that, under these particular circumstances, language clarity affects retention differently than it affects attitude change. Research using a different analysis for each measure does not allow any such conclusion. Further discussion of this point is probably better suited to a late-night session at a convention bar than to a book on persuasion.

Aesthetic language. Considering the present state of this area, any discussion of the effect of aesthetic language in persuasion can be no more than a call for research. There has been much speculation regarding the pleasantness of language, but essentially no attempts to find objective answers to the two major questions: "What factors make language pleasing to an audience?" and "Under what circumstances does the pleasantness of language affect persuasion?" Such an approach suggests the use of measures of audience **attitude toward the language** in the message, which should not be too difficult to devise. The real difficulty, of course, will be in determining the characteristics of language which are responsible for differences in audience attitude toward language and thence responsible for differences in attitude toward the speaker and the concept.

Language intensity. One type of experiment which seems clearly relevant to persuasion and which has typically used measures of attitude change is the study dealing with the effect of language **intensity.** Bowers (1963) initially defined language intensity as "the quality of language which indicates the degree to which the speaker's attitude toward a concept deviates from neutrality." He composed persuasive speeches and then deleted all words which seemed to reveal the speaker's attitude toward the concept. He then provided a number of alternative words to replace each deletion, and asked a group of judges to rate the intensity of each word (as defined above) in the context in which it was to be placed. He reports elsewhere (Bowers, 1964) that these words were rated as more intense if they contained more syllables (the correlation was only .10, but significant), if they were "more obscure," if they were preceded by enhancing qualifiers, and if they were highly metaphorical. In fact, insofar as the terms could be classified as "sex" or "death" metaphors, the correlations with intensity were perfect.

Bowers then composed versions of each speech which contained language of either high or low intensity. His principal finding was that listeners changed attitude more in response to language of low intensity. He offered a number of explanations for this finding. One of these was that his listeners seemed frustrated or hostile. Carmichael and Cronkhite (1965) tested the hypothesis that Bowers' results were limited to listeners who were frustrated. They deliberately frustrated one group of listeners and "ego-satisfied" another group. Half of each group then heard two of Bowers' highly intense speeches while the other half heard the speeches of low intensity. The finding was replicated for subjects who were frustrated: Frustrated subjects who heard the speeches using language of high intensity were significantly less favorable toward the concepts than were subjects who heard the speeches using language of low intensity. This effect did not appear among ego-satisfied listeners, however. In fact, there were no significant differences among subjects who were ego-satisfied and those who were frustrated but heard the speeches of low intensity. The interaction was accounted for by the fact that the frustrated subjects who heard the highly intense speeches responded significantly less favorably than any other subjects.

Carmichael and Cronkhite hypothesize that the negative response of this particular group of listeners may have been due to the fact that being highly aroused, they reacted negatively to language designed to push them to even higher levels of arousal. A second possibility is that the frustration combined with the intense language produced a level of arousal so high as to interfere with the rather complex task of listening and responding to a persuasive message.

These findings, however, must be qualified by those of Bowers and Osborn (1966). In this study two speeches were composed. All subjects heard both speeches, but some heard "literal" conclusions and some heard intense "metaphorical" conclusions, one of which was an extended death metaphor while the other was an extended sex metaphor. In both cases, the metaphorical conclusions produced greater attitude change. This finding appears to contradict those of Bowers and of Carmichael and Cronkhite. There are at least two possible explanations. One of these is that Osborn writes better metaphorical than literal conclusions. A second less trivial possibility is that audiences tolerate, expect, and possibly even long for highly intense language in the **conclusions** of argumentative speeches.

Franzwa (1967) has done the most recent study in this area. She used language which was rated favorably or unfavorably on semantic differential evaluative scales, and dynamic or nondynamic on activity and potency scales. She found that speakers who are favorable toward a concept use more favorable language, which is no great surprise, but she also found that speakers who anticipate facing a hostile audience use less dynamic language than do those who anticipate speaking to a partisan audience. Regarding the effect of dynamic language on the audience, however, her findings did not support the thesis that listeners respond differently to language which differs in dynamism.

The conclusion to be drawn from these studies seems to be that the speaker runs the risk of alienating his audience by using language of high intensity, at least in the body of his speech, although such language may be used effectively in the conclusion. Needless to say, there is room for more research.

Effects of delivery

There is some research regarding the role of delivery in message clarity. Insofar as the persuader wishes his message to be clearly perceived by the listener, that research is relevant to persuasion. However, it is the extent to which various styles of delivery contribute to the listeners' perceptions of the speaker which is really central to persuasion, and that is what I wish to deal with here.

Two books in this area are especially recommended: one by Joel

Davitz, titled **The Communication of Emotional Meaning,** and another edited by Peter Knapp, titled **Expression of the Emotions in Man.** In addition, a section titled "Nonverbal Interaction" in Dean Barnlund's book, **Interpersonal Communication,** and a section on nonverbal symbols in the book **Communication and Culture** by Alfred G. Smith contain important papers. The area is broad enough that the present discussion can only suggest some directions for research; the interested reader should consult one of these recommended sources.

The clearest thesis that arises from studies in this area is that the potential persuader is well-advised to be sincere or avoid a personal appearance. Audiences are surprisingly perceptive in their judgments of emotion reflected in **each** of a number of nonverbal modalities, and when they have several of those modalities available to reinforce their judgments, it will take a very clever speaker to deceive them. Further, the nonverbal cues of emotion are very difficult for a speaker to control consciously and simultaneously, and it will take only a few inconsistencies during the course of a speech to give the listener a sense of insincerity. Most importantly, it is apparent that much emotional meaning is transmitted by cues of which neither the speaker nor the listener is aware.

Facial expressions, for example, can be judged with a fair degree of accuracy, even though most of the research has probably yielded spuriously low estimates of accuracy because the stimuli have generally been **still** photographs, out of context, of people with whom the judges were not familiar, often posed by actors. Schlosberg (1954) has classified facial expressions on three dimensions: pleasantness-unpleasantness, attention-rejection, and activity-inactivity. The emotions that judges have the greatest difficulty identifying seem to be those most closely associated on those dimensions. The difficulty seems to be in identifying the facial cues by which observers make such judgments. Certainly the research attempting to specify the areas of the face from which such cues emanate has been quite fruitless. Some work by Hess on pupillary dilation suggests how complex such judgments may be. The finding that pupillary dilation is indicative of an individual's interest is now fairly well known. More relevant to our present concern is the fact that male subjects shown photographs of girls whose pupils were either dilated or not dilated chose the photographs in which the pupils were dilated, and were not able to explain their choices. If facial cues are of this sort—not under the control of the person generating the expression and not consciously recognized by the observer—the speaker will do well to avoid attempts to manipulate them artificially. In the theatre, given that the audience engages in some "willing suspension of disbelief," the actor may rely upon less subtle and more stereotyped means of communicating the emotions he is supposed to be experiencing, but that is a different world. Even there, one of the most successful schools of acting technique recommends that the actor actually feel the emotion he is attempting to portray.

Vocal cues seem to be of the same sort. There is evidence that emotion can be judged beyond chance expectation even from a whisper (Knower, 1941) in the presence of noise (Pollack, Rubenstein, and Horowitz, 1960), and from speech samples shorter than one-tenth of a second (Pollack, Rubenstein, and Horowitz, 1960). Again, identifying the vocal correlates of these judgments has been more difficult. Davitz (1964) found that loudness, pitch, timbre, and rate were significantly correlated with judgments of a speaker's activity, but not with judgments of his affect or potency. Fairbanks and Hoaglin (1941) found that some emotional states can be differentiated on the basis of vocal rate, ratio of pause time to phonation time, pitch range, and rate of pitch change; and Skinner (1935) reported that the pitch of "happy" speech was reliably higher than that of sad or neutral speech. Again, the speaker is hardly advised to try to "fake" such vocal nuances. Davitz, discussing his failure to find vocal correlates of affect and potency, speculates that those aspects of emotional meaning "are probably communicated by subtler, and perhaps more complex, vocal patterns of inflection, rhythm, etc. . . ."

The research on the role of postural and gesticulatory cues has shown that there are patterns in such behavior which are to some extent similar from one individual to another, somewhat more under the control of the speaker, and more clearly recognizable by observers. Even here, however, a split-second delay or anticipation in timing can reveal a damning insincerity or ludicrous planning on the part of the speaker. It is not that the speaker is advised not to smile, use pitch variety, and gesture—it is only suggested that these aspects of his delivery will be most effective if they are generated by real emotion rather than by a desire to convey emotion. Whatever one's beliefs about the ethical necessity for sincerity, it can certainly be an aid to delivery.

REFERENCES

Adams, H. F. "The Effects of Climax and Anti-Climax Order," **Journal of Applied Psychology,** 4 (1920), 330–338.

Allyn, Jane, and Leon Festinger. "The Effectiveness of Unanticipated Persuasive Communications," **Journal of Abnormal and Social Psychology,** 62 (1961), 35–40.

Andersen, Kenneth. "An Experimental Study of the Interaction of Artistic and Nonartistic Ethos in Persuasion." Unpublished doctoral dissertation, University of Wisconsin, 1961.

———, and Theodore Clevenger, Jr. "A Summary of Experimental Research in Ethos," **Speech Monographs,** 30 (1963), 59–78.

Anderson, D. C. "The Effect of Various Uses of Authoritative Testimony in Persuasive Speaking." Unpublished master's thesis, Ohio State University, 1958.

Anderson, L., and William J. McGuire. "Prior Reassurance of Group Consensus as a Factor in Producing Resistance to Persuasion," **Sociometry,** 28 (1965), 44–56.

Apsler, Robert, and David O. Sears. "Warning, Personal Involvement, and Attitude Change," **Journal of Personality and Social Psychology,** 9 (1968), 162–166.

Argyle, M. and J. Dean. "Eye Contact, Distance, and Affiliation," **Sociometry,** 28 (1965), 289–304.

———, and A. Kendon. "The Experimental Analysis of Social Performance," **Advances in Experimental Social Psychology.** L. Berkowitz, ed. New York: Academic Press, 1967.

Aronson, Elliot, and Burton W. Golden. "The Effect of Relevant and Irrelevant Aspects of Communicator Credibility on Opinion Change," **Journal of Personality,** 30 (1962), 135–146.

Barnlund, Dean C., ed. **Interpersonal Communication.** Boston: Houghton Mifflin, 1968.

Bauer, Raymond A. "The Obstinate Audience: The Influence Process from the Point of View of Social Communication," **American Psychologist,** 19 (1964), 319–328.

Beighley, Kenneth C. "An Experimental Study of the Effect of Four Speech Variables on Listener Comprehension," **Speech Monographs,** 19 (1952), 249–258.

Berkowitz, L., and D. R. Cottingham. "The Interest Value and Relevance of Fear-Arousing Communications," **Journal of Abnormal and Social Psychology,** 60 (1960), 37–43.

Berkowitz, and Louise R. Daniels. "Responsibility and Dependency," **Journal of Abnormal and Social Psychology,** 66 (1963), 429–436.

———. "Affecting the Salience of the Social Responsibility Norm: Effects of Past Help on the Response to Dependency Relationships," **Journal of Abnormal and Social Psychology,** 68 (1964), 275–281.

Berkowitz, Sharon Klanderman, and R. Harris. "Effects of Experimental Awareness and Sex of Subject and Experimenter on Reactions to Dependency Relationships," **Sociometry,** 27 (1964), 327–337.

Berlo, David K. "An Empirical Test of a General Construct of Credibility." Paper presented at the convention of the Speech Association of America, New York City, December 1961.

———, James B. Lemert, and Robert J. Mertz. **Dimensions for Evaluating the Acceptability of Message Sources.** East Lansing: Department of Communication, Michigan State University, 1966.

Berscheid, E. "Opinion Change and Communicator-Communicatee Similarity and Dissimilarity," **Journal of Personality and Social Psychology,** 4 (1966), 670–680.

Bettinghaus, Erwin P., Jr. "The Relative Effect of the Use of Testimony in a Persuasive Speech Upon the Attitudes of Listeners." Unpublished master's thesis, Bradley University, 1953.

———. "The Operation of Congruity in an Oral Communication Situation." Unpublished doctoral dissertation, University of Illinois, 1959.

Biddle, Phillips R. "An Experimental Study of Ethos and Appeal for Overt Behavior in Persuasion." Unpublished doctoral dissertation, University of Illinois, 1966.

Black, John W. "Accompaniments of Word Intelligibility," **Journal of Speech and Hearing Disorders,** 17 (1952), 409–417.

———. "Aural Reception of Sentences of Different Lengths," **Quarterly Journal of Speech,** 47 (1961), 51–53.

Bowers, John. "Language Intensity, Social Introversion, and Attitude Change," **Speech Monographs,** 30 (1963), 345–352.

———. "Some Correlates of Language Intensity," **Quarterly Journal of Speech,** 50 (1964), 415–520.

———, and Michael M. Osborn. "Attitudinal Effects of Selected Types of Concluding Metaphors in Persuasive Speeches," **Speech Monographs,** 33 (1966), 147–155.

Brock, Timothy C. "Communicator-Recipient Similarity and Decision Change," **Journal of Personality and Social Psychology,** 1 (1965), 650–654.

———, and Lee Becker. "Ineffectiveness of 'Overheard' Counterpropaganda," **Journal of Personality and Social Psychology,** 2 (1965), 654–660.

Burnstein, E., E. Stotland, and Alvin Zander. "Similarity to a Model and Self-

Evaluation," **Journal of Abnormal and Social Psychology,** 62 (1961), 257–264.

Byrne, Donn. "The Influence of Propinquity and Opportunity for Interaction on Classroom Relations," **Human Relations,** 14 (1961), 63–69.

———. "Interpersonal Attraction and Attitude Similarity," **Journal of Abnormal and Social Psychology,** 62 (1961), 713–715.

———. "Interpersonal Attraction as a Function of Affiliation Need and Attitude Similarity," **Human Relations,** 14 (1961), 281.

———. "Response to Attitude Similarity-Dissimilarity as a Function of Affiliation Need," **Journal of Personality,** 30 (1962), 164–177.

———, William Griffitt, and Carole Golightly. "Prestige as a Factor in Determining the Effect of Attitude Similarity-Dissimilarity on Attraction," **Journal of Personality,** 34 (1966), 441–442.

Byrne, and Don Nelson. "Attraction as a Function of Attitude Similarity-Dissimilarity: The Function of Topic Importance," **Psychonomic Science,** 1 (1964), 93–94.

———. "Attraction as a Linear Function of Positive Reinforcement," **Journal of Personality and Social Psychology,** 1 (1965), 659–663.

Byrne, and Ray Rhamey. "Magnitude of Positive and Negative Reinforcements as a Determinant of Attraction," **Journal of Personality and Social Psychology,** 2 (1965), 884–889.

Byrne, and Terry Wong. "Racial Prejudice, Interpersonal Attraction, and Assumed Dissimilarity of Attitudes," **Journal of Abnormal and Social Psychology,** 65 (1962), 246–253.

Carmichael, Carl, and Gary Cronkhite. "Frustration and Language Intensity," **Speech Monographs,** 32 (1965), 107–111.

Carroll, John B. "Vectors of Prose Style," **Style in Language.** Thomas A. Sebeok, ed. New York: Wiley, 1960, pp. 283–292.

Carter, R. "Writing Controversial Stories for Comprehension," **Journalism Quarterly,** 32 (1955), 319–328.

Cartier, Francis A. "Listenability and Readability," **Speech Monographs,** 22 (1955), 53–56.

Cathcart, Robert S. "An Experimental Study of the Relative Effectiveness of Four Methods of Presenting Evidence," **Speech Monographs,** 22 (1955), 227–233.

Clore, Gerald L., and Barbara Baldridge. "Interpersonal Attraction: The Role of Agreement and Topic Interest," **Journal of Personality and Social Psychology,** 9 (1968), 340–346.

Cohen, Arthur R. "Need for Cognition and Order of Communications as Determinants of Opinion Change," **The Order of Presentation in Persuasion.** Carl I. Hovland, ed. New Haven: Yale University Press, 1957, pp. 102–120.

————. **Attitude Change and Social Influence.** New York: Basic Books, 1964.

Cook, Thomas D., and Chester A. Insko. "Persistence of Attitude Change as a Function of Conclusion Re-exposure: A Laboratory-Field Experiment," **Journal of Personality and Social Psychology,** 9 (1968), 322–328.

Costley, D. L. "An Experimental Study of the Effectiveness of Quantitative Evidence in Speeches of Advocacy." Unpublished master's thesis, University of Oklahoma, 1958.

Cromwell, Harvey. "The Relative Effect on Audience Attitude of the First versus the Second Argumentative Speech of a Series," **Speech Monographs,** 17 (1950), 105–122.

Cronkhite, Gary. "Identification and Persuasion," **Central States Speech Journal,** 15 (1964), 57–59.

Dabbs, James M., Jr. "Self-Esteem, Communicator Characteristics, and Attitude Change," **Journal of Abnormal and Social Psychology,** 69 (1964), 173–181.

Dale, E., and J. S. Chall. "A Formula for Predictive Readability," **Educational Research Bulletin,** 27 (1945), 11–20, 28, 37–54.

Daniels, Louise R., and L. Berkowitz. "Liking and Response to Dependency Relationships," **Human Relations,** 16 (1963), 141–148.

Darnell, Donald K. "The Relation Between Sentence Order and Comprehension," **Speech Monographs,** 30 (1963), 97–100.

Davis, K. E., and E. E. Jones. "Changes in Interpersonal Perception as a Means of Reducing Cognitive Dissonance," **Journal of Abnormal and Social Psychology,** 61 (1960), 402–410.

Davitz, Joel R. "Auditory Correlates of Vocal Expressions of Emotional Meanings," **The Communication of Emotional Meaning.** Joel R. Davitz, ed. New York: McGraw-Hill, 1964.

————, ed. **The Communication of Emotional Meaning.** New York: McGraw-Hill, 1964.

Dawes, Robyn M. "Cognitive Distortion," **Psychological Reports,** 14 (1964), 443–459.

Deaux, Kay K. "Variations in Warning, Information Preference, and Anticipatory Attitude Change," **Journal of Personality and Social Psychology,** 9 (1968), 157–161.

DeSoto, Clinton B. "Learning a Social Structure," **Journal of Abnormal and Social Psychology,** 60 (1960), 417–421.

————. "The Predilection for Single Orderings," **Journal of Abnormal and Social Psychology,** 60 (1962), 16–23.

————, Marvin London, and Stephen Handel. "Social Reasoning and Spatial Paralogic," **Journal of Personality and Social Psychology,** 2 (1965), 513–521.

DeWolfe, D. S., and C. N. Governale. "Fear and Attitude Change," **Journal of Abnormal and Social Psychology,** 69 (1964), 119–123.

Doob, J. W. "Effects of Initial Serial Position and Attitude Upon Recall Under Conditions of Low Motivation," **Journal of Abnormal and Social Psychology,** 44 (1953), 199–205.

Dresser, W. R. "Éffects of 'Satisfactory' and 'Unsatisfactory' Evidence in a Speech of Advocacy," **Speech Monographs,** 30 (1963), 302–306.

Duncan, Margaret. "Fear-Arousing Appeals in Persuasion." Paper submitted in a seminar in theories of persuasion conducted at the University of Illinois, Summer 1966.

Efran, Jay S. "Looking for Approval: Effects on Visual Behavior of Approbation from Persons Differing in Importance," **Journal of Personality and Social Psychology,** 10 (1968), 21–25.

————, and A. Broughton. "Effect of Expectancies for Social Approval on Visual Behavior," **Journal of Personality and Social Psychology,** 4 (1966), 103–107.

Ellsworth, Phoebe C., and J. Merrill Carlsmith. "Effects of Eye Contact and Verbal Content on Affective Response to a Dyadic Interaction," **Journal of Personality and Social Psychology,** 10 (1968), 15–20.

Exline, R., D. Gray, and D. Schuette. "Visual Behavior in a Dyad as Affected by Interview Content and Sex of Respondent," **Journal of Personality and Social Psychology,** 1 (1965), 201–210.

Exline, R., and L. C. Winters. "Affective Relations and Mutual Glances in Dyads," **Affect, Cognition, and Personality,** S. Tomkins and C. Izard, eds. New York: Springer, 1965.

Fairbanks, Grant, and L. W. Hoaglin. "An Experimental Study of the Durational Characteristics of the Voice During Expression of Emotion," **Speech Monographs,** 8 (1941), 85–90.

Feather, N. T. "Subjective Probability and Decision Under Uncertainty," **Psychological Review,** 66 (1959), 150–164.

Fishbein, Martin. This explanation was suggested in a lecture in a seminar in attitude change conducted at the University of Illinois, Spring 1965.

Flesch, Rudolph. "A New Readability Yardstick," **Journal of Applied Psychology,** 32 (1943a), 221–233.

————. **Marks of Readable Style.** New York: Columbia University Teachers College Bureau of Publications, 1943b.

————. **The Art of Plain Talk.** New York: Harper, 1946.

Franzwa, Helen H. "The Use and Effectiveness of Evaluative-Dynamic Language in Persuasion." Unpublished doctoral dissertation, University of Illinois, 1967.

Freedman, Jonathan L., and David O. Sears. "Warning, Distraction, and Resistance to Influence," **Journal of Personality and Social Psychology,** 1 (1965), 262–266.

Fulton, Barry. "Attitude Change: A Homeostatic Model of the Listener." Unpublished doctoral dissertation, University of Illinois, 1968.

Gilkinson, Howard, Stanley F. Paulson, and Donald E. Sikkink. "Effects of Order and Authority in an Argumentative Speech," **Quarterly Journal of Speech,** 40 (1954), 183–192.

Gilson, Charlotte, and Robert P. Abelson. "The Subjective Use of Inductive Evidence," **Journal of Personality and Social Psychology,** 2 (1965), 301–310.

Glass, D. C. "Changes in Liking as a Means of Reducing Discrepancies Between Self-Esteem and Aggression," **Journal of Personality,** 32 (1964), 531–549.

Goldstein, M. "The Relationship Between Coping and Avoiding Behavior and Response to Fear-Arousing Propaganda," **Journal of Abnormal and Social Psychology,** 48 (1959), 247–252.

Golightly, Carole, and Donn Byrne. "Attitude Statements as Positive and Negative Reinforcements," **Science,** 146 (1964), 798–799.

Gray, W. S., and B. E. Leary. **What Makes a Book Readable?** Chicago: University of Chicago Press, 1935.

Greenberg, Bradley S., and Gerald R. Miller. "The Effects of Low-Credible Sources on Message Acceptance," **Speech Monographs,** 33 (1966), 127–136.

Gulley, Halford E., and David K. Berlo. "Effect of Intercellular and Intracellular Speech Structure on Attitude Change and Learning," **Speech Monographs,** 23 (1956), 288–297.

Haaland, Gordon A., and M. Venkatesan. "Resistance to Persuasive Communications: An Examination of the Distraction Hypothesis," **Journal of Personality and Social Psychology,** 9 (1968), 167–170.

Harwood, Kenneth A., "Listenability and 'Human Interest,'" **Speech Monographs,** 22 (1955), 49–52.

Helmreich, Robert, and Barry E. Collins. "Studies in Forced Compliance: Commitment and Magnitude of Inducement to Comply as Determinants of Opinion Change," **Journal of Personality and Social Psychology,** 10 (1968), 75–81.

Hess, Eckhart H. "Attitude and Pupil Size," **Scientific American** (1965), 46–65.

Hewgill, Murray A., and Gerald R. Miller. "Source Credibility and Response to Fear-Arousing Communications," **Speech Monographs,** 32 (1965), 95–101.

Hollander, E. P. "Conformity, Status, and Idiosyncrasy Credit," **Psychological Review,** 65 (1958), 117–127.

Hovland, Carl I., *et al.* **The Order of Presentation in Persuasion.** New Haven: Yale University Press, 1957.

Hovland, A. A. Lumsdaine, and F. D. Sheffield. **Experiments on Mass Communication (Studies in Social Psychology in World War II,** Vol. 3.) Princeton: Princeton University Press, 1949.

Hovland, and W. Mandell. "An Experimental Comparison of Conclusion-Drawing by the Communicator and by the Audience," **Journal of Abnormal and Social Psychology,** 47 (1952), 581–588.

Hovland, and H. Pritzker. "Effect of Opinion Change as a Function of Amount of Change Advocated," **Journal of Abnormal and Social Psychology,** 54 (1957), 257–261.

Hovland, and W. Weiss. "The Influence of Source Credibility on Communication Effectiveness," **Public Opinion Quarterly,** 15 (1951), 635–650.

Husek, T. R. "Persuasive Impacts of Early, Late, or No Mention of a Negative Source," **Journal of Personality and Social Psychology,** 2 (1965), 125–128.

Insko, Chester A. "Primacy versus Recency in Persuasion as a Function of the Timing of Arguments and Measures," **Journal of Abnormal and Social Psychology,** 69 (1964), 381–391.

Janis, Irving L. "Psychological Effects of Warnings," **Man and Society in Disaster.** C. W. Baker and D. W. Chapman, eds. New York: Basic Books, 1962, pp. 55–92.

———, and Seymour Feshbach. "Effects of Fear-Arousing Communications," **Journal of Abnormal and Social Psychology,** 48 (1953), 78–92.

———. "Personality Differences Associated With Responsiveness to Fear-Arousing Communications," **Journal of Personality,** 23 (1954), 154–166.

Janis, and Howard Leventhal. "Human Reactions to Stress," **Handbook of Personality Theory and Research,** E. Borgatta and W. Lambert, eds. Boston: Rand McNally, 1967.

Janis, and Harry C. Milholland. "The Influence of Threat Appeals on Selective Learning of the Content of a Persuasive Communication," **Journal of Psychology,** 37 (1954), 75–80.

Janis, and Robert F. Terwilliger. "An Experimental Study of Psychological Responses to Fear-Arousing Communications," **Journal of Abnormal and Social Psychology,** 65 (1962), 403–410.

Jellison, Jerald M., and Judson Mills. "Effect of Similarity and Fortune of the Other on Attraction," **Journal of Personality and Social Psychology,** 5 (1967), 459–463.

Jersild, A. "Primacy, Recency, Frequency, and Vividness," **Journal of Experimental Psychology,** 12 (1929), 58–70.

Jones, E. E., and B. N. Daugherty. "Political Orientation and the Perceptual Effects of an Anticipated Interaction," **Journal of Abnormal and Social Psychology,** 59 (1959), 340–349.

Kelman, Herbert C., and Carl I. Hovland. "Reinstatement of Communicator in Delayed Measurement of Opinion Change," **Journal of Abnormal and Social Psychology,** 48 (1953), 327–335.

Kendon, A. "Some Functions of Gaze Direction in Social Interaction," **Acta Psychologica,** 26 (1967), 22–63.

Kerrick, Jean S. "The Effect of Relevant and Non-Relevant Sources on Attitude Change." **Journal of Social Psychology,** 47 (1958), 15–20.

Kiesler, Charles A., and Sara B. Kiesler. "Role of Forewarning in Persuasive Communications," **Journal of Abnormal and Social Psychology,** 68 (1964), 547–549.

Knapp, Peter H., ed. **Expression of the Emotions in Man.** New York: International Universities Press, 1963.

Knower, Franklin H. "Analysis of Some Experimental Variations of Simulated Vocal Expressions of the Emotions," **Journal of Social Psychology,** 14 (1941), 369–372.

Kraus, Sidney, Elaine El-Assel, and Melvin DeFleur. "Fear-Threat Appeals in Mass Communication: An Apparent Contradiction," **Speech Monographs,** 33 (1966), 23–29.

Lemert, Jim. "Dimensions of Source Credibility." Paper presented at the convention of the Association for Education in Journalism, August 1963.

Lerner, Melvin J. "The Effect of Responsibility and Choice on a Partner's Attractiveness Following Failure," **Journal of Personality,** 33 (1965a), 178–187.

————. "Evaluation of Performance as a Function of Performer's Reward and Attractiveness," **Journal of Personality and Social Psychology,** 1 (1965b), 355–360.

————, and Carolyn H. Simmons. "Observer's Reaction to the 'Innocent Victim': Compassion or Rejection?" **Journal of Personality and Social Psychology,** 4 (1966), 203–210.

Leventhal, Howard, and P. Niles. "A Field Experiment on Fear-Arousal with Data on the Validity of Questionnaire Measures," **Journal of Personality,** 32 (1964), 459–479.

————. "Persistence of Influence for Varying Durations of Exposure to Threat Stimuli," **Psychological Reports,** 16 (1965), 223–233.

Leventhal, and Sidney I. Perloe. "A Relationship Between Self-Esteem and Persuasibility," **Journal of Abnormal and Social Psychology,** 64 (1962), 385–388.

Leventhal, and Robert P. Singer. "Affect Arousal and Positioning of Recommendations in Persuasive Communications," **Journal of Personality and Social Psychology,** 4 (1966), 137–146.

Leventhal, Singer, and S. Jones. "Effects of Fear and Specificity of Recommendation Upon Attitudes and Behavior," **Journal of Personality and Social Psychology,** 2 (1965), 20–29.

Leventhal, and J. C. Watts. "Sources of Resistance to Fear-Arousing Communications on Smoking and Lung Cancer," **Journal of Personality,** in press.

Levinger, George, and James Breedlove. "Interpersonal Attraction and Agreement," **Journal of Personality and Social Psychology,** 3 (1966), 367–372.

Lorge, I. "Predicting Reading Difficulty of Selections for Children," **Elementary English Review,** 16 (1939), 229–233.

McCroskey, James C. "Scales for the Measurement of Ethos," **Speech Monographs,** 33 (1966), 65–72.

——. **Studies of the Effects of Evidence in Persuasive Communication.** Mimeographed publication. East Lansing: Speech Communication Research Laboratory, Department of Speech, Michigan State University, 1967.

——. "A Summary of Experimental Research on the Effects of Evidence in Persuasive Communication," **Quarterly Journal of Speech,** in press.

McGuire, William J. "A Syllogistic Analysis of Cognitive Relationships," **Attitude Organization and Change,** M. J. Rosenberg, et al. eds. New Haven: Yale University Press, 1960.

——. "The Effectiveness of Supportive and Refutational Defenses in Immunizing and Restoring Beliefs Against Persuasion," **Sociometry,** 24 (1961a), 184–197.

——. "Resistance to Persuasion Conferred by Active and Passive Prior Refutation of the Same and Alternative Counterarguments," **Journal of Abnormal and Social Psychology,** 63 (1961b), 326–332.

——. "Persistence of the Resistance to Persuasion Induced by Various Types of Prior Belief Defenses," **Journal of Abnormal and Social Psychology,** 64 (1962b), 241–248.

——. **Effectiveness of Fear Appeals in Advertising.** New York: Advertising Research Foundation, 1963.

——. "Attitudes and Opinions," **Annual Review of Psychology,** 17 (1966), 475–514.

——. "Immunization Against Persuasion." Unpublished manuscript, 1962a. Cited by Chester A. Insko, **Theories of Attitude Change.** New York: Appleton-Century-Crofts, 1967.

——. "Personality and Attitude Change: A Theoretical Housing," **Attitude Change Theory and Research,** A. G. Greenwald et al., eds. New York: Academic Press, 1968.

——, and Susan Millman. "Anticipatory Belief Lowering Following Forewarning of a Persuasive Attack," **Journal of Personality and Social Psychology,** 2 (1965), 471–479.

——, and Demetrius Papageorgis. "The Relative Efficacy of Various Types of Prior Belief-Defense in Producing Immunity Against Persuasion," **Journal of Abnormal and Social Psychology,** 62 (1961), 327–337.

————. "Effectiveness of Forewarning in Developing Resistance to Persuasion," **Public Opinion Quarterly,** 26 (1962), 24–34.

Manion, O. G. "An Application of Readability Formulas to Oral Communication." Unpublished doctoral dissertation, University of Michigan, 1952.

Manis, Melvin. "Immunization, Delay, and the Interpretation of Persuasive Messages," **Journal of Personality and Social Psychology,** 1 (1965), 541–550.

————, and Joan P. Blake. "Interpretation of Persuasive Messages as a Function of Prior Immunization," **Journal of Abnormal and Social Psychology,** 66 (1963), 225–230.

Marlowe, David, Kenneth J. Gergen, and Anthony N. Doob. "Opponent's Personality, Expectation of Social Interaction, and Interpersonal Bargaining," **Journal of Personality and Social Psychology,** 3 (1966), 206–213.

Mason, Harry M. "Improvement of Listener Performance in Noise," **Speech Monographs,** 13 (1946), 41–46.

May, Mark A., and Arthur A. Lumsdaine. **Learning from Films.** New Haven: Yale University Press, 1958.

Mehrabian, Albert. "Relationship of Attitude to Seated Posture, Orientation, and Distance," **Journal of Personality and Social Psychology,** 10 (1968), 26–30.

Miller, Gerald R. "Studies on the Use of Fear Appeals: A Summary and Analysis," **Central States Speech Journal,** 14 (1963), 117–125.

Miller, Neal, and Donald T. Campbell. "Recency and Primacy in Persuasion as a Function of the Timing of Speeches and Measurements," **Journal of Abnormal and Social Psychology,** 59 (1959), 1–9.

Miller, Norman, D. T. Campbell, Helen Twedt, and Edward J. O'Connell. "Similarity, Contrast, and Complementarity in Friendship Choice," **Journal of Personality and Social Psychology,** 3 (1966), 3–12.

Millman, Susan. "Anxiety, Comprehension, and Susceptibility to Social Influence," **Journal of Personality and Social Psychology,** 9 (1968), 251–256.

Mills, Judson. "Opinion Change as a Function of the Communicator's Desire to Influence and Liking for the Audience," **Journal of Experimental Social Psychology,** 2 (1966), 152–159.

————, and Elliot Aronson. "Opinion Change as a Function of the Communicator's Attractiveness and Desire to Influence," **Journal of Personality and Social Psychology,** 1 (1965), 173–177.

Mills, and Jerald M. Jellison. "Effect on Opinion Change of Similarity Between the Communicator and the Audience Addressed," **Journal of Personality and Social Psychology,** 9 (1968), 153–156.

Minnick, Wayne C. **The Art of Persuasion.** Boston: Houghton Mifflin, 1957.

Moltz, H., and D. L. Thistlethwaite. "Attitude Modification and Anxiety Reduction," **Journal of Abnormal and Social Psychology,** 50 (1955), 231–237.

Moser, Henry M. "Intelligibility Related to Routinized Messages," **Speech Monographs,** 13 (1946), 47–49.

Newton, Kenneth C. "Placement of Affirmative Plan: Attitude Change and Information Gain." Unpublished master's thesis, Illinois State University, 1968.

Nichols, Alan C. "Apparent Factors Leading to Errors in Audition Made by Foreign Students," **Speech Monographs,** 31 (1964), 85–91.

Niles, P. "The Relationship of Susceptibility and Anxiety to Acceptance of Fear-Arousing Communications." Unpublished doctoral dissertation, Yale University, 1964.

Norman, Warren T. "Toward an Adequate Taxonomy of Personality Attributes: Replicated Factor Structures in Peer Nomination Personality Ratings," **Journal of Abnormal and Social Psychology,** 66 (1963), 574–583.

Osgood, Charles E. and Percy H. Tannenbaum. "The Principle of Congruity in the Prediction of Attitude Change," **Psychological Review,** 62 (1955), 42–55.

Ostermeier, T. H. "An Experimental Study on the Type and Frequency of Reference as Used by an Unfamiliar Source in a Message and its Effect Upon Perceived Credibility and Attitude Change." Unpublished doctoral dissertation, Michigan State University, 1966.

Papageorgis, Demetrius, and William J. McGuire. "The Generality of Immunity to Persuasion Produced by Pre-Exposure to Weakened Counterarguments," **Journal of Abnormal and Social Psychology,** 62 (1961), 475–481.

Payne, Donald E., ed. **The Obstinate Audience.** Ann Arbor, Michigan: Foundation for Research on Human Behavior, 1965.

Petrie, Charles R., Jr. "Informative Speaking: A Summary and Bibliography of Related Research," **Speech Monographs,** 30 (1963), 79–91.

Pollack, I., H. Rubenstein, and A. Horowitz. "Communication of Verbal Modes of Expression," **Language and Speech,** 3 (1960), 121–130.

Redding, W. Charles. "The American Value System: Premises for Persuasion," **Western Speech,** 26 (1966), 83–91.

Robbins, P. R. "An Application of the Method of Successive Intervals to the Study of Fear-Arousing Information." **Psychological Reports,** 11 (1962), 757–760.

Schlossberg, H. "Three Dimensions of Emotion," **Psychological Review,** 61 (1954), 81–88.

Schopler, John and Nicholas Bateson. "The Power of Dependence," **Journal of Personality and Social Psychology,** 2 (1965), 247–254.

Schunk, John. "Probability and Desirability Determinants of Relationships Among Beliefs in Rhetorical Propositions." Unpublished doctoral dissertation, University of Illinois, 1967.

Sharp, Harry, Jr., and Thomas McClung. "Effects of Organization on the Speaker's Ethos," **Speech Monographs,** 33 (1966), 182–183.

Sikkink, Donald E. "An Experimental Study of the Effects on the Listener of Anti-Climax Order and Authority in an Argumentative Speech," **Southern Speech Journal,** 22 (1956), 73–78.

Singer, Robert P. "The Effects of Fear-Arousing Communications on Attitude Change and Behavior." Unpublished doctoral dissertation, University of Connecticut, 1965.

Skinner, E. Ray. "A Calibrated Recording and Analysis of the Pitch, Force and Quality of Vocal Tones Expressing Happiness and Sadness; and a Determination of the Pitch and Force of the Subjective Concepts of Ordinary, Soft and Loud Tones," **Speech Monographs,** 2 (1935), 81–137.

Smith, Alfred G., ed. **Communication and Culture.** New York: Holt, Rinehart, and Winston, 1966.

Smith, A. J. "Similarity of Values and Its Relation to Acceptance and the Projection of Similarity," **Journal of Psychology,** 43 (1957), 251–260.

Smith, Raymond G. "An Experimental Study of the Effects of Speech Organization Upon Attitudes of College Students," **Speech Monographs,** 18 (1951), 292–301.

Sommer, R. "Small Group Ecology," **Psychological Bulletin,** 67 (1967), 145–151.

Speisman, Joseph C., et al. "Experimental Reduction of Stress Based on Ego-Defense Theory," **Journal of Abnormal and Social Psychology,** 68 (1964), 367–380.

Sponberg, Harold. "A Study of the Relative Effectiveness of Climax and Anti-Climax Order in an Argumentative Speech," **Speech Monographs,** 13 (1946), 35–44.

Stachowiak, J., and C. Moss. "Hypnotic Alterations of Social Attitudes," **Journal of Personality and Social Psychology,** 2 (1965), 77–83.

Stass, John W., and Frank N. Willis, Jr. "Eye Contact, Pupil Dilation, and Personal Preference," **Psychonomic Science,** 7 (1967), 375–376.

Steiner, Ivan D., and H. Johnson. "Relationships Among Dissonance Reducing Responses," **Journal of Abnormal and Social Psychology,** 68 (1964), 38–44.

————, and E. D. Rogers. "Alternative Responses to Dissonance." **Journal of Abnormal and Social Psychology,** 66 (1963), 128–136.

Tannenbaum, Percy H. "Effect of Serial Position on Recall of Radio News Stories," **Journalism Quarterly,** 31 (1954), 319–323.

————. "Mediated Generalization of Attitude Change via the Principle of Congruity," **Journal of Personality and Social Psychology,** 3 (1966), 493–500.

————, and R. Gengel. "Generalization of Attitude Change Through Congruity

Principle Relationships," **Journal of Personality and Social Psychology,** 3 (1966), 299–304.

Tannenbaum, J. Macauley, and E. Norris. "Principle of Congruity and Reduction of Persuasion," **Journal of Personality and Social Psychology,** 3 (1966), 233–238.

Thistlethwaite, Donald L., Joseph Kamenetsky, and Hans Schmidt. "Refutation and Attitude Change," **Speech Monographs,** 23 (1956), 14–25.

Thomas, Gordon L. "Oral Style and Intelligibility," **Speech Monographs,** 23 (1956), 46–54.

Thompson, E. "An Experimental Investigation of the Relative Effectiveness of Organization Structure in Oral Communications," **Southern Speech Journal,** 26 (1960), 59–69.

Thompson, Wayne N. **Quantitative Research in Public Address and Communication.** New York: Random House, 1967.

Uhlmann, Frank W., and Eli Saltz. "Retention of Anxiety Material as a Function of Cognitive Differentiation," **Journal of Personality and Social Psychology,** 1 (1965), 55–62.

Walster, E. "Assignment of Responsibility for an Accident," **Journal of Personality and Social Psychology,** 3 (1966), 73–79.

Walster, Elaine, and Leon Festinger. "The Effectiveness of "Overheard' Persuasive Communications," **Journal of Abnormal and Social Psychology,** 65 (1962), 395–402.

Weiss, Robert F., Harve E. Rawson, and Benjamin Pasamanick. "Argument Strength, Delay of Argument, and Anxiety in the 'Conditioning' and 'Selective Learning' of Attitudes," **Journal of Abnormal and Social Psychology,** 67 (1963), 157–165.

Weiss, W. "Opinion Congruence with a Negative Source on one Issue as a Factor Influencing Agreement on Another Issue," **Journal of Abnormal and Social Psychology,** 54 (1957), 180–186.

Wilson, Warner, and Howard Miller. "Repetition, Order of Presentation, and Timing of Arguments and Measures as Determinants of Opinion Change," **Journal of Personality and Social Psychology,** 9 (1968), 184–188.

Wittich, W. A., and J. G. Fowlkes. **Audio-Visual Paths to Learning.** New York: Harper, 1946.

Woodworth, R. S., and H. Schlosberg. **Experimental Psychology.** New York: Holt, 1954.

Index